Bayard Taylor

Travels in South Africa

Vol. 1

Bayard Taylor

Travels in South Africa
Vol. 1

ISBN/EAN: 9783337309039

Printed in Europe, USA, Canada, Australia, Japan

Cover: Foto ©Andreas Hilbeck / pixelio.de

More available books at **www.hansebooks.com**

*ILLUSTRATED LIBRARY OF TRAVEL,
EXPLORATION, AND ADVENTURE.*

TRAVELS IN

SOUTH AFRICA.

COMPILED AND ARRANGED BY

BAYARD TAYLOR.

NEW YORK:
SCRIBNER, ARMSTRONG, AND CO.,
SUCCESSORS TO
CHARLES SCRIBNER AND CO.
1872.

CONTENTS.

CHAPTER I.
SOUTH AFRICA.—ITS DISCOVERY AND SETTLEMENT . . PAGE 1

CHAPTER II.
THE NATIVE TRIBES OF SOUTH AFRICA 13

CHAPTER III.
MOFFAT'S MISSIONARY JOURNEYS 25

CHAPTER IV.
LIVINGSTONE'S DISCOVERY OF LAKE NGAMI . . 41

CHAPTER V.
LIVINGSTONE'S FIRST JOURNEY TO THE ZAMBESI . . 54

CHAPTER VI.
ANDERSON'S JOURNEY TO THE OVAMPO LAND AND LAKE NGAMI 68

CHAPTER VII.
ANDERSON'S JOURNEY TO THE OKAVANGO RIVER . . 82

CHAPTER VIII.
LIVINGSTONE'S JOURNEY ACROSS THE CONTINENT.—
I.–TO THE MAKOLOLO COUNTRY 99

CONTENTS.

CHAPTER IX.
LIVINGSTONE'S JOURNEY ACROSS THE CONTINENT.—
II.-VOYAGE UP THE ZAMBESI RIVER . . . 122

CHAPTER X.
LIVINGSTONE'S JOURNEY ACROSS THE CONTINENT.—
III.-UP THE LEEBA RIVER 143

CHAPTER XI.
LIVINGSTONE'S JOURNEY ACROSS THE CONTINENT.—
IV.-FROM SHINTE TO LOANDA 177

CHAPTER XII.
LIVINGSTONE'S JOURNEY ACROSS THE CONTINENT.—
V.-RETURN TO THE MAKOLOLO COUNTRY . . 204

CHAPTER XIII.
LIVINGSTONE'S JOURNEY ACROSS THE CONTINENT.—
VI.-DOWN THE ZAMBESI TO THE EASTERN COAST . 234

CHAPTER XIV.
MAGYAR'S JOURNEY TO BIHE 253

CHAPTER XV.
MAGYAR'S JOURNEYS IN THE INTERIOR . . . 269

CHAPTER XVI.
LIVINGSTONE'S EXPEDITION TO LAKE NYASSA . . 284

CHAPTER XVII.
LIVINGSTONE'S LAST JOURNEY 301

LIST OF ILLUSTRATIONS.

	PAGE
DAVID LIVINGSTONE	*Frontispiece.*
CAPE TOWN	6
NAMAQUA MUSICIAN	16
MOSHECH, CHIEF OF BASSUTOS	20
THABA BOSSIN	24
HIPPOPOTAMUS TRAP	40
LIVINGSTONE ATTACKED BY A LION	44
ANDERSON STARTING OUT	68
SOUTH AFRICAN WATERING-PLACE	77
ANDERSON'S JOURNEY ACROSS THE BURNING PRAIRIE	88
"BEHOLD! A WHITE MAN"	95
A HIPPOPOTAMUS FAMILY	120
MOONLIGHT DANCE OF THE NATIVES	140
HALT UNDER THE BAOBAB	176
PASS OF PUNGO ADONGO	200
HEAD-DRESSES OF LONDA	215
HIPPOPOTAMUS UPSETTING A BOAT	228
VILLAGE OF SKULLS	231
FALLS OF THE ZAMBESE	239
ST. PAUL DE LOANDA	254
MAGYAR'S ASCENT OF THE COAST RANGE	261
AN EXPEDITION FROM BIHE	281
ZANZIBAR	302

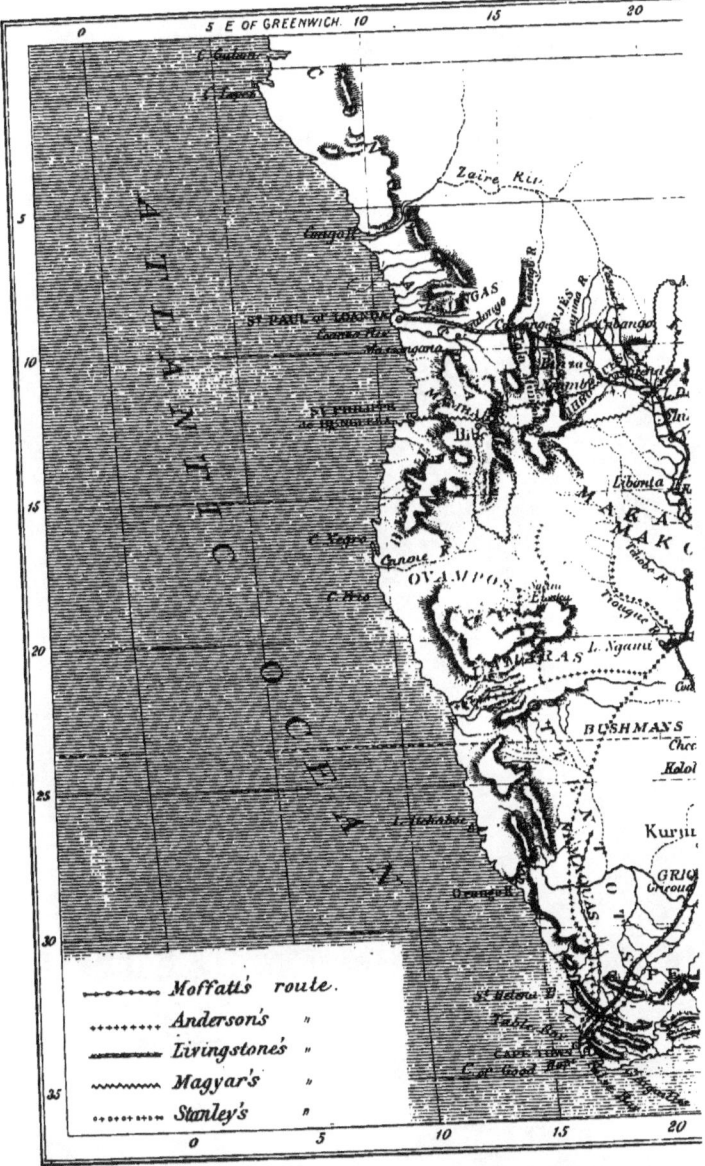

TRAVELS IN SOUTH AFRICA.

CHAPTER I.

SOUTH AFRICA.—ITS DISCOVERY AND SETTLEMENT.

THE fact that the northern part of Africa was well known to the civilized nations of antiquity gave rise to very early attempts to explore the dimensions of that continent. The first authentic record of such an attempt is given by Herodotus, who relates that Pharaoh Necho (about 600 years before the Christian era) sent an expedition down the Red Sea, with orders to sail around what was then considered to be an island, reaching to the latitude of the Equator. The vessels sailed until the autumn, landed, sowed grain, waited until they had reaped the harvest, and then sailed further. In the third year of their voyage they reached the Pillars of Hercules (Gibraltar), and returned to Egypt with the intelligence, which Herodotus utterly discredits, that they had seen the sun in the north. This circumstance, alone, seems to be sufficient proof that the Egyptians really circumnavigated Africa.

The second attempt, of which we have a more particular description, was made by the Carthaginians, about the year 500 B. C., when the famous Admiral Hanno set out on his voyage of colonization, some account of which is preserved to us in the fragments of his *Periplus*. He sailed with sixty vessels, carrying three thousand colonists of both sexes, with a rich store of provisions and implements of labor. Coasting for two days southward from the Straits of Gibraltar, he founded the first colony, and built, upon a wooded headland near it, a stately temple to Neptune. Still further to the south,—but at what point we cannot now ascertain,—he found a large lake, frequented by elephants and other wild beasts, and, beyond this, founded four other colonies. Near this place the great river "Lixus," coming down from the Atlas mountains, emptied into the ocean.

After a further voyage of three days along a desert coast, he reached a bay with an island, and there established the last colony, which was named Cerne. He reckoned that its distance from the Pillars of Hercules was about the same as from that point to Carthage. From Cerne, as a starting-point, voyages of exploration were made still further to the south. They found great rivers, tenanted by the crocodile and the hippopotamus; savage negro tribes, partly clothed with the skins of beasts; great forests, from which flame arose at night, and where they heard the sound of cymbals and drums; and finally, on an island near the shore, strange, hairy creatures, resembling men, to which they gave the name of *gorillas*. These monsters fled as they approached, clambered upon the rocks and hurled stones upon the explorers. The latter captured three females, which were so ferocious that they were obliged to kill them; but their skins were sent to Carthage.

Modern geographers are divided in opinion as to the furthest point reached by Hanno, some limiting his explorations to the southern boundary of Morocco, while others extend them to the Bight of Benin. The evidence is tolerably conclusive that he must have penetrated as far, at least, as the Gambia River.

The next attempt was made about the year 130 B. C. by a Greek navigator, named Eudoxus. On his trading voyages to India he had seen the eastern coast of Africa, where it trends to the south-west, beyond Cape Gardafui; and he naturally imagined (being also familiar, probably, with the account of the Egyptian expedition given by Herodotus) that it might be but a short journey around the continent to Gibraltar. His plan was heartily encouraged by the merchants of Marseilles and Cadiz, then important trading-ports; two large vessels were furnished, and a crowd of volunteers offered themselves for the expedition. But the latter resisted the efforts of Eudoxus to sail at a safe distance from the land; they compelled him to keep near the coast, and the larger of the two vessels was soon stranded, as he had predicted. The crew and cargo were rescued, and from the fragments of the vessel he constructed a smaller one, with which he continued the voyage until he reached a tribe of people who apparently spoke the same language as those he had seen on the eastern coast. Here, however, he was obliged to return. He succeeded in fitting out a second expedition, but there is no record whatever of its results, and Eudoxus is only mentioned by Strabo as a fantastic adventurer—a Munchausen of the ancient times.

The knowledge of the eastern coast of Africa extended, as the commerce with India increased. The trade in ivory led the vessels which navigated the Red Sea ever further to the south, until, from the relations of Ptolemy, it seems probable that they reached the mouth of the Zambesi River, and may possibly have attained the southern extremity of the continent, without being aware of the discovery.

The trade in ivory, gold, and slaves, along the eastern coast, was kept up by the Arabs during the Middle Ages. There is a great deal of evidence to show that they had a regular intercourse with the regions of Zanzibar and Mozambique, which was afterward extended to Caffraria. Indeed, the intellectual superiority of the Kaffers over the other native tribes of South Africa, is attributed by some ethnologists to a mixture of Arabic blood. Their language still contains words of Arabic origin.

But the complete exploration of the African coast was reserved for Portugal. The rapid growth of Portuguese commerce, about the beginning of the fifteenth century, together with the wars with Morocco, which occasioned the sending out of naval expeditions, led to the rediscovery of the Canary Islands in 1420, and made the navigators familiar with the mainland, as far as Cape Bojador. This point was looked upon as one of the ends of the world; and when, in 1433, the intrepid Gilianez, sailed beyond it, his achievement excited almost as much wonder and enthusiasm as the great discovery of Columbus, sixty years afterwards.

In ten years more the Portuguese had reached

Cape Blanco, and made a settlement on an island near it. Furnished by the Pope with authority to possess themselves of all the lands beyond Cape Bojador, they very soon found the fertile regions of Senegal, and were stimulated by the double prospect of enriching themselves with gold-dust and ivory, and of extending their rule over new tribes, who must first, of course, be forcibly converted to Christianity. The death of Prince Henry the Navigator, whose interest in these undertakings had contributed so greatly to their success, checked the advance of exploration,—but only for a short time. Fernando Gomez was commissioned by the king to extend the line of explored coast one hundred miles a year, for five years, and thereby reached the Gold Coast in 1471. The island of Fernando Po was reached soon afterwards, and in 1484 Diego Cam sailed into the mouth of the great Congo River, established friendly relations with the kingdom of that name, and introduced Christianity. During nearly two centuries, Congo and Angola appeared to be thoroughly Christianized, but they have since relapsed into their former condition of pagan barbarism.

The line of Portuguese exploration was very gradually pushed southward, until Bartholomew Diaz first saw the great mountain-cape with which Africa fronts the Southern Ocean. Terrified by the stormy sky, the furious winds, and the great waves formed by the meeting of two strong ocean-currents, he turned back, naming the headland the Cape of Storms, and hastened with his shattered vessels to Portugal. The king, however, changed the name to the Cape of Good Hope, rightly believing that the ocean-road to India was at last found. In 1498 his belief was justified by Vasco de Gama, who doubled the dreaded Cape, followed the eastern coast to Mozambique and Melinda, and reached India.

The commercial spirit of the Portuguese, however, was only attracted by the regions on the eastern and western coasts of Africa, which supplied their trade in gold, ivory, and slaves. The extreme southern part of the continent, with its wild shores, bare plains, and savage Hottentot inhabitants, did not tempt them to colonize it. Their vessels on the voyage to and from India, occasionally touched at the Cape for fresh water and cattle, but they had little intercourse with the natives, except of a hostile character.

The Dutch, who had become, in the course of another century, the commercial rivals of the Portuguese in the Indies, were the first to perceive the importance of establishing a permanent station at the southern extremity of Africa, where their ships could find supplies on the long voyage to the East. In 1630, Van Riebeck built a fort on Table Bay, which was the first germ of the present Capetown. His only object was to establish a stopping-place for Dutch vessels, and the garrison took pains to conciliate the native tribes, since they found the intercourse exceedingly profitable. Little by little, however, the Dutch embraced in their claim the land surrounding the fort, began raising their own herds of cattle, cultivating the soil, and even forcibly making slaves of the natives. By the beginning of the last century they had obtained possession of several thousand miles of territory. The boundaries of this colony were subjected to constant attacks, but

CAPE TOWN.

the weaker races were wasted in the warfare, and slowly receded, as on our own western frontier.

After a time, farmers and mechanics began to emigrate from Holland to the settlement, and in 1685, many of the Huguenots who were driven from France, found their way thither. The discovery was made that a district near Capetown was remarkably favorable to the growth of the vine, and those vineyards were planted which have since then produced the famous Constantia wine. The growth of the colony, nevertheless, was restricted to the narrow belt of fertile country south of the mountain ranges, which cross South Africa in a line nearly parallel to its southern coast. The broad, barren table-land of the Karroo seemed to be a bar to settlement in that direction, and the great valley of the Orange River, beyond, had not then been discovered.

The Orange River was first discovered by Capt. Gordon, in 1777. The English, who had long cast covetous eyes upon the Cape-land, captured Capetown and the adjacent territory in 1795. Although they relinquished this acquisition in the Treaty of Amiens, they retook it in 1806, and held possession, until by the peace of 1815, they secured it permanently. Under their rule, the work of exploration went forward more rapidly, partly by means of adventurers who sought fields of future gain, and partly by the missionaries sent from Scotland. The course and extent of the Orange River was soon ascertained, and the land of the Bechuanas beyond, with its capital of Lattakoo, was reached in 1813 by the missionary John Campbell. The area of colonized territory was also slowly extended to the eastward and northward, and other towns were founded along or near the coast.

The Dutch population, who, after a century of settlement, had fallen into their own traditional habits of life, were greatly dissatisfied with the new rule. After the possession of the territory had been assured to England, officials were sent out who were ignorant of the condition and needs of the country, and whose chief aim was to enrich themselves as speedily as possible. The old order of things was roughly overturned: the natives were treated according to a different system, and finally, the abolition of Hottentot slavery, in in 1829, seemed to the *Boers* (farmers) a fatal blow to their prosperity. Moreover, those living on the frontier were forbidden to carry on their old warfare against the assaults of the savage tribes, yet no equivalent military protection was furnished to them.

All these causes of dissatisfaction led to a movement which, in the end, greatly hastened the exploration of Southern Africa. The Dutch farmers determined to withdraw themselves from English rule. They sold their cultivated farms to English settlers and speculators, often at a small fraction of their real value, equipped themselves for emigration, and in 1836 set out, several thousand in number, to seek a new home beyond the Orange River. They knew of the fertile regions stretching from the upper valley of that river towards Delagoa Bay on the eastern coast,—regions which had been almost entirely depopulated in the wars of the native tribes,—and also of nearer districts, on the eastern slopes of the Winterberg. As this great body of emigrants penetrated towards the north, they found few difficulties in their way; but those who turned eastward came into conflict with the fierce Kaffer tribes. In the following year, however, Prætorius, one of the Dutch leaders, defeated the Kaffer chief Dingaan, took possession of his land and organized the Free State of Natal. The Boers who had settled on the western slopes of the mountain chain formed a separate government, which they called the Republic of the Orange River.

The success of the Boers in establishing two independent States attracted the attention of the English Government, which determined to bring them again under its rule. From the circumstance that an English settlement had been made in Natal (although it was afterwards given up), the Government laid claim to the possession of that territory, appointed officials of all kinds, and sent them with ships of war to enforce their authority. The Dutch both protested and actively resisted, but they were finally overcome, some accepting the English rule, while others left their homes a second time and withdrew into the wilderness. In November, 1843, Natal was declared to be a British colony.

Soon afterwards, the English applied the same plan of annexation to the Orange River Republic, but the civil officers they sent to replace the republican government which the Dutch had established were immediately driven away. Then an armed force followed: the Dutch, under Prætorius, resisted, until, in August, 1848, at the battle of Boom-Plats, the latter were defeated with much slaughter. The same results followed, as in the case of Natal; some submitted to the conquering power, while others, with Prætorius at their head, wandered away to the north, crossed the Vaal River, the main branch of the Orange, took possession of the mountainous region, dividing its waters from those of the Limpopo, and founded that independent State which is now known as the Transvaal Republic.

In 1854 the English Government wisely decided to give up the Orange River sovereignty, as it was termed, and restore its independence to the little republic. Thus the heroic Boers, after their long wanderings and their desperate struggle for liberty to regulate their own affairs, were at last successful; but their subsequent history has been less favorable to their character. After the death of President Prætorius, the Transvaal Republic, in 1858, broke out into open hostility against that of Orange River; party hatred and jealousy seem to be as great in these little communities as in large nations, and at this day, although both have increased in population and prosperity, there has been little improvement in the character of their inhabitants, who are charged by the English with continual violence and cruelty towards the native tribes. It should be remembered, however, that the Dutch in South Africa, after an intercourse of a hundred and fifty years with the latter, cannot avoid retaining some of their characteristics. Their own development has been retarded, and they have been rendered less accessible to the influences of modern civilization. The recent discovery of the diamond fields, which lie chiefly within the territories of the two republics, and of the rich gold region beyond the Limpopo, will no doubt greatly hasten their growth, and gradually wear away the bitter mutual prejudice between them and their English neighbors.

The last fifty years, it will be seen, have contributed more to the opening of South Africa, as a home for civilized man, than the three centuries of Portuguese and Dutch rule, after the voyage of Vasco de Gama. The English colony of the Cape increases much more slowly than those in Australia, New Zealand, and other parts of the world, especially since communication with the latter colonies has been more speedily made by way of Suez and Panama; but its growth appears to be steady and healthy. It claims possession of the coast from Whale Bay around to Delagoa Bay on the east, and of the interior territory, with the exception of a few small Kaffer or Bushmen sovereignties. Capetown has become a stately, well-built place of 30,000 inhabitants, while Georgetown, Grahamstown, and Port Natal are all flourishing towns. The entire population of the colony is about 225,000.

The two Dutch republics open a communication far into the interior, and greatly facilitate its exploration. That of Orange River embraces the broad region between the upper valley of that river and its main tributary, the Vaal,—great plains of grass, broken with ridges of naked rock. It is a lofty, irregular table-land, with a healthy and equable climate. The Boers devote themselves principally to the raising of sheep and cattle on the plains; in the valleys nearer the mountains there are large plantations of grain and orchards of fruit. The capital of the republic, Bloemfontain, is a well-built town of about 200 houses, and 2,500 inhabitants; but the whole population of the republic is not much more than 20,000 at present, including 5,000 natives.

The territory of the Transvaal Republic is much more extensive. Towards the north it reaches the Limpopo River, but there is no fixed frontier, and it will probably be pushed onward towards the Zambesi, with the growth of the country. Commencing near the Vaal, with the same grassy plains as in the southern republic, the land rises into ranges of hills, between which lie broad valleys, with thickets, woods, and abundant streams. The soil is equally adapted for pasturage and tillage. On account of the greater mildness of the climate, all kinds of fruit, especially grapes and oranges, attain an unusual perfection. Beyond the mountains to the northward the climate becomes tropical and unhealthy, and the *tsetse*—that fly whose bite is fatal to cattle—is found. Of late years the cultivation of sugar and coffee has been successfully introduced, and the population somewhat increased by an immigration of farmers and herdsmen from Scotland; but it is still scanty, Potschefstrom, the capital, containing only about a thousand souls. Trade is carried on chiefly with the settlement on Delagoa Bay, which is a little nearer than Port Natal.

The discovery of diamond-fields and coal-mines in the Transvaal Republic, and of a gold region to the north of the Limpopo, promises to change the character of the country in a very short time. Indeed, these new sources of wealth have already given a fresh importance to South Africa, and will hasten the complete exploration of the regions first penetrated by Moffat, Anderson, and Livingstone.

CHAPTER II.

THE NATIVE TRIBES OF SOUTH AFRICA.

ALTHOUGH the various native tribes of Africa, from the Atlas to the Cape of Good Hope, possess so many common peculiarities of language and of physical structure, that they may be all classed as belonging to the same original stock, yet those which inhabit the southern end of the Continent exhibit many curious and interesting features. The influences of climate and habits of life have greatly modified their character and appearance, while they have remained in the same state of barbarism as the tropical tribes.

The primitive inhabitants of the Cape country were the Hottentots, who are still scattered over the whole colony, gradually diminishing like the Indians and Polynesians, through their intercourse with civilized races. The name "Hottentot," which was given to them by the early settlers, does not seem to belong to any particular tribe; the general designation which they use among themselves, is "Anaqua." They have long been held by the civilized world, and hardly with injustice, to be the very ideals of human ugliness, and some ethnologists place them lowest in the scale of races.

The pure-blooded Hottentot is a weak, dwarfish creature, rarely five feet high, with a spine so curved towards the base that it gives him a half-stooping attitude. His skull is flattened and retreating, and the head is sprinkled with little twists of short, thin wool, —a feature so comical, that it suggested to the Dutch settlers the nickname of "pepper-heads." The nose is so short and flat that it hardly can be called one, although the nostrils are very large, and the thick, projecting lips frequently cover one-third of the face. Nevertheless, their hands and feet are remarkably delicate and beautiful; full-grown Hottentots easily wear the gloves and shoes of European children of eight or nine years old.

The race is characterized by a peculiar and exceedingly disagreeable odor, so powerful that it may often be noticed in a room hours after a Hottentot has left it. For this reason they cannot be employed as house-servants, and all familiar intercourse with Europeans is prevented, except with the missionaries to whom such intercourse is a duty. As a natural consequence, the Hottentots are painted in very different colors by the latter and by English or Dutch colonists, the former affirming that the work of conversion and civilization is succeeding among them, while the settlers say that they are still lazy, dishonest, and attached to the lowest features of their former life.

The truth probably lies midway between these two representations. The Hottentot is good-natured, social, and fond of music; therefore capable of a certain degree of civilization. On the other hand, he is indolent, capricious, servile under force, and impudent under kindness. He is a child who requires a steady, strict, and humane discipline from the stronger race; but this is not to be expected from any colonial government.

A superior tribe, called the Griquas, has been produced from the mixture of the Hottentots with the early Dutch settlers. They formed, at first, a nomadic race; but about the beginning of this century took possession of the territory along the Orange River, and gradually attached themselves to the soil. The missionaries who had accompanied them in their wanderings taught them to add agriculture to cattle-raising, to establish themselves in villages, and organize a primitive system of government. The settlement has now a capital, Griqua City, and a population of more than 20,000, which is rapidly increasing.

The Griquas are taller and more vigorous than the Hottentots; their skin has a lighter color, and their hair is more abundant. They are comparatively steady and industrious, less given to drunkenness, and their condition is regularly, if slowly, improving. In their settlement of Philippolis, on a branch of the Orange River, they have churches and schools, and cultivate large wheat-farms. Those of the tribe who retain more of the Hottentot blood and character, wander with their herds of cattle over the less fertile districts to the north of the river, where they have partly affiliated themselves with another native tribe, the Koranas, who somewhat resemble them. The latter are also herdsmen, but cultivate maize, melons, and tobacco, and carry on a considerable trade with the Cape, in cattle, hides and ostrich-feathers. Their former propensity for war and plunder has been extinguished by the efforts of the missionaries who live among them.

The western coast of South Africa, on both sides of the Orange River, is called "Namaqua-Land," from the large tribe of the Namaquas—a branch of the original Hottentot race—who inhabit it. Their home is found in those great sandy plains, which extend far inland, dotted with small oases, where scanty springs of water appear or disappear, according to the season. The greater part of the territory belongs to the Cape Colony, but the Government exercises little or no authority over the Namaquas. They wander over the desert with their herds of dwarf cattle, said to be the smallest in the world, seeking the scanty tracts of pasturage. Sometimes there is no rain for four or five years, and they are then compelled to approach the more fertile regions to the eastward. The Namaquas are taller than the Hottentots, astonishingly lean, with strongly projecting cheek-bones, oblique eyes, and have little woolly knobs instead of hair. Their language is considered the purest of the Hottentot dialects.

The last and lowest branch of this race is the Bushmen, as they are called by the settlers, their own name being *Saab*. The Bushman seems to be the native African savage, whom even the ruder civilization of his neighbors has left untouched, one of the lowest, most miserable and persecuted of the races of men. His home is in those desolate tracts of country which all other tribes have rejected as unfit for habitation. There are plenty of these tracts scattered over South Africa, and the Bushmen may therefore be found from the Karroo, or the Snowy Mountains, in the south, to Lake Ngami in the north, ranging from

NAMAQUA MUSICIAN.

will or necessity over hundreds of miles of territory. Their condition was the same as at present when the Dutch landed in Table Bay: they were looked upon as savages and outlaws by their Hottentot relatives.

The Bushman is only 4 feet high, but rather symmetrical in form. His skin is jet-black, and only appears gray from its permanent coating of dust and ashes. His woolly hair hangs in short twists over his forehead and ears, and one of his greatest delights is to grease these twists and decorate them with feathers, shells, or pieces of bone. His clothing consists of a skin over the shoulders, and a thin leather girdle around the loins. His dwelling, whenever he happens to have one, is of the very simplest kind. He will sleep under a bush, in a hedge-hog's hole, beside an ant-hill, in the cleft of a rock; but sometimes he bends a few sticks in a semicircular form, fastens their ends in the earth, covers them with grass and creeps under them.

The language of the tribe, originally Hottentot, has become so changed in their wandering life that it now scarcely appears to be an articulate speech. It is a continual clucking of the tongue against the teeth or the roof of the mouth, mixed with snorts through the nose. For a long time it was supposed that the Bushmen were incapable of being improved, but many of them have learned the Dutch language, and their children have even been taught to read and write.

These savages live upon whatever they find in their way. They prefer beef, and are arrant robbers to obtain it: they shoot antelopes, gnus, hyenas, with small poisoned arrows; grasshoppers and worms are welcome to them, and even the desert supplies a variety of plants and roots which they eat raw. The Bushman wandering over the bare, burning sand, sees perhaps a single dried blade which no other eye than his own would detect; he thrusts his bony finger into the soil, scoops out a rough bulb, and eats it as a delicious morsel. When he has slain a large animal, he so fills himself that he can afterwards go without food for a week. This mode of life, however, soon exhausts his vital forces; he is old, withered and gray at the age of forty, if, indeed, the bullet of a settler or the lance of a Kaffer has not pierced him long before that age.

Not only the Dutch and English colonists, but every native tribe in South Africa, wage war upon the Bushmen. The latter, it is true, provoke this continual hostility by their thefts of cattle from the outlying settlements. In former times it was customary to organize expeditions for the pursuit and slaughter of the Bushmen, and even now, after all the efforts made by missionaries, by the Government and by private individuals, but very little change has been effected. Almost the only successful attempt to improve the condition of the tribe was made by one of the Bechuana chiefs, who collected a number of Bushmen together, gave them cattle and persuaded them to cultivate the soil. The descendants of these people, it is said, have entirely lost their nomadic instincts, and now resemble the other branches of the Hottentot race.

The eastern half of South Africa, and a portion of the central region, is mainly inhabited by a very different race of natives, all apparently related to each other, though now divided into distinct tribes, the Bechuanas, Bassutos, and the various branches of the Kaffers. The former inhabit the territory stretching from the upper waters of the Orange River northward to the Kalihari Desert and towards the Zambesi; the Bassutos live on the western slopes of the Dragon Mountains, and the Kaffers (where they have not been forced into the interior by English settlement) have possession of the eastern coast.

The Bechuanas have been made familiar to us by the missionary labors of Mr. Moffatt, one of the first and boldest explorers of the interior. They are a race superior to the Hottentots, both in physical structure and in their natural capacity for improvement. They live chiefly in *kraals*, or villages, cultivate the soil, and have a rude patriarchal form of government. Like their relatives, the Kaffers, they have produced many men of unusal energy and intelligence.

The region inhabited by the Bassutos was an unknown land thirty or forty years ago. The Griquas and Koranas gave the first intimation of the existence of the race, and the zealous missionaries, guided by them, set out for this new field of labor. The chief of the Bassutos, Moshesh, who is still living, sent word that he desired a visit from some of the "men of prayer," in the hope that he might be protected by them from the forays of the Griquas. After a long and wearisome journey up the Caledon River, one of the southern branches of the Orange, the missionaries saw at last the picturesque chain of the Dragon Mountains. The rolling and ascending table-land over which they had travelled gave way to a singularly wild and broken country. Isolated mountains, or masses of sandstone rock, five or six hundred feet in height, and sometimes several miles in circumference, studded the region; the vegetation was rich and strange, semi-tropical in character, and game was abundant. Between the peaks opened deep basins, or long, trough-like valleys, watered with beautiful streams.

They found the chief Moshesh at his residence of Thaba Bossiu, a singular table-mountain, which the Bassutos had made inaccessible to their enemies. Owing to the security of the place, the valley was partly cultivated, and the adjacent region was dotted with villages and herds. The rains, which fall regularly on the mountains from October to April, nourish a rich vegetation, and those wild people, under the direction of their heroic chief, had already begun the cultivation of wheat and fruits.

For a number of years the missionaries, who were French Protestants, worked among the Bassutos with encouraging success. The people learned to read and write, showed an unusual quickness of understanding, and were deeply impressed by the Bible narratives. Moshesh took the lead in these changes; the printing of the Bible in the native language was commenced, and there was every prospect of the complete conversion of the tribe, when the emigration of the Dutch Boers and the establishment of their Orange River Republic interrupted the good work. The Bassuto territory was invaded, wars arose, the English Government supported the petty chiefs in a revolt against Moshesh, the natives lost their faith in the efficacy of Christian

MOSHECH, CHIEF OF THE BASSUTOS

doctrines, and in four years had relapsed into worse than their former condition. Of late years the work has been resumed, since the establishment of a fixed boundary between the Boers and the Bassutos secures a season of peace.

The Bassutos, like the Bechuanas, are tall, strong, well-built, and often strikingly handsome in form, and quick and graceful in their movements. There is very little of the negro character in their faces, and some have the appearance of dark-brown Caucasians. They live in small straw-huts, shaped like bee-hives, and arranged in a circle, where their herds are kept at night. The chief's house stands alone, upon an elevated point, near which there is an inclosure where the elders of the village meet to discuss matters of general interest, decide disputes, and punish crimes. The people live almost entirely in the open air, only entering their huts when it rains, or in case of sickness. They have some mechanical skill, manufacturing their own knives, baskets, household implements, and even a kind of felt cloth. Like the Hottentots, they are lazy and thievish, the only employment which they relish being the herding of their cattle. The Bassuto will pass whole days sitting on his heels and talking with his neighbor, or smoking hemp until he is stupid, or lying on the ground in the sun, while his wife performs all the necessary household labors.

The old chief Moshesh, in 1859, visited the settlement of Aliwal, on Orange River, in order to pay his respects to Prince Alfred and Governor Grey. He was accompanied by three thousand Bassuto horsemen, five hundred of whom wore skins of lions and leopards. The wild war-dance which they performed must have been the most remarkable spectacle seen by the Prince on his voyage around the world. The old chief wore the European costume, with a high black hat and a heavy military cloak. On the top of his natural fortress of Thaba Bossiu he has built an English house, and filled it with modern furniture, but still lives in a little native hut, smears his body with a mixture of fat and red clay, and hangs around his neck every trinket which he can beg from a chance visitor.

The Kaffers—a name derived from the Arabic *kafir*, a heretic—inhabit all the country from the Snowy and Dragon Mountains to the Indian Ocean, while the same race is found between the Limpopo and the Zambesi Rivers, and, according to Livingstone, in the upper valley of that river. They are, in many respects, a remarkable race, showing a strange mixture of the native African and the Caucasian in their features, their habits of life and their intellectual qualities. For this reason some have conjectured that they are of mixed blood, produced—like the Griquas, in later times—by the intercourse of the Arabs with the natives of the eastern coast, during the Middle Ages. Although divided into many detached tribes, the essential characteristics of the race are found in all. Proud, independent, courageous, and dignified in their bearing, they form the strangest possible contrast with the Hottentots; and they have many natural virtues which might have carried them far towards civilization, but for the wars into which they have been plunged by the rapacity of the Dutch and English settlers. These wars have not only greatly diminished their numbers, but kept alive a feeling of implacable hatred towards the white race, which the missionaries have only mitigated, not subdued.

The Amakosa Kaffers, inhabiting the beautiful and fertile terraces of the eastern coast, furnish, perhaps, the best type of the race. Favored by soil and climate, they have developed an unusual degree of beauty and symmetry. Although their hair is woolly, and their lips and cheek-bones suggest the negro, the Caucasian character is predominant, both in the features and the form of the skull. The forehead indicates intelligence, and the aquiline nose and clear, brilliant eyes are thoroughly Semitic. These Kaffers are quick of apprehension, cunning, noble-minded and firm of character, yet cautious in manner, and with a certain expression of pride and reserve. Towards strangers their bearing is cold, almost contemptuous, and only slowly changes when their confidence has been secured. They are strong and active, and naturally averse to an indolent habit of life. Their activity, however, is rather manifested in war and the chase than in useful labor. In their public assemblies and debates they exhibit a genuine oratorical power, and the keenness and closeness of their reasoning is quite remarkable. They have both a local attachment, and a strong patriotic, or national, feeling, in which respect they differ favorably from almost all other native African tribes.

The Kaffers are herdsmen, without being nomads. The fortunate chara ter of the territory where they settled long ago, after having, according to their traditions, migrated from the north, gives them continual pastures, without changing their homes. The eastern coast of Africa, for a breadth of fifteen or twenty miles, is tropical: then it gradually rises to a height of 2,000 feet above the sea,—a broad table-land, warm yet temperate, with a soil which produces all varieties of grain and fruit; and finally, twenty miles further, there is a second elevation of 2,000 feet, beyond which there are grand forests, and inexhaustible pastures. On these rising plateaux the Kaffers have lived for centuries, developing a simple yet sufficient form of government, a rude religion, and a highly imaginative and picturesque literature.

The races of South Africa thus divide themselves into two families, the limits of which are tolerably well defined. A line drawn north and south, through the centre of this extremity of the continent, would leave the Hottentot tribes on the west and the Kaffer tribes on the east. By bearing in mind the peculiar characteristics of each, and their differences, the reader will more readily comprehend the difficulties which surrounded each special field of exploration.

TIABA BOSSIN.

CHAPTER III.

MOFFAT'S MISSIONARY JOURNEYS.

AS we have already indicated, the Protestant missionaries were really the first explorers of South Africa, for the exploration of the interior (beyond the discovery of the Orange River) did not commence until after the Cape Colony had passed into the hands of England. To comprehend how much those missionaries dared, in their zeal for the conversion of the native tribes, we must remember how the hostility between the Dutch Boers and the Hottentots, especially the Namaquas and Bushmen, had been confirmed by generations of warfare. It was a settled, chronic enmity, and the suspicion which it engendered could only be overcome by slow degrees.

The first missionaries sent to the Cape of Good Hope had, therefore, a far more serious task before them than the successors for whom they prepared the way. The patience, zeal and integrity of the Scotch character was admirably adapted to this arduous work, and in the annals of missionary enterprise there are no more deserving names than those of Campbell, Moffat, and Livingstone. The first of these greatly increased our knowledge of the native tribes, but did not accomplish a great deal in the way of exploration. Robert Moffat, who was sent out by the London Missionary Society in

1817, and labored steadily in the field for nearly forty years, then transferring his mantle to the shoulders of his son-in-law, Livingstone, was the first to penetrate into the unknown regions beyond the Orange River, as far as the Bamangwato Mountains, north of the headwaters of the Limpopo. His work, "Missionary Scenes and Labors in Southern Africa," published in London in 1842, is not a connected narrative of his journeys, but a series of incidents, observations and reflections, which, nevertheless, contains much geographical information that was new and valuable at the time.

Mr. Moffat's first years were spent in what is called Great Namaqua-land, on the western coast, north of the Orange River, a country of sand and stones, with a thinly-scattered population, always suffering from the lack of water. The region is traversed by the Fish and Oup Rivers and their tributaries—or, rather, the glowing beds wherein those rivers flow, when there happens to be any water. "Sometimes," he says, "for years together, they are not known to run; when, after the stagnant pools are dried up, the natives congregate to their beds and dig holes, or wells, in some instances to the depth of twenty feet from which they draw water, generally of a very inferior quality. They place branches of trees in the excavation, and with great labor, under a hot sun, hand up the water in a wooden vessel and pour it into an artificial trough, to which the panting, lowing herds approach, partially to satiate their thirst. Thunder-storms are eagerly anticipated, for by these only rain falls; and frequently these storms will pass over with tremendous violence, striking the inhabitants with awe, while not a single drop of rain descends to cool and fructify the parched waste.

"When the heavens let down their watery treasures, it is generally in a partial strip of country which the electric cloud has traversed, so that the traveller will frequently pass, almost instantaneously, from ground on which there is not a blade of grass, into tracts of luxuriant green, sprung up after a passing storm. Fountains are indeed few and far between, the best very inconsiderable, frequently very salt, and some of them hot springs, while the surrounding soil is generally so impregnated with saltpetre, as to crackle under the feet like hoar-frost, and it is with great difficulty that any kind of vegetable can be made to grow. Much of the country is hard and stony, interspersed with plains of deep sand. There is much granite, and quartz is so abundantly scattered, reflecting such a glare of light from the rays of the sun, that the traveller, if exposed at noonday, can scarcely allow his eyelids to be sufficiently open to enable him to keep his course."

The inhabitants of this region were the Namaqua branch of the Hottentots, who have already been described. Their chief at this time was a native named Africaner, who had been a slave to a Dutch farmer, but, having been treated with cruelty, murdered his master, led his tribe beyond the Orange River, and thenceforth made such forays into the colony that his very name had become a terror. He was victorious over all native enemies, successful over all the plots made to destroy him, and his power seemed to interpose an insurmountable obstacle to any further advance into the interior. The missionary, Campbell, however, conciliated his favor by a friendly letter; his colleague, Ebner, followed, and succeeded in converting Africaner and his family to Christianity.

On Moffat's arrival at the Cape, he found Mr. Ebner, who had just returned from Africaner's land, and he determined, at once, to accompany him thither. It was a proper beginning for his later labors. On approaching the northern borders of the Cape Colony, he says: "It was evident to me, that the farmers, who, of course, had not one good word to say of Africaner, were skeptical to the last degree about his reported conversion, and most unceremoniously predicted my destruction. One said he would set me up as a mark for his boys to shoot at; another that he would strip off my skin and make a drum of it to dance to; and another most consoling prediction was that he would make a drinking-cup of my skull. I believe they were serious, and especially a kind, motherly lady, who, wiping the tears from her eyes, bade me farewell, saying: 'Had you been an old man, it would have been nothing, for you must soon have died, whether or no; but you are young, and going to become a prey to that monster.'"

Moffat safely reached Africaner's village, but the people were reserved, suspicious and unfriendly. The chief did not immediately visit him, but when he had done so, and learned that Moffat had been sent out by the London Missionary Society, he expressed his satisfaction, and added that as he was a young man he hoped he should live long with him and his people. He then ordered a number of women to come, an attention which somewhat puzzled the missionary, until the women arrived, bearing bundles of native mats and long poles, like fishing-rods. Africaner pointed to a spot of ground, and said: "You must build there a house for the missionary." A circle was instantly formed, the women fixed the poles, tied them down in a hemispheric form, and covered them with mats, all ready for habitation, in the space of little more than half an hour.

Mr. Moffat confesses, however, that a Hottentot house is not very comfortable. "I lived," he says, "nearly six months in this native hut, which very frequently required tightening and fastening after a storm. When the sun shone, it was unbearably hot, when the rain fell, I came in for a share of it; when the wind blew I had frequently to decamp to escape the dust; and in addition to these little inconveniences, any hungry cur of a dog that wished a night's lodging, would force itself through the frail wall, and not unfrequently deprive me of my meal for the coming day; and I have more than once found a serpent coiled up in a corner. Nor were these all the contingencies of such a dwelling, for, as the cattle belonging to the village had no fold, I have been compelled to start up from a sound sleep, and try to defend myself and my dwelling from being crushed to pieces by the rage of two bulls which had met to fight a nocturnal duel."

It was soon evident that Africaner's conversion was as genuine as his limited intelligence would admit. He attended seriously to Mr. Moffat's instructions, treated him in the most friendly manner, and even, at times, manifested a sensibility in regard to moral impressions, which could hardly have been expected in one of his degraded race. "One day, when seated together," the missionary relates, "I happened, in absence of mind, to be gazing steadfastly on him. It arrested his attention, and he modestly inquired the cause. I replied, 'I was trying to picture to myself your carrying fire and sword through the country, and I could not think how eyes like yours could smile at human woe!' He answered not, but shed a flood of tears! He zealously seconded my efforts to improve the people in cleanliness and industry, and it would have made any one smile to have seen Africaner and myself superintending the school children, now about a hundred and twenty, washing themselves at the fountain."

The place which Africaner had selected for his village was not well adapted for a permanent habitation; so, accompanied by Moffat, he set out to examine the country to the northward. The record of this journey, however, relates rather to the natives than to the geographical character of the region. Failing to find the requisite supply of water, they returned, and we can only guess that they must have penetrated as far as the tropical line. Several months afterwards, Moffat undertook to visit the Griqua country, further up the Orange River, in the interest of Africaner, who was desirous of settling in some locality where his tribe could be permanently subsisted.

This second journey was successful in its object, but, before commencing the migration, Moffat found it necessary to visit Capetown, and he proposed that Africaner should accompany him. As a reward of a thousand dollars had been offered for the chief's head, both he and his people objected to the plan; since, although he might not be molested by the Government, he could hardly escape the vengeance of the colonists, through whose territory they must pass. It was finally arranged that Africaner should go in disguise, as Moffat's servant, and the latter set out on his return to civilization. He relates an interesting incident which occurred after reaching the settlements:

"On approaching the place, which was on an eminence, I directed my men to take the wagon to the valley below, while I walked towards the house. The farmer, seeing a stranger, came slowly down the descent to meet me. When within a few yards, I addressed him in the usual way, and stretching out my hand, expressed my pleasure at seeing him again. He put his hand behind him, and asked me, rather wildly, who I was. I replied that I was Moffat, expressing my wonder that he should have forgotten me. 'Moffat!' he rejoined, in a faltering voice; 'it is your *ghost!*' and moved some steps backward. 'I am no ghost,' I said. 'Don't come near me!' he exclaimed, 'you have been long murdered by Africaner.' 'But *I am* no ghost,' I said, feeling my hands, as if to convince him, and myself too, of my materiality; but his alarm only increased. 'Everybody says you were murdered, and a man told me he had seen your bones;' and he continued to gaze at me, to the no small astonishment of the good wife and children, who were standing at the door, as also to that of my own people, who were looking on from the wagon below. At length he extended his trembling hand, saying, 'When did you rise from the dead?'

"As he feared my presence would alarm his wife, we bent our steps towards the wagon, and Africaner was the subject of our conversation. I gave him in a few words my views of his present character, saying: 'He is now a truly good man,'—to which he replied: 'I can believe almost anything you say, but *that* I cannot credit.' By this time we were standing with Africaner at our feet; on his countenance sat a smile, he well knowing the prejudices of some of the farmers. The man closed the conversation by saying, with much earnestness, 'Well, if what you assert be true respecting that man, I have only one wish, and that is, to see him before I die; and when you return, as sure as the sun is over our heads, I will go with you to see him, though he killed my own uncle.' I was not before aware of this fact, and now felt some hesitation whether to discover to him the object of his wonder; but knowing the sincerity of the farmer and the goodness of his disposition, I said, 'This, then, is Africaner.' He started back, looking intensely at the man as if he had just dropped from the clouds. 'Are you Africaner?' he exclaimed. The chief arose, doffed his old hat, and making a polite bow, answered, 'I am.' The farmer seemed thunder-struck; but when, by a few questions, he had assured himself of the fact, that the former bugbear of the border stood before him, now meek and lamb-like in his whole deportment, he lifted up his eyes and exclaimed, 'O God, what a miracle of thy power! what cannot thy grace accomplish!' The kind farmer and his no less hospitable wife, now abundantly supplied our wants; but we hastened our departure lest the intelligence might get abroad that Africaner was with me, and bring unpleasant visitors."

On arriving at Capetown, Africaner was received with much kindness by the Governor, Lord Charles Somerset. His presence produced a great sensation among the people, who were only gradually convinced of the sincerity of his conversion; but at a public meeting, which was held for the purpose, he displayed a surprising familiarity with the Gospel narratives and teachings. This first success encouraged Mr. Moffat to continue his labors, and in 1821 he established himself at Kuruman, in the Bechuana country. He was forced to contend with great difficulties, on account of the lazy and thievish habits of the natives, and their indifference to instruction, unless it was accompanied by some material advantage. The vegetables, which the missionaries had raised with great labor, would be stolen from their gardens; their houses were pilfered during service on the Sabbath; and the conduct of even the converted natives was so careless and irreverent that the teachers were greatly discouraged. After five years of the greatest patience they had made so little impression on the minds of the people, that their position among them seemed as insecure as at the beginning. The incident which revealed this insecurity is a curious illustration of the superstitions of the Bechuanas.

"Years of drought had been severely felt," says Moffat, "and the natives, tenacious of their faith in the potency of a man, held a council, and passed resolutions to send for a rain-maker of renown from the Bahurutsi tribe, two hundred miles north-east of the Kuruman station. Rain-makers have always most honor among a strange people, and therefore they are generally foreigners. The heavens had been as brass,—scarcely a cloud had been seen for months, even on the distant horizon. Suddenly a shout was raised, and the whole town was in motion: the rain-maker was approaching. Every voice was raised to the highest pitch, with acclamations of enthusiastic joy. He had sent a harbinger to announce his approach, with peremptory orders for all the inhabitants to wash their feet. Every one seemed to fly in swiftest obedience to the adjoining river. Noble and ignoble, even the girl who attended to our kitchen-fire, ran; old and young ran; all the world could not have stopped them. By this time the clouds began to gather, and a crowd went out to welcome the mighty man, who, as they imagined, was now collecting in the heavens his stores of rain.

"Just as he was descending the height into the town, the immense concourse danced and shouted, so that the very earth rang, and at the same time the lightnings darted, and the thunders roared in awful grandeur. A few heavy drops fell, which produced the most thrilling ecstacy in the deluded multitude, whose shoutings baffled all description. Faith hung upon the lips of the impostor, while he proclaimed aloud that this year the women must cultivate gardens on the hills and not in the valleys, for the latter would be deluged. After the din had somewhat subsided, a few individuals came to our dwellings to treat us and our doctrines with derision. 'Where is your God?' one asked with a sneer. We were silent, because the wicked were before us. 'Have you not seen our

Morimo? Have you not beheld him cast from his arm the fiery spears, and rend the heavens? Have you not heard with your ears his voice in the clouds?' adding with an interjection of supreme disgust, 'You talk of Jehovah and Jesus, what can they do?' Never in my life do I remember a text being brought home with such power as the words of the Psalmist, 'Be still, and know that I am God : I will be exalted among the heathen.'

"The rain-maker found the clouds in our country rather harder to manage than those he had left. He complained that secret rogues were disobeying his proclamations. When urged to make repeated trials, he would reply, 'You only give me sheep and goats to kill, therefore I can only make goat-rain; give me fat slaughter-oxen, and I shall let you see ox-rain.' One day, as he was taking a sound sleep, a shower fell, on which one of the principal men entered his house to congratulate him, but to his utter amazement found him totally insensible to what was transpiring. 'Halloo, by my father! I thought you were making rain,' said the intruder; when the magician arising from his slumbers, and seeing his wife sitting on the floor, shaking a milk-sack, in order to obtain a little butter, to anoint her hair, he replied, pointing to the operation of churning, 'Do you not see my wife churning rain as fast as she can?' This reply gave entire satisfaction, and it presently spread through the length and breadth of the town, that the rain-maker had churned the shower out of a milk-sack. The moisture caused by this shower was dried up by a scorching sun; many long weeks followed without a single cloud, and when they did appear, they were sometimes seen, to the great mortification of the conjurer, to discharge their watery treasures at an immense distance.

"The rain-maker had recourse to numerous expedients and stratagems, and continued his performances for many weeks. All his efforts, however, proving unsuccessful, he kept himself very secluded for a fortnight, and, after cogitating how he could make his own cause good, he appeared in the public fold, and proclaimed that he had discovered the cause of the drought. All were now eagerly listening; he dilated some time, until he had raised their expectation to the highest pitch, when he revealed the mystery. 'Do you not see, when clouds come over us, that Hamilton and Moffat look at them?' This question receiving a hearty and unanimous affirmation, he added that our white faces frightened away the clouds, and they need not expect rain so long as we were in the country. This was a home-stroke, and it was an easy matter for us to calculate what the influence of such a charge would be on the public mind. We were very soon informed of the evil of our conduct, to which we plead guilty, promising that as we were not aware that we were doing wrong, being as anxious as any of them for rain, we would willingly look to our chins, or the ground all the day long, if it would serve their purpose. It was rather remarkable, that much as they admired my long black beard, they thought that in this case it was most to blame. However, this season of trial passed over to our great comfort, though it was followed for some time with many indications of suspicion and distrust."

For a number of years Mr. Moffat continued his missionary labors, gradually extending his journeys further into the interior. He made the acquaintance of the Barolong tribe, who live to the north of the Bechuana, among the Bawangwato Mountains, which divide the waters of the Orange River from the Kalihari Desert. His accounts of the character and customs of the native tribes are very thorough and complete; and if he gives us few geographical details, he at least opened the way for geographical explorers.

His account of the manner in which the conversion of the natives is preceded or accompanied by external signs, entirely corresponds with the later observations of Livingstone. "For a long period," he says, "when a man was seen to make a pair of trowsers for himself, or a woman a gown, it was a sure indication that we might expect additions to our inquirers. Abandoning the custom of painting the body, and beginning to wash with water, was with them what cutting off the hair was among the South-Sea islanders,—a public renunciation of heathenism. In the progress of improvement during the years which followed, and by which many individuals who made no profession of the Gospel were influenced, we were frequently much amused. A man might be seen in a jacket with but one sleeve, because the other was not finished, or he lacked material to complete it; another in a leathern or duffle jacket, with the sleeves of different colors, or of fine printed cotton. Gowns were seen like Joseph's coat of many colors, and dresses of such fantastic shapes as were calculated to excite a smile in the gravest of us."

In the course of time the missionary stations were pushed as far as the village of Kolobeng, on the headwaters of the Limpopo, in Lat. 24° S., and consequently near the tropical line. The unknown territory to the north-east of this point, lying between the Limpopo and Zambesi rivers, was inhabited by the Matsebele, a branch of the Kaffers, whose chief, Mosilikatse, had acquired great renown through South Africa, carrying his hostile inroads in all directions, even as far as the Orange River. In 1829 two messengers of the chief visited the country of the Bechuanas, and Mr. Moffat determined to accompany them on their return. It was a hazardous journey, but the intrepid missionary was not to be turned aside from his purpose. On the way, he fell in with a tribe of natives which no white man had ever before seen.

On reaching the first cattle outposts of the Matsebele tribe, they encamped beside a fine rivulet. "My attention," says Mr. Moffat, "was arrested by a beautiful and gigantic tree, standing in a defile leading into an extensive and woody ravine, between a high range of mountains. Seeing some individuals employed on the ground under its shade, and the conical points of what looked like houses in miniature protruding through its evergreen foliage, I proceeded thither, and found that the tree was inhabited by several families of Bakones, the aborigines of the country. I ascended by the notched trunk, and found, to my amazement, no less than seventeen of these aerial abodes, and three others unfinished. On reaching the topmost hut, about thirty feet from the ground, I entered and sat down. Its only furniture was the hay which covered the floor, a spear, a spoon, and a bowl-full of locusts. Not having eaten anything that day, and, from the novelty of my situation, not wishing to return immediately to the wagons, I asked a woman, who sat at the door with a babe at her breast, permission to eat. This she granted with pleasure, and soon brought me more, in a powdered state. Several more females came from the neighboring roosts, stepping from branch to branch to see the stranger, who was as great a curiosity to them as the tree was to him. I then visited the different abodes, which were on several principal branches. The structure of these houses was very simple. An oblong scaffold, about seven feet wide, is formed of straight sticks; on one end of this platform a small cone is formed, also of straight sticks, and thatched with grass. A person can nearly stand upright in it; the diameter of the floor is about six feet. The house stands on the end of the oblong, so as to leave a little square space before the door. On the day previous I had passed several villages, some containing forty houses, all built on poles about seven or eight feet from the ground, in the form of a circle; the ascent and descent are by a knotty branch of a tree placed in front of the house. In the centre of the circle there is always a heap of the bones of the game they have killed. Such were the domiciles of the impoverished thousands of the aborigines of the country, who, having been scattered and peeled by Mosilikatse, had neither herd nor stall, but subsisted on locusts, roots, and the chase. They adopted this mode of architecture to escape the lions which abound in that country."

Mr. Moffat was kindly received by the chief, Mosilikatse, who patiently listened to his instructions, but does not appear to have profited by them. He returned in safety to the Bechuana country, and finally, in the years 1837 and 1838, had the satisfaction of seeing a great and wide-spread movement among the natives to adopt Christianity and accustom themselves to settled and industrious habits of life.

More than any other man, Mr. Moffat opened the interior of South Africa, from the Orange River to the tropical line, and when he relaxed from his long and arduous task, there was another ready to take it up and carry it so far that we may safely say that no other individual has contributed so much to our knowledge of the unknown interior of Africa. This man, who took Moffat's daughter as his wife, and made her the companion of his first journeys of exploration, was David Livingstone.

HIPPOPOTAMUS TRAP.

CHAPTER IV.

LIVINGSTONE'S DISCOVERY OF LAKE NGAMI.

DR. LIVINGSTONE, in the opening chapter of his "Travels and Researches in South Africa," gives an interesting description of his youth, and the manner in which he educated himself for the missionary field, not then anticipating a life of discovery. His father was a small tradesman in a village near Glasgow, and his own early years were spent in a cotton factory, where he acquired the scanty means which were necessary for a limited education. He studied Latin at night, read all books upon which he could lay his hands, preferring scientific works and books of travel, and finally, having been brought up by his parents under strict religious influences, determined to qualify himself for the office of missionary among the Chinese.

While working as a cotton-spinner, at the age of nineteen, he contrived to carry on his studies in Greek, divinity and medicine, and without aid from any one succeeded in graduating in the latter branch. At this time some friends advised him to apply to the London Missionary Society, on account of its unsectarian character. The opium war, which was then raging, interfered with his original plan of going to China, and, after having been accepted by the London Society, and prepared himself still further by a course of theology in England, he was induced to look upon South Africa as the field of his future labors. In 1840 he sailed from England, a young man of twenty-two, full of health, strength, hope, and courage.

The general instructions which he received from the Directors of the London Missionary Society led him, as soon as he had reached Kuruman, which was then their farthest inland station from the Cape, to turn his attention to the regions lying north of that point. He therefore lost no time in visiting the Bakwain country and making the acquaintance of the chief Sechele. The result of this trip was that he established himself in a spot, fifteen miles from the chief's residence; and there, in order to obtain an accurate knowledge of the language, cut himself off from all European society for six months. He thus gained an insight into the habits, ways of thinking, laws and language of that section of the Bechuanas called Bakwains, which proved to be of incalculable advantage in his later travels. During a journey to the north in 1842, he was, without knowing it, within ten days of the waters flowing into Lake Ngami, and might then have discovered that lake, if discovery had been his object.

Having finally selected the beautiful valley of Mabotsa (in Lat. 25° 14' S.) as the site of a new missionary station, he settled there in 1843. Here an occurrence took place, which came near putting an end to his adventurous career. The neighborhood was infected with lions, which even attacked the herds of the natives in open day. This was so unusual an occurrence that the people believed they were bewitched, that is, given into the power of the lions by a neighboring tribe. What followed must be given in Livingstone's own words:

"It is well known that if one of a troop of lions is killed, the others take the hint and leave that part of the country. So, the next time the herds were attacked, I went with the people, in order to encourage them to rid themselves of the annoyance by destroying one of the marauders. We found the lions on a small hill about a quarter of a mile in length, and covered with trees. A circle of men was formed round it, and they gradually closed up, ascending pretty near to each other. Being down below on the plain with a native schoolmaster, named Mebálwe, a most excellent man, I saw one of the lions sitting on a piece of rock within the now closed circle of men. Mebálwe fired at him before I could, and the ball struck the rock on which the animal was sitting. He bit at the spot struck, as a dog does at a stick or stone thrown at him; then leaping away, broke through the opening circle and escaped unhurt. The men were afraid to attack him, perhaps on account of their belief in witchcraft. When the circle was re-formed, we saw two other lions in it; but we were afraid to fire lest we should strike the men, and they allowed the beasts to burst through also. If the Bakatla had acted according to the custom of the country, they would have speared the lions in their attempt to get out. Seeing we could not get them to kill one of the lions, we bent our footsteps toward the village; in going round the end of the hill, however, I saw one of the beasts sitting on a piece of rock as before, but this time he had a little bush in front. Being about thirty yards off, I took a good aim at his body through the bush, and fired both barrels into it. The men then called out, 'He is shot, he is shot!' Others cried, 'He has been shot by another man too; let us go to him!' I did not see any one else shoot at him, but I saw the lion's tail erected in anger behind the bush, and, turning to the people, said, 'Stop a little, till I load again.' When in the act of ramming down the bullets, I heard a shout. Starting, and looking half round, I saw the lion just in the act of springing upon me. I was upon a little height; he caught my shoulder as he sprang, and we both came to the ground below together. Growling horribly close to my ear, he shook me as a terrier dog does a rat. The shock produced a stupor similar to that which seems to be felt by a mouse after the first shake of the cat. It caused a sort of dreaminess, in which there was no sense of pain nor feeling of terror, though quite conscious of all that was happening. It was like what patients partially under the influence of chloroform describe, who see all the operation, but feel not the knife. This singular condition was not the result of any mental process. The shake annihilated fear, and allowed no sense of horror in looking round at the beast. This peculiar state is probably produced in all animals killed by the carnivora; and if so, is a merciful provision by our benevolent Creator for lessening the pain of death. Turning round to relieve myself of the weight, as he had one paw on the back of my head, I saw his eyes directed to Mebálwe, who was trying to shoot him at a distance of ten or fifteen yards. His gun, a flint one, missed fire in both

LIVINGSTONE ATTACKED BY A LION.

barrels; the lion immediately left me, and, attacking Mebálwe, bit his thigh. Another man, whose life I had saved before, after he had been tossed by a buffalo, attempted to spear the lion while he was biting Mebálwe. He left Mebálwe and caught this man by the shoulder, but at that moment the bullets he had received took effect, and he fell down dead. The whole was the work of a few moments, and must have been his paroxysms of dying rage. In order to take out the charm from him, the Bakatla on the following day made a huge bonfire over the carcass, which was declared to be that of the largest lion they had ever seen. Besides crunching the bone into splinters, he left eleven teeth wounds on the upper part of my arm.

"A wound from this animal's tooth resembles a gun-shot wound; it is generally followed by a great deal of sloughing and discharge, and pains are felt in the part periodically ever afterward. I had on a tartan jacket on the occasion, and I believe that it wiped off all the virus from the teeth that pierced the flesh, for my two companions in this affray have both suffered from the peculiar pains, while I have escaped with only the inconvenience of a false joint in my limb. The man whose shoulder was wounded showed me his wound actually burst forth afresh on the same month of the following year. This curious point deserves the attention of inquirers."

Livingstone was as successful with the chief Sechele as Moffat had been with Africaner. He converted him and his family, and acquired so much influence with the people, that he persuaded them to settle upon the Kolobeng River, and cultivate the soil. For years the colony was visited by a terrible drought, and annoyed by the hostility of the Boers of the Transvaal Republic, who were now their near neighbors, and who retained their old habits of compelling the natives to labor for them without pay. Livingstone's endeavors to protect the people only brought upon himself the jealousy and enmity of the Boers, who finally devastated the settlement at Kolobeng and plundered his house, during his absence in 1852.

The projected journey into the Kalihari Desert, and the search for the great lake Ngami, accounts of which had been received from the natives long before, was delayed for some years by these troubles. The Bechuanas, also, had a superstitious terror of the desert, and it was not easy to induce them to accompany the expedition. But early in 1849, two English gentlemen, Messrs. Oswell and Murray, offered to join Livingstone, and he immediately made preparations for the journey. He had married the daughter of Moffat some years before, and determined to take his wife and children with him. It was a fortunate circumstance, that, while they were preparing, a party of natives from the neighborhood of the lake came to Kolobeng, with an invitation to Livingstone from their chief.

The party started on the 1st of June, and after travelling five or six days towards the Bamangwato Mountains, struck off northward into the Kalihari Desert. This is not a sandy region, destitute of vegetable and animal life, for it is covered with grass and a great variety of creeping plants; besides which there are large patches of bushes, and even trees. It is flat, but occasionally crossed by the beds of ancient rivers, and the abundant grass supports immense herds of antelopes, who require little or no water. The number of tuberous-rooted plants is very great, and many varieties of them supply both food and drink to the wandering tribes. One of these, indicated on the surface only by a thin, grass-like blade, has a root the size of a child's head, at the depth of eighteen inches; the rind is filled with a cool, juicy pulp, with a flavor like that of a turnip. After rains, great tracts of the desert are covered with wild watermelons and scarlet cucumbers, some of which are intensely bitter and poisonous, while others are entirely sweet and wholesome.

At a station called Seroti, the travellers were obliged to dig trenches in the soil, and wait until they slowly filled with water for their oxen, since there was a waterless tract, seventy miles in breadth, to be crossed. But the soil was sandy, and the progress of the wagons very slow; at the end of three days they had only made forty-four miles. The horses were sent in advance with some natives, but the latter lost their way, and rejoined the thirsty caravan. From this state of suffering they were relieved by the discovery of a pool of rain-water, and soon afterwards reached the dry bed of a river named Mokoko. They again lost their way, and were guided to a watering-place by a lonely Bushwoman whom they found in the desert. Beyond this they crossed saline plains, where the mirage constantly cheated them into the belief that they had found Lake Ngami, although it was still three hundred miles distant.

On the 4th of July they reached the Zouga River, which flowed in a north-easterly direction. The natives assured them that the water came from the lake. Here two men of the Bamangwato tribe, who had accompanied them, started in advance, up the river, circulating reports among the natives that the object of the strangers was to plunder them. This might have occasioned much difficulty, had not one of the men been stricken with fever, and soon died. The people connected his death in some way with the fact that he was trying to injure the strangers, and, although they were armed at first, they soon became friendly and confiding.

"When we had gone up the bank of this beautiful river about ninety-six miles from the point where we first struck it," says Livingstone, "and understood that we were still a considerable distance from the Ngami, we left all the oxen and wagons, except Mr. Oswell's, which was the smallest, and one team, at Ngabisáne, in the hope that they would be recruited for the home journey, while we made a push for the lake. The Bechuana chief of the Lake region, who had sent men to Sechele, now sent orders to all the people on the river to assist us, and we were received by the Bakóba, whose language clearly shows that they bear an affinity to the tribes in the north. They call themselves Bayeiye, *i. e.*, men; but the Bechuanas call them Bakoba, which contains somewhat of the idea of slaves. They have never been known to fight, and indeed have a tradition that their forefathers, in their first essays at war, made their bows of the Palma Christi, and, when these broke, they gave up fighting altogether. They have invariably submitted to the rule of every horde which has overrun the countries adjacent to the rivers on which they specially love to dwell. They are thus the Quakers of the body politic in Africa.

"The canoes of these inland sailors are truly primitive craft: they are hollowed out of the trunks of single trees by means of iron adzes; and if the tree has a bend, so has the canoe. I liked the frank and manly bearing of these men, and, instead of sitting in the wagon, preferred a seat in one of the canoes. I found they regarded their rude vessels as the Arab does his camel. They have always fires in them, and prefer sleeping in them while on a journey to spending the night on shore. 'On land you have lions,' say they, 'serpents, hyænas, and your enemies; but in your canoe, behind a bank of reed, nothing can harm you.' Their submissive disposition leads to their villages being frequently visited by hungry strangers. We had a pot on the fire in the canoe by the way, and when we drew near the villages devoured the contents. When fully satisfied ourselves, I found we could all look upon any intruders with perfect complacency, and show the pot in proof of having devoured the last morsel.

"Twelve days after our departure from the wagons at Ngabisane we came to the north-east end of Lake Ngami; and on the 1st of August, 1849, we went down together to the broad part, and, for the first time, this fine looking sheet of water was beheld by Europeans. The direction of the lake seemed to be N.N.E. and S.S.W. by compass. The southern portion is said to bend round to the west, and to receive the Teoughe from the north at its northwest extremity. We could detect no horizon where we stood looking S.S.W., nor nor could we form any idea of the extent of the lake, except from the reports of the inhabitants of the district; and, as they profess to go round it in three days, allowing twenty-five miles a day would make it seventy-five, or less than seventy geographical miles in circumference. Other guesses have been made since as to its circumference, ranging between seventy and one hundred miles. It is shallow, for I subsequently saw a native punting his canoe over seven or eight miles of the north-east end; it can never, therefore, be of much value as a commercial highway. In fact, during the months preceding the annual supply of water from the north, the lake is so shallow that it is with difficulty cattle can approach the water through the boggy, reedy banks. These are low on all sides, but on the west there is a space devoid of trees, showing that the waters have retired thence at no very ancient date. This is another of the proofs of desiccation met with so abundantly throughout the whole country. A number of dead trees lie on this space, some of them imbedded in the mud, right in the water. We were informed by the Bayeiye, who live on the lake, that when the annual inundation begins, not only trees of great size, but antelopes, are swept down by its rushing waters; the trees are gradually driven by the the winds to the opposite side, and become imbedded in mud.

"The water of the lake is perfectly fresh when full, but brackish when low; and that coming down the Tamunakle we found to be so clear, cold, and soft, the higher we ascended, that the idea of melting snow was suggested to our minds. We found this region, with regard to that from which we had come, to be clearly a hollow, the lowest point being Lake Kumadau; the point of the ebullition of water, as shown by one of Newman's barometric thermometers, was only between $207\frac{1}{2}°$ and $206°$, giving an elevation of not much more than two thousand feet above the level of the sea. We had descended above two thousand feet in coming to it from Kolobeng. It is the southern and lowest part of the great river system beyond, in which large tracts of country are inundated annually by tropical rains.

"My chief object in coming to the lake was to visit Sebituane, the great chief of the Makololo, who was reported to live some two hundred miles beyond. We had now come to a half-tribe of the Bamangwato, called Batauana. Their chief was a young man named Lechulatebe. Sebituane had conquered his father Morémi, and Lechulatebe received part of his education while a captive among the Bayeiye. His uncle, a sensible man, ransomed him; and, having collected a number of families together, abdicated the chieftainship in favor of his nephew. As Lechulatebe had just come into power, he imagined that the proper way of showing his abilities was to act directly contrary to everything that his uncle advised. When we came, the uncle recommended him to treat us handsomely, therefore the hopeful youth presented us with a goat only. It ought to have been an ox. So I proposed to my companions to loose the animal and let him go, as a hint to his master. They, however, did not wish to insult him. I, being more of a native, and familiar with their customs, knew that this shabby present was an insult to us. We wished to purchase some goats or oxen; Lechulatebe offered us elephants' tusks. 'No, we cannot eat these; we want something to fill our stomachs.' 'Neither can I; but I hear you white men are all very fond of these bones, so I offer them; I want to put the goats into my own stomach.' A trader, who accompanied us, was then purchasing ivory at the rate of ten good large tusks for a musket worth thirteen shillings. They were called 'bones;' and I myself saw eight instances in which the tusks had been left to rot with the other bones where the elephant fell. The Batauana never had a chance of a market before; but, in less than two years after our discovery, not a man of them could be found who was not keenly alive to the great value of the article.

"On the day after our arrival at the lake, I applied to Lechulatebe for guides to Sebituane. As he was much afraid of that chief, he objected, fearing lest other white men should go thither also, and give Sebituane guns; whereas, if the traders came to him alone, the possession of fire-arms would give him such a superiority, that Sebituane would be afraid of him. It was in vain to explain that I would inculcate peace between them—that Sebituane had been a father to him and Sechele, and was as anxious to see me, as he, Lechulatebe, had been. He offered to give me as much ivory as I needed without going to that chief; but when I refused to take any, he unwillingly consented to give me guides. Next day, however, when Oswell and I were prepared to start, with the horses only, we received a senseless refusal; and like Sekomi, who had thrown obstacles in our way, he sent men to Bayeiye with orders to refuse us a passage across the river. Trying hard to form a raft at a narrow part, I worked many hours in the water; but the dry wood was so worm-eaten that it would not bear the weight of a single person. I was not then aware of the number of alligators which exist in the Zouga, and never think of my labor in the water, without feeling thankful that I escaped their jaws. The season was now far advanced; and as Mr. Oswell, with his wonted generous feelings, volunteered, on the spot, to go down to the Cape and bring up a boat, we resolved to make our way south again."

The Makololo tribe, of which Livingstone speaks, were destined to play a very important part in his later explorations. Although disappointed in his first attempt to visit them, he had at least found a practicable way by which the interior of the continent might be reached. The discovery of Lake Ngami was received in Europe with great interest, and this success encouraged the London Missionary Society to employ Livingstone thenceforth in that work of exploration, which must, to some extent, precede the labors of the missionary. The immense numbers of elephants, also, which the travellers found on descending the Zouga River, drew the attention of sportsmen and traders to this region, and hastened the opening of the entire region to the southward and westward of the lake.

The return journey was accomplished without accident, and the party reached Kolobeng towards the close of the year 1849.

CHAPTER V.

LIVINGSTONE'S FIRST JOURNEY TO THE ZAMBESI.

IN April, 1850, Livingstone again left Kolobeng with his wife, three children, and the chief Sechele, their object being to cross the Zouga at its lower end, follow the northern bank until they reached the other river, and then ascend the latter until they should find the Makololo country. The journey was prosecuted without much difficulty until, at the confluence of the Zouga with the Tamunakle, the appearance of the fly called *tsetse* obliged them to cross the former river in order to save their oxen. Here Livingstone learned that a party of Englishmen, who had come to the lake in search of ivory, were lying ill of fever, and turned aside for a time to take care of them.

The result of the undertaking, which promised so favorably, up to the last moment, will be best given in Livingstone's own words: "Sechele used all his powers of eloquence with Lechulatebe to induce him to furnish guides that I might be able to visit Sebituane on ox-back, while Mrs. Livingstone and the children remained at Lake Ngami. He yielded at last. I had a very superior London-made gun, the gift of Lieutenant Arkwright, on which I placed the greatest value, both on account of the donor and the impossibility of my replacing it. Lechulatebe fell violently in love with it, and offered whatever number of elephants' tusks I might ask for it. I, too, was enamored with Sebituane; and as he promised in addition that he would furnish Mrs. Livingstone with meat all the time of my absence, his arguments made me part with the gun. Though he had no ivory at the time to pay me, I felt the piece would be well spent on those terms, and delivered it to him. All being ready for our departure, I took Mrs. Livingstone about six miles from the town, that she might have a peep at the broad part of the lake. Next morning we had other work to do than part, for our little boy and girl were seized with fever. On the day following, all our servants were down, too, with the same complaint. As nothing is better in these cases than change of place, I was forced to give up the hope of seeing Sebituane that year; so, leaving my gun as part payment for guides next year, we started for the pure air of the Desert.

"Some mistake had happened in the arrangement with Mr. Oswell, for we met him on the Zouga on our return, and he devoted the rest of this season to elephant-hunting, at which the natives universally declare he is the greatest adept that ever came into the country. He hunted without dogs. It is remarkable that this lordly animal is so completely harassed by the presence of a few yelping curs, as to be quite incapable of attending to man. He makes awkward attempts to crush them by falling on his knees; and sometimes places his forehead against a tree ten inches in diameter; glancing on one side of the tree and then on the other, he pushes it down before him, as if he thought thereby to catch his enemies. The only danger the huntsman has to apprehend is the dogs running toward him, and thereby leading the elephant to their master. Mr. Oswell has been known to kill four large old male elephants a day. The value of the ivory in these cases would be one hundred guineas. We had reason to be proud of his success, for the inhabitants conceived from it a very high idea of English courage; and when they wished to flatter me, would say, 'If you were not a missionary you would just be like Oswell; you would not hunt with dogs either.' When, in 1852, we came to the Cape, my black coat eleven years out of fashion, and without a penny of salary to draw, we found that Mr. Oswell had most generously ordered an outfit for the half-naked children, which cost about £200, and presented it to us, saying he thought Mrs. Livingstone had a right to the game of her own preserves.

"Foiled in this second attempt to reach Sebituane, we returned again to Kolobeng, whither we were soon followed by a number of messengers from that chief himself. When he heard of our attempts to visit him, he dispatched three detachments of his men with thirteen brown cows to Lechulatebe, thirteen white cows to Sekomi, and thirteen black cows to Sechele, with a request to each to assist the white men to reach him. Their policy, however, was to keep him out of view, and act as his agents in purchasing with his ivory the goods he wanted. This is thoroughly African; and that continent being without friths and arms of the sea, the tribes in the centre have always been debarred from European intercourse by its universal prevalence among all the people around the coasts."

Setting out for the third time with his family and Mr. Oswell, Livingstone reached the last wells in the neighborhood of the Zouga River, and then, instead of turning westward towards Lake Ngami, as on the first and second journeys, pushed on in a northern course towards the Makololo country, guided by a Bushman who knew the way. They entered upon a hot, level region, studded with glittering deposits of salt, where all the springs were more or less brackish. After several days of weary travel, they reached a place called "The Links" by the natives, where they found a number of wells of fresh water. Here there was a settlement of Bushmen, of taller stature and darker color than those of the Kalihari Desert.

One of these Bushmen, named Shobo, consented to be their guide over the unknown waste between those springs and the land of Shebituane, the Makalolo chief. Nevertheless, he informed them that they would not reach water again in less than a month. Yet by a species of Providence, in a very short time they came upon a number of pools of rain-water. "It is impossible," says Livingstone, "to convey an idea of the dreary scene on which we entered after leaving this spot. The only vegetation was a low scrub in deep sand; not a bird or insect enlivened the landscape. It was, without exception, the most uninviting prospect I ever beheld; and, to make matters worse, our guide Shobo wandered on the second day. We coaxed him on at night, but he went to all points of the compass on the trails of elephants which had been here in the rainy season, and then would sit down in the path, and in his broken Sichuána say, 'No water, all country only; Shobo sleeps; he breaks down; country only;' and then coolly curl himself up and go to sleep. The oxen were terribly fatigued and thirsty; and on the morning of the fourth day, Shobo, after professing ignorance of everything, vanished altogether. We went on in the direction in which we last saw him, and about eleven o'clock began to see birds; then the trail of a rhinoceros. At this we unyoked the oxen, and they, apparently knowing the sign, rushed along to find the water in the River Mahábe, which comes from the Tamunakle, and lay to the west of us. The supply of water in the wagons had been wasted by one of our servants, and by the afternoon only a small portion remained for the children. This was a bitterly anxious night; and next morning the less there was of water, the more thirsty the little rogues became. The idea of their perishing before our eyes was terrible. It would almost have been a relief to me to have been reproached with being the entire cause of the catastrophe; but not one syllable of upbraiding was uttered by their mother, though the tearful eye told the agony within. In the afternoon of the fifth day, to our inexpressible relief, some of the men returned with a supply of that fluid of which we had never before felt the true value.

"The cattle, in rushing along to the water in the Mahábe, probably crossed a small patch of trees containing *tsetse*, an insect which was shortly to become a perfect pest to us. Shobo had found his way to the Bayeiye, and appeared, when we came up to the river, at the head of a party; and, as he wished to show his importance before his friends, he walked up boldly and commanded our whole calvalcade to stop, and to bring forth fire and tobacco, while he coolly sat down and smoked his pipe. It was such an inimitably natural way of showing off, that we all stopped to admire the acting, and, though he had left us previously in the lurch, we all liked Shobo, a fine specimen of that wonderful people, the Bushmen."

The next day they came to the village of a new tribe, called the Banajoa. Their huts were built on poles, and fires were kindled under them during the night, to drive away the musquitos which abound in the country. But a more dangerous scourge was the *tsetse*, which now began to attack their cattle. It is thus described: "It is not much larger than the common house-fly, and is nearly of the same brown color as the common honey-bee; the after part of the body has three or four yellow bars across it; the wings project beyond this part considerably, and it is remarkably alert, avoiding most dextrously all attempts to capture it with the hand at common temperatures; in the cool of the mornings and evenings it is less agile. Its peculiar buzz when once heard can never be forgotten by the traveller whose means of locomotion are domestic animals; for it is well known that the bite of this poisonous insect is certain death to the ox, horse, and dog. In this journey, though we were not aware of any great number having at any time lighted on our cattle, we lost forty-three fine oxen by its bite. We watched the animals carefully, and believe that not a score of flies were ever upon them.

"A most remarkable feature in the bite of the *tsetse* is its perfect harmlessness in man and wild animals, and even calves, so long as they continue to suck the cows. We never experienced the slightest injury from them ourselves, personally, although we lived two months in their *habitat*, which was in this case as sharply defined as in many others, for the south bank of the Chobe was infested by them, and the northern bank, where our cattle were placed, only fifty yards distant, contained not a single specimen. This was the more remarkable, as we often saw natives carrying over raw meat to the opposite bank with many *tsetse* settled upon it.

"The mule, ass, and goat enjoy the same immunity from the *tsetse* as man and the game. Many large tribes on the Zambesi can keep no domestic animals except the goat, in consequence of the scourge existing in their country. Our children were frequently bitten, yet suffered no harm; and we saw around us numbers of zebras, buffaloes, pigs, pallahs, and other antelopes, feeding quietly in the very habitat of the *tsetse*, yet as undisturbed by its bite as oxen are when they first receive the fatal poison. There is not so much difference in the natures of the horse and zebra, the buffalo and ox, the sheep and antelope, as to afford any satisfactory explanation of the phenomenon. Is a man not as much a domestic animal as a dog? The curious feature in the case, that dogs perish though fed on milk, whereas the calves escape so long as they continue sucking, made us imagine that the mischief might be produced by some plant in the locality, and not by *tsetse;* but Major Vardon, of the Madras Army, settled that point by riding a horse up to a small hill infested by the insect without allowing him time to graze, and though he only remained long enough to take a view of the country, yet in ten days afterwards the horse was dead."

Crossing a marshy country to the Chobe, a large branch of the Zambesi River, the travellers at last met the Makololo, by whom they were well received. The chief, Sebituane, was about twenty miles further down the river, and Livingstone and Oswell proceeded in canoes to his residence. He had come one hundred miles southward from his capital, to meet the first white men who had ever reached his country. "He was upon an island," says Livingstone, "with all his principal men around him, and engaged in singing when we arrived. It was more like church music than the sing-song ē ē ē, æ æ æ, of the Bechuanas of the south, and they continued the tune for some seconds after we approached. We informed him of the difficulties we had encountered, and how glad we were that they were all at an end by at last reaching his presence. He signified his own joy, and added, 'Your cattle are all bitten by the *tsetse*, and will certainly die; but never mind, I have oxen, and will give you as many as you need.' We, in our ignorance, then thought that as so few *tsetse* had bitten them no great mischief would follow. He then presented us with an ox and a jar of honey as food, and handed us over to the care of Mahále, who had headed the party to Kolobeng, and would now fain appropriate to himself the whole credit of our coming. Prepared skins of oxen, as soft as cloth, were given to cover us through the night; and, as nothing could be returned to this chief, Mahále became the owner of them. Long before it was day Sebituane came, and sitting down by the fire, which was lighted for our benefit behind the hedge where we lay, he narrated the difficulties he had himself experienced, when a young man, in crossing that same desert which we had mastered long afterward. As he has been most remarkable in his career, and was unquestionably the greatest man in all that country, a short sketch of his life may prove interesting to the reader.

"Sebituane was about forty-five years of age; of a tall and wiry form, an olive or coffee-and-milk color, and slightly bald; in manner cool and collected, and more frank in his answers than any other chief I ever met. He was the greatest warrior ever heard of beyond the colony; for, unlike Mosilikatse, Dingaan, and others, he always led his men into battle himself. When he saw the enemy, he felt the edge of his battle-axe, and said, 'Aha! it is sharp, and whoever turns his back on the enemy will feel its edge.' So fleet of foot was he, that all his people knew there was no escape for the coward, as any such would be cut down without mercy. In some instances of skulking he allowed the individual to return home; then calling him, he would say, 'Ah! you prefer dying at home to dying in the field, do you? You shall have your desire.' This was the signal for his immediate execution."

This famous chief came from a tribe much further to the south, and had conquered his kingdom by his own courage and energy. Thirty years before, he had fought the Griquas at Kuruman; and many years of wandering, of fighting, of danger and poverty had intervened, before he established his sovereignty on the Zambesi. His wars with the chief Mosilikatse completely broke up the latter's power throughout the central region, and thus opened the way to explorers. He knew of the commerce carried on with white men on the eastern and western coasts of the continent, and appears to have made several attempts to establish intercourse with them, before sending the invitation to Livingstone.

Unfortunately the end of his adventurous career was near at hand. "He was much pleased," says Livingstone, "with the proof of confidence we had shown in bringing our children, and promised to take us to see his country, so that we might choose a part in which to locate ourselves. Our plan was, that I should remain in the pursuit of my objects as a missionary, while Mr. Oswell explored the Zambesi to the east. Poor Sebituane, however, just after realizing what he had so long ardently desired, fell sick of inflammation of the lungs, which originated in and extended from an old wound got at Melita. I saw his danger, but, being a stranger, I feared to treat him medically, lest, in the event of his death, I should be blamed by his people. I mentioned this to one of his doctors, who said, 'Your fear is prudent and wise; this people would blame you.' He had been cured of this complaint, during the year before, by the Barotse making a large number of free incisions in the chest. The Makololo doctors, on the other hand, now scarcely cut the skin. On the Sunday afternoon in which he died, when our usual religious service was over, I visited him with my little boy Robert. 'Come near,' said Sebituane, 'and see if

I am any longer a man. I am done.' He was thus sensible of the dangerous nature of his disease, so I ventured to assent, and added a single sentence regarding hope after death. 'Why do you speak of death?' said one of a relay of fresh doctors; 'Sebituane will never die.' If I had persisted, the impression would have been produced that by speaking about it I wished him to die. After sitting with him some time, and commending him to the mercy of God, I rose to depart, when the dying chieftain, raising himself up a little from his prone position, called a servant, and said, 'Take Robert to Manku (one of his wives), and tell her to give him some milk.' These were the last words of Sebituane.

"We were not informed of his death until the next day. The burial of a Bechuana chief takes place in his cattle-pen, and all the cattle are driven for an hour or two around and over the grave, so that it may be quite obliterated. We went and spoke to the people, advising them to keep together and support the heir. They took this kindly; and in turn told us not to be alarmed, for they would not think of ascribing the death of their chief to us; that Sebituane had just gone the way of his fathers; and though the father had gone, he had left children, and they hoped that we would be as friendly to his children as we intended to have been to himself.

"He was decidedly the best specimen of a native chief I ever met. I never felt so much grieved by the loss of a black man before; and it was impossible not to follow him in thought into the world of which he had just heard before he was called away, and to realize somewhat of the feelings of those who pray for the dead. The deep, dark question of what is to become of such as he, must, however, be left where we find it, believing that, assuredly, the 'Judge of all the earth will do right.'

"At Sebituane's death the chieftainship devolved, as her father intended, on a daughter named Ma-mochisane. He had promised to show us his country and to select a suitable locality for our residence. We had now to look to the daughter, who was living twelve days to the north, at Naliele. We were obliged, therefore, to remain until a message came from her; and when it did, she gave us perfect liberty to visit any part of the country we chose. Mr. Oswell and I then proceeded one hundred and thirty miles to the north-east, to Sesheke; and in the end of June, 1851, we were rewarded by the discovery of the Zambesi, in the centre of the continent. This was a most important point, for that river was not previously known to exist there at all. The Portuguese maps all represent it as rising far to the east of where we now were; and if every anything like a chain of trading stations had existed across the country between the latitudes 12° and 18° south, this magnificent portion of the river must have been known before. We saw it at the end of the dry season, at the time when the river is about at its lowest, and yet there was a breadth of from three hundred to six hundred yards of deep flowing water. Mr. Oswell said he had never seen such a fine river, even in India. At the period of its annual inundation it rises fully twenty feet in perpendicular height, and floods fifteen or twenty miles of lands adjacent to its banks.

"The country over which we had travelled from the Chobe was perfectly flat, except where there were large ant-hills, or the remains of former ones, which had left mounds a few feet high. These are generally covered with wild date-trees and palmyras, and in some parts there are forests of mimosæ and mopane. Occasionally the country between the Chobe and Zambesi is flooded, and there are large patches of swamps lying near the Chobe, or on its banks. The Makololo were living among these swamps for the sake of the protection the deep reedy rivers afforded them against their enemies.

"As we were the very first white men the inhabitants had ever seen, we were visited by prodigious numbers. Among the first who came to see us was a gentleman who appeared in a gaudy dressing-gown of printed calico. Many of the Makololo, besides, had garments of blue, green, and red baize, and also of printed cottons; on inquiry, we learned that these had been purchased, in exchange for boys, from a tribe called Mambári, which is situated near Bihé."

Livingstone gives no account of the return journey, and we only know that it was performed without accident, though probably not without much privation. As there was then no hope of the Boers allowing the peaceable instruction of the natives at Kolobeng, he resolved to send his family to England, and to return alone to the Makololo country, with a view to explore it in search of a healthy district that might prove a future centre of civilization, and open up the interior by a path to either the east or west coast. This plan led him to the Cape in April, 1852, being the first time during eleven years that he had visited civilization. "Our route to Capetown," he says, "led us to pass through the centre of the colony during the twentieth month of a Kaffer war; and if those who periodically pay enormous sums for these inglorious affairs wish to know how our little unprotected party could quietly travel through the heart of the colony to the capital with as little sense or sign of danger as if we had been in England, they must engage a '*Times* Special Correspondent' for the next outbreak to explain where the money goes, and who have been benefited by the blood and treasure expended.

"Having placed my family on board a homeward-bound ship, and promised to rejoin them in two years, we parted, for, as it subsequently proved, nearly five years. The Directors of the London Missionary Society signified their cordial approval of my project by leaving the matter entirely to my own discretion; and I have much pleasure in acknowledging my obligations to the gentlemen composing that body for always acting in an enlightened spirit, and with as much liberality as their constitution would allow."

CHAPTER VI.

ANDERSON'S JOURNEY TO THE OVAMPO LAND AND LAKE NGAMI.

BEFORE following Livingstone on his great journey of four years into and across South Africa from sea to sea, let us turn to other explorations of the regions below the parallel of Lake Ngami, which have almost completed our knowledge of the geography of that part of the continent. Some important information has also been contributed by Gordon Cumming, Baldwin, and other professional sportsmen; but their object was game and not discovery, and the explorations they made were only incidental and fragmentary.

Livingstone's visit to Lake Ngami, and his report of the immense herds of elephants on the Zouga River, created much excitement throughout the Cape Colony. Among others who determined to follow in his tracks was the Swedish naturalist Anderson, who had come to South Africa to prosecute his scientific studies. In company with an Englishman, named Galton, he fitted out a small expedition, intending to take the direct route to the lake, through the interior; but the breaking out of hostilities between the Boers and the native tribes compelled them to give up this plan. They returned to the coast and made their way to Whale Bay, a port in lat. 22° S., whence the actual distance to the lake was not greater than from Kuru-

ANDERSON STARTING OUT.

man, but the intervening territory was almost wholly unknown.

The Namaqua Hottentots inhabit the territory bordering the ocean, and several German missionary stations—those of Rehoboth and New-Barmen being the chief—have been established among them, but without much effect upon the habits of the people. So long as the latter receive food and clothing from the missionaries, they gather about them and listen to their instruction; but when the gifts cease, they turn their backs in indifference, or insult their benefactors. The success of the missions has further been somewhat jeopardized by the forays which the Namaquas have made, in late years, into the land of the Damaras, who inhabited the region to the north. These Damaras are a comparatively fine-looking race of men: they are nomads, and wander about with enormous herds of cattle, leaving the country bare behind them wherever they go. They appear to have come from the eastward, driving the aboriginal tribes, who were probably Hottentots, into the mountains, where a small remnant of them still exists.

The Damaras are tall, strong and symmetrically formed. They are well armed with the assagay (a sort of lance), bow and arrow, and club; but their inclinations are peaceful, and their faces have a gentle expression. They resemble the other native tribes in their scanty clothing, in the habit of smearing their bodies with fat, and in the fondness of the women for a burden of rings, plates and other metallic ornaments. The men wind their strips of leather, sometimes several hundred feet in length, around their loins, and carry their clubs and pipes therein. They are so skilful in throwing the *kerri*, a stick with a knob on one end, that they will even bring down birds on the wing.

The missionaries, thus far, have accomplished very little towards civilizing the Damaras. When they first settled themselves in the country, the latter quietly withdrew with their herds, and left the strangers to procure their food as they best could. The idea of a pure human interest being incomprehensible to them, they suspected some hostile intention, and at first debated whether they should not exterminate them. In the course of time they became more friendly, but to this day a Damara in good circumstances keeps aloof from the teaching of the missionaries; while the poorer people, who support themselves chiefly by cultivating tobacco, are learning to understand the advantage of settling in the neighborhood of the mission stations.

When Anderson and Galton landed at Whale Bay, they had no definite plan of travel. After reaching Barmen, however, they heard of a great lake of fresh water, called "Omanbonde," lying some distance to the northward. The region was entirely unknown, and the Damaras who inhabited it were represented to them by the natives as fierce, unfriendly and treacherous. Nevertheless they undertook the journey, and after several weeks of slow progress, encountering the usual dangers, difficulties and delays, reached the famed lake, which the natives had described to them as being "as large as the sky." But their disappointment was great, at finding only a great reedy marsh, without any water! There were indications, it is true, that a lake of considerable extent had formerly existed there; but in drying it had banished the herds of elephants and other wild beasts which they had hoped to find.

Having penetrated so far, however, the travellers determined to go on. They had heard of a people still further to the north, who had permanent habitations, who cultivated the soil, and were industrious, peaceful and hospitable. They were called the Ovampo (or Ovambo), which denoted agriculturists, and carried on a trade with the Damaras, giving them in exchange for cattle implements of iron. They were said to be very numerous, and to be governed by a king who was of gigantic stature. In regard to the distance of the country, and the character of the region to be traversed in order to reach it, the Damaras could only give very uncertain and fabulous accounts. Although it seemed probable that the journey would occupy several months, Anderson decided to make the venture, and left the unfortunate Lake Omanbonde behind him. There was no longer any desert, at least; the road must be forced through high grass, thickets, and occasional forests. Water was found in abundance, and there was so much game that the party never lacked food. In a few days after leaving the lake, they were surprised to find groves of fan-palm covering the landscapes.

They had barely reached the last settlement of the Damaras when the axle of their large wagon broke, and there were no means of mending it. Therefore they determined to leave the vehicles, and push on by means of pack and saddle oxen. But the native chief not only refused to furnish them with a guide, he would give them no information whatever, and all they could extort from him was the promise that they might join a caravan which was expected from the Ovampo land. Fortunately, this caravan soon arrived: it consisted of twenty-three tall, strong, very dark-colored men, of serious demeanor, and of a type very different from that of the Damaras. They brought lance-heads, knives, rings, and beads of copper and iron—all their own workmanship—which they sold dearly enough; as, for instance, a lance-head for an ox.

The Ovampos agreed that the strangers might accompany them back to their country, and when the caravan was ready to start it numbered 170 persons, for many Damaras—among them seventy or eighty girls—decided to join it. The Ovampos had collected a fine herd of cattle by their trading, and they declared that fourteen long days' journeys would bring them to their own country. The pleasant scenery soon disappeared; thorny thickets and dreary plains followed; the watering-places were few and far apart, and the travellers now recognized how difficult it would have been to cross such a region without a skilful guide. Here, as elsewhere, they encountered parties of the wild Bushmen, and they noticed with pleasure that these outcasts, so despised by all other tribes, were kindly treated by the Ovampos.

After a journey of eight days, the caravan reached the first pasture-lands of the tribe, and there rested for a few days. The welcome of the country, which they received, consisted in having their faces thickly smeared with butter. Messengers were sent in advance to announce the coming of the strangers to the king, Nangaro, and then the travel was resumed,—at first across great salt-pans, surrounded with a girdle of forests, and afterwards over boundless, grassy savannas. So much the more agreeable was the surprise of Anderson and Galton, when they saw before them the fertile, well-cultivated fields of Ondonga, the central part of the Ovampo land. Instead of the never-ending thickets and sandy tracts, they beheld immense fields of grain, dotted over with peaceful dwellings, isolated forest or fruit trees, and groves of palm. It seemed to them like a veritable paradise, and these attractive features multiplied as they advanced.

There were no villages; each family has its own patriarchal home, in the midst of the fields it cultivates. The houses are surrounded with strong palisades, for even these peaceable farmers have hostile neighbors, and are sometimes compelled to defend their possessions. Their grain is lentils and millet, which grow to the height of eight or nine feet. At harvest they simply cut off the ripe heads, and then turn their cattle into the fields to devour the straw. They have extensive pasture-grounds at some distance from the cultivated region, and are said to raise a breed of pigs of an enormous size. The travellers were unable to ascertain the exact extent of the country, or the number of the inhabitants.

On the second day they reached the residence of the terrible Nangaro, but without being admitted: a group of trees, near at hand, was pointed out to them as the place where they should wait. This is the custom of African as of European courts, and in their case it lasted three days. Finally, they were taken before his Majesty, whom they found to be a giant, truly, but only in a horizontal direction. He was an exceedingly thick, ugly man, yet every inch a king in the eyes of his subjects, with whom corpulency was a royal attribute, and all the more to be admired, since it would have been unpardonable in themselves. The only answer which the stout king made to the brilliant address of the travellers was, that he now and then gave a grunt of assent or dissent, as the case might be.

Neither the king nor his people had a correct knowledge of fire-arms. They imagined that if one should blow into the barrel, the weapon could do no harm. The effect of a rifle, loaded with conical ball, so startled them that many fell flat upon their faces at each shot. The king presently demanded that they should shoot for him one of the elephants which occasionally devastated his fields. Anderson refused, from the suspicion that the king would not only keep the ivory for himself, but possibly retain them in the country as long as there were any elephants to shoot. Nevertheless, they were very kindly and hospitably treated. The king furnished them with food, and a kind of beer, and every evening there was a native ball, where the young people danced to the sound of tom-toms and a sort of guitar. The girls, when young, have coarse but not disagreeable features, but afterwards become heavy and muscular, partly from carrying so many heavy metal rings on their arms and legs, and partly, in consequence of their unremitting labor. Both sexes work in the fields from sunrise until sunset. The women increase the circumference of their woolly locks by stiffening them with a mixture of fat and red ochre, with which they also plaster their bodies.

The principal food of the Ovampo is a kind of coarse meal porridge, which is always served hot, with butter or sour milk. Although they are also very fond of a flesh diet, and their herds are large, yet they slaughter cattle but sparingly, and appear to keep their herds rather for pleasure than use or profit. Inside of their stockades they have a number of detached buildings,—dwellings for owners and servants, stables, granaries, and pens for pigs and fowls. The houses are tent-shaped, circular, and not more than six feet in height; the granaries are huge baskets of woven palm-leaves, each sheltered by a conical roof.

A good characteristic of the Ovampo, which distinguishes them above all other African tribes, is, that they not only do not steal, but they consider theft a crime worthy of being punished by death. While the travellers with all their watchfulness could not prevent the Damaras from plundering them, here they could leave their possessions unguarded, knowing that not the slightest article would be taken. The king has the sole power of punishment, and order is preserved throughout the land by persons whom he appoints, and who report to him all crimes and disputes. Moreover, the Ovampo take excellent care of all sick, crippled or superannuated persons, instead of driving them into the jungle to perish, like the Damaras.

They are passionately attached to their country, and are very proud of its advantages. It is an offence to them when a stranger inquires the number of their chiefs, and they answer: "We acknowledge but one king; among the Damaras each one thinks he is a chief, as soon as he owns a few cows." Fugitives from other tribes are accepted, and allowed to marry among them, but afterwards they are compelled to remain in the land. Polygamy prevails among them, as elsewhere in South Africa: each man is allowed to take as many wives as he is able to buy. One of small means can get a wife for two oxen and a cow, while those who are wealthier must pay a higher price. The king, alone, is not obliged to buy his wives, the honor of being connected with him being considered a full equivalent. The stout Nangaro had already collected 106 spouses from the various quarters of his realm.

After the travellers had spent several weeks in the Ovampo land, they prepared to continue their journey. They were told that only four days to the north there was a large beautiful river, with inhabited shores. [This was certainly the Kunene, a river which has since been partly explored. It flows into the sea near Great Fish Bay, on the southern border of Benguela.] But the king positively refused to permit them to visit it, saying that they had refused to shoot an elephant for him, and therefore he would not favor their plans. They then decided to return southward, and with all the more speed, since they were uncertain how the wagons and cattle they had left behind had fared among the Damaras. The journey to the mission-station at Barmen occupied six weeks, and was accompanied with many privations, since it was winter, the nights were cold, water and pasture dried up, and game very scarce.

Anderson now returned to his original design of reaching Lake Ngami. Still accompanied by Galton, he set out, and after encountering many difficulties and

A SOUTH AFRICAN WATERING-PLACE.

embarrassments, at the end of five months reached a point called Tunobis, about two hundred miles from the lake. This is a watering-place surrounded with forests, where a few Bushmen hide, and where great quantities of elephants and other beasts collect. It was a pleasant spot in the wilderness; but the party had suffered intensely from heat and thirst, and the fatigues of the journey; the oxen were worn to skeletons, and the Bushmen assured Anderson that a thorny desert lay before him where no water could be found for several days. So much time had been lost in forcing their way to this point, that the prospect ahead decided them to turn about and retrace their weary steps.

Mr. Galton was by this time quite satisfied with African exploration, and, on reaching Whale Bay, took passage for England. Anderson remained to make another attempt, after the rainy season was over; and, in order to supply himself with materials for barter with the natives, bought a herd of cattle and drove them down the coast to Capetown. The speculation was tolerably successful: he procured the necessary supplies, sailed to Whale Bay, organized his caravan, and struck into the desert.

By the time he reached Tunobis, his turning-point the former year, his party was in a very dilapidated condition. The men had suffered greatly from hunger, on account of the unexpected scarcity of game, and it now seemed as hazardous to return as to go onwards. The natives declared that the direct way to the lake was through a desolate, waterless wilderness, and quite impassable; but that if he would travel a few days to the eastward, following a dry river-bed called Otjambinde, and then turn to the left, he might succeed.

It was only by making the greatest exertions that Anderson could induce both men and beasts to go further. The latter were as obstinate as the former; he was obliged to take both in hand, drill them anew, and compel them to his authority. Setting out about the middle of June, they followed the empty river-bed, plodding over wastes of glaring white sand. Here and there, however, they found grass and luxuriant vegetation, and little slimy pools of rain-water, sometimes swarming with reptiles, or turned into liquid mud by the feet of elephants. They found, also, a number of ancient and skilfully-constructed wells, some of which were damp at the bottom, and, by thrusting a reed into the soil, in the manner of the Bushmen, they could suck up moisture enough to allay their thirst. These wells indicated that the now desolate region had been formerly inhabited by a race civilized enough to secure themselves a constant supply of water.

After several days of this travel, it was time to leave the old river-bed and strike out northward on the dry and stony plains. Anderson had already sent out messengers in advance, to announce his coming to the chief, Lechulatebe, whom Livingstone had found on the borders of Lake Ngami. A few days afterwards, in the desert, a troop of Bechuanas suddenly appeared; it was the escort which the chief had sent to meet them. The stately appearance of the men, with their shields and assagays, made a favorable impression upon Anderson, who found that they resembled the Damaras. The two tribes, in fact, were not strangers; for the Damaras had formerly penetrated as far as the lake, and had often come into collision with the Bechuanas. With these new guides, the caravan toiled forwards, making directly for the lake, through deep sands, and thickets of the thorny acacia, with here and there a giant tree. In spite of the wild and wooded character of the region, there were rich pastures, and old wells gave evidence that it had once had permanent inhabitants. Yet a few days more, and the cry "Ngami!" was heard at the head of the caravan. Anderson had at last reached the goal of so much toil and privation: a beautiful, apparently boundless, expanse of water spread out before him. Although sick, and almost a cripple from his encounters with rhinoceros and elephant, he forgot all his sufferings at this view. But as he drew near, and their route skirted the shores, the reality proved to be less pleasant. The water was bitter and disagreeable, and could only be reached at a few points, the mud and reeds elsewhere barring all approach to it.

The chief, whose residence was at that time on the banks of the Zuoga, refused, at first, to allow Anderson to pass through his land. After a few days, however, he suddenly furnished canoes and boatmen for a voyage on the lake. He was so unexpectedly willing that Anderson immediately suspected some covert design, and the result proved that he was right. The boatmen were quite skilful in the use of poles and oars, but did not venture far from the shore, and it was two days before they reached the mouth of the Tioge River, at the northern extremity of the lake.

The animal life around Lake Ngami is wonderfully rich and varied. The elephant, rhinoceros, hippopotamus, buffalo and giraffe have their settlements, with many kinds of antelopes, of which Anderson shot so many that his native envoy was soon increased by volunteers to the number of sixty or seventy. The water swarmed with crocodiles, some of which were of enormous size. The first part of the voyage up the Tioge was very monotonous. The river had overflowed its banks in many places, and nothing was to be seen but wide marshes, out of which rose groups of palm-trees. On the fourth day, the landscape changed; the river-banks were higher, and covered with the richest growth of trees—palms, mimosas, sycamores, and many entirely new varieties, some of which bore delicious fruits. The scenery was so charming that Anderson would have willingly lingered there for days, but he well knew the danger of breathing that fever-laden atmosphere, and hastened onward.

After a voyage of twelve days he reached a large village, the residence of the principal chief of the Bayeiye tribe, which is subject to the chief Lechulatebe, on Lake Ngami. It was a most picturesque spot: on an island in the river, more than a hundred houses were grouped in the shade of large fan-palms, while on either side the water spread out like a lake. Here, however, the natives who accompanied him declared that their chief had given orders that he should have no further boats or guides. It was not until he declared that he was ready to return, that they assisted him in any way. His object had been to follow the river to a place called Libebe, the capital of an agricultural tribe called

Bavicko, of which he had heard many interesting reports.

In his annoyance at the disappointment, Anderson supposed that the raft which was given to him for his return down the Tioge, instead of the boats, was intended as an insult. But he soon found that it was an agreeable mode of transportation. The rafts are made of palm-leaves, or reeds, laid crosswise, and not even bound together; the traveller's weight prevents them from separating. The descent of the river occupied nine days, and after an absence of four weeks Anderson returned to his encampment beside the lake, where he found everything in good order, except that his people complained bitterly of the thievishness of the Bechuanas and the meddlesomeness of the chief.

In order to convey to Capetown his collection of objects of natural history, and the ivory which he had procured by barter and the chase, it was necessary to have a wagon. Anderson thereupon travelled across the wilderness to the Namaqua land, and returned to the lake, in the space of four months. He travelled on foot, on horse-back or ox-back, sometimes entirely alone, sometimes with a single companion. Hunger and thirst were more dangerous enemies to him than the lion or the hyena. On one occasion he was without food for two days, and could only drink once in twenty-four hours. His indomitable energy and great powers of endurance enabled him to overcome all impediments, and successfully bring back his spoils.

CHAPTER VII.

ANDERSON'S JOURNEY TO THE OKAVANGO RIVER.

IN 1856, three or four years after Anderson's attempt to reach the town called Libebe, on the Tioge River, the journey was successfully made by Mr. Green, the celebrated elephant-hunter. He overcame many difficulties in penetrating to that point, and was not able to remain long enough to make any important observations. His account of the beauty of the scenery and the luxuriance of the vegetation along the Tioge corresponds with that given by Anderson.

The reports of the Kunene River, brought back from the Ovampo land, had in the meantime led to several unsuccessful attempts to reach it. The Portuguese in Benguela, recognizing the value of this river to their inland trade, if it should prove to be navigable, sent vessels along the coast, which failed to discover its mouth; but an expedition by land finally succeeded. The region where the river reaches the sea proved to be a sandy desert, and the mouth is cut off from navigation by a long sand-bank. Advancing inland, the Portuguese found that the stream was narrow and broken by cataracts, whereupon they gave up all further exploration.

In May, 1857, the German missionaries, Hahn and Rath set out from New-Barwèn, well provided with wagons, oxen and sheep, with the intention of passing through the Ovampo land to the Kunene. In ten days they reached a vast shallow plain, with no distinct water-courses. It seemed to be a basin where the rains collected, without any channel of discharge. The soil was covered with high grass, out of which rose the black trunks of mimosa trees. It was a melancholy region, where the only paths were those made by elephants, and where the ant-hills were frequently 40 feet in diameter and 15 in height. The former population had been almost entirely exterminated by the forays of the Demaras, and only a few were found, living in hidden nooks, and reduced almost to the condition of Bushmen.

After passing lat. 20°, early in June, the travellers found the fan-palm, at first as a bush, but soon as a splendid tree, 50 feet high. Near a river called Omuramba they found herds of elephants, and here fell in with Mr. Green, who joined their party. The journey beyond was rendered difficult by the increasing density of the forests, through which they were often obliged to hew a way for the wagons. The line of their course led to the eastward of the Ovampo country, but early in July their negro guides represented that a waterless desert was before them, and it would be impossible to reach the Kunene without turning westward. Ten days after changing their direction, they came suddenly upon a beautiful lake, nearly thirty miles in circumference, called by the natives Onandova. Here they met with many of the Ovampo, who were returning from a neighboring mountain-range, laden with copper ore which they had mined there.

The missionaries had sent messengers to the king Nangaro, at Odongo, to announce their approach; but they now learned that the men had been guided, instead, to the king's younger brother, Chipanga, who had risen in rebellion against him, and established an independent sovereignty of his own. This was an unfortunate mistake, and led them to expect an unfriendly reception from Nangaro.

On the 22d of July they issued from the jungles, and saw before them the broad plain of Odongo, which seems to have made a very different impression on them from that recorded by Anderson and Galton. "We saw," they write, "some heaps of black twigs and reeds, perhaps four feet high, and some high poles planted in the soil, the use of which we could not discover. We asked for houses, and they pointed to the heaps of reeds: we then approached and examined them. The stakes and twigs are stuck in the earth, so as to form a multitude of passages and compartments for various purposes,—stalls for sheep, goats, cattle, granaries, which are only large baskets, and finally the dwellings. The latter have walls two feet high, a door eighteen inches square, a diameter of five feet, and a height, in the middle, of six feet. The entire establishment is about 120 feet in circumference. These residences are scattered over the whole country, near each other, and each surrounded by its own fields."

Their intercourse with king Nangaro was equally unfortunate. After they had refused to accompany and assist him in one of his forays for plunder, he forbade them to pass further through his territory.

At the end of a week they decided to return, but had hardly started on their way, when a loud war-cry was raised in the king's hut, and immediately echoed from all the huts scattered over the plain. In a short time the little party, only 30 in number, was surrounded and attacked by 800 Ovampo warriors. The former were, fortunately, well-armed, and defended themselves so desperately, that after a fight of several hours the natives retreated. The travellers now pushed rapidly forward, avoiding the inhabited portions of the country, without guides, in a waterless wilderness, for three days, when they reached a well, and could rest without fear of a new attack. Beyond this point they ventured to resume the regular route, and on the 11th of September arrived safely at New-Barwen.

They afterwards learned that King Nangaro's hostility to them had proved fatal to himself. The vigorous defence which the party made, and the terror and loss occasioned to his people by fire-arms, enraged him to such a degree that he was stricken with apoplexy, and died almost immediately, his great corpulence hastening the catastrophe.

The following spring, 1858, Anderson, who had returned to South Africa, fitted out a new expedition, in order to make a more thorough exploration of the country north of the Damara land. He furnished all his own wagons and supplies, depending on a good harvest of ivory for payment of his losses by the way. He had two servants, a Portuguese named Mortar, and Pereira, a half-breed from Malabar, both faithful and fearless men, and eight natives. He took seventy sheep and goats for provision, extra oxen, a horse and four asses for riding, and a pack of dogs for hunting. His main hope was to reach the Kunene River, and explore, if possible, its whole course.

He set out in a northerly direction, but in a line which would have taken him to the westward of the Ovampo country. After crossing the Omarurn River, which flows into Whale Bay, he entered a plain covered with those thorny thickets which are the curse of a great part of South Africa. It was a terrible labor to break a way for the wagons. In order to give some idea of the toil and patience which the explorer must exercise, Anderson calculated that, for every 900 feet of distance, 170 bushes must be cut away, each bush having four tough stems, varying in thickness from the size of a man's finger to that of his leg. On an average, each bush required twelve strokes of the axe, making nearly 10,000 strokes to the mile; and when we reflect that this labor must be carried on for a distance of 120 miles, we can then first fully comprehend its magnitude.

After twenty-three days Anderson's patience was rewarded by seeing the last of the thorns (the acacia *detinens!*) behind him, and before him a forest of lofty trees, clear of undergrowth. Beyond this there were thorns again, but in narrower belts; and the way was made difficult by gulleys, deep lateral valleys, and dry water-courses, which always ran east and west, therefore at right angles to their course. Yet a few days, and he came upon a magnificent limestone wall, like that of a giant fortress, with bastions, ramparts and towers, twelve miles in length. At its base there was a little stream, nearly dry, but still nourishing a rich vegetation. In the distance a chain of mountains, 2000 feet in height, rose above the plains.

At a place called Otjidambi, where there were five springs, Anderson found the first sign of human life: there were evidences that a large number of natives had recently been there. The country is a table-land, from two to four thousand feet above the sea-level, bounded on the west by a range of granite mountains near the coast, about 500 miles in length, and running nearly due north and south. The table-land is crossed, at right angles to this chain, by hills of sandstone or limestone, while now and then an isolated granite peak, from one to three thousand feet in height, crops out. The face of the country is partly bare and stony, partly covered with thickets of the thorny mimosa. The valleys which lie below the general level have running streams during the rainy season, but during the dry months these shrink into pools or marshy spots, where water may be found by digging.

In some of these valleys, the Damaras had settled with their herds, and lived quietly until their retreats were discovered by the Namaquas, who made an incursion into the country, the year before Anderson's journey, and, in spite of the gallant resistance of the Damaras, carried off many of their cattle. Anderson's caravan, therefore, was looked upon with suspicion, and the natives hid themselves at his approach. As he was suffering for want of water, he made a hunt for men instead of elephants, and succeeded in capturing a man and his wife. The terrified creatures received presents, instead of the death they expected; they guided the caravan to the nearest spring, and then, still mistrustful of the character of the strangers, made their escape by night.

Nevertheless, the hidden natives were enticed, by the presents which the two had received, to come forth, and some of them willingly offered their services as guides. With their aid, the journey was continued, in a series of zigzags to the right and left, for between three and four hundred miles. This distance, in a straight line, would have taken Anderson beyond the Kunene River; but it was not yet reached. Meanwhile, his condition was becoming hazardous: for two days no water had been found, and the guides declared that they had lost the way to the next spring. Men were sent out in all directions to look for signs of water, but, as the night came on, one after another returned, without having been successful. Two men still remained absent, but their absence was not an encouraging sign, and Anderson was obliged, without much time for reflection, to retrace his steps.

Now, however, a new and unexpected danger threatened the caravan. The Damara herdsmen are accustomed to set fire to the dry grass, in order to hasten the growth of a fresh pasturage for their cattle. Anderson had frequently seen these fires in the distance, without paying any particular attention to them; but now, on the return, almost perishing from thirst, he suddenly saw the lines of flame approaching in front, and still closing in as they came, until the whole country became like a sea of fire. There was no escape; but he discovered a kind of channel where the grass was thin, and the oxen made their way through covered with showers of sparks, and scorched by the

ANDERSON'S JOURNEY ACROSS THE BURNING PRAIRIE.

falling branches of burning trees. When, finally, at midnight, he reached a place where water could be obtained by digging, all the cattle, which had not had a drop for six days, broke loose and dashed away, following their certain instinct, to the nearest Damara camping-place. While Anderson and his men were resting here, the two missing natives arrived, having actually found water after long search.

But the whole party had suffered too much, and escaped too many dangers, to think of turning about again. They made their way slowly back towards the nearest mission-station, and Anderson sent Pereira with the broken wagon, to have it repaired and then rejoin him further to the eastward. Meantime, he devoted himself to elephant-hunting, to replenish his diminishing resources. While thus engaged he met a caravan of 400 Damaras, on their way to the Ovampo land. Many of them were women-porters carrying loads of beads and shells, to be bartered for articles of copper and iron. Anderson, however, suspected that trade was not the only object of the caravan. He noticed among the people several subjects of the Nawaque robber-chief, Yonker Africaner, and rightly guessed that they meant to spy out the land and report to their master the probable success of a plundering expedition.

At the end of August, Pereira arrived with the wagon, and Anderson set out for the lake Omanbonde, which had so disappointed him and Galton when they discovered it in 1850. Now, however, instead of a mere swamp, he found a fine sheet of water four or five miles in circumference, with another of the same size near it. The shores of both swarmed with wild animals; the elephants came in herds of a hundred, and he was able to kill a great many of the old male animals, which furnished the most ivory.

Anderson describes those nightly watches, hidden behind a high ant-hill, or in a dense thicket, awaiting the coming of the unsuspecting beasts in the full light of the moon, and sometimes witnessing their combats or amorous sports, as the highest delight which a true hunter can anywhere enjoy. He was sometimes obliged to bring into play all his courage and self-possession, when, after a close shot, the wounded animal turned upon him, or the whole herd put themselves in battle array. There were also lions, rhinocerosses, zebras, gnus and antelopes, so that his table was always well supplied. He asserts that lion-steaks are very good and nutritious, the taste being very much like that of veal.

He writes, in his journal: "During my wanderings in South Africa, I have learned every variety of hunting, whether by night, on the borders of a lake or a salt-lick, or by day, on foot or horseback,—and I must affirm that an ambush by moonlight, near a pool frequented by herds of wild beasts, far surpasses all else. In the first place, there is something mysterious and exciting in the knowledge that one is the hidden, unsuspected witness of the movements, habits, and instincts of the members of a great natural menagerie—a menagerie wherein over-feeding, the iron bars of cages, and the brutal energy of the keepers has not tamed the fierceness of animal life, or blunted their elastic strength, their abandonment to passion and play.

And then the intense interest with which the arrival of every new animal is awaited! The distant footstep, which is always distinctly heard on the stony soil, then the strain of the ear when the beast crosses a softer strip of soil, the effort to determine whether it is an antelope or an elephant, a wild bear or a rhinoceros, a gnu or a giraffe, a jackal or a lion! Moreover, there are constant opportunities for observing the habits and peculiarities of all, to an extent which would be impossible by daylight. I do not exaggerate when I say that I have learned more from the *tableau vivant* of a single night, than from months of observation in the sunshine."

In a short time so much ivory had been collected that Pereira was sent back to the mission with a large wagon-load, and meanwhile Anderson made an excursion to the most eastern point which he had reached in the expedition of 1850, with Galton. When he had returned to the lake, and was awaiting his attendant's return, the Damara caravan arrived. When they reached the borders of the Ovampo country, the inhabitants of the first village refused to allow them to proceed further, until the present chief, Chipanga, should send a special permission. The Damaras therefore halted, and sent messengers forward; but they soon returned with the news that, under no circumstances, could the caravan be allowed to enter the country. At the same time the Ovampo had inquired what Anderson's plans were, declaring that they were disgusted with the conduct of the white men, in using weapons different from their own. Their defeat by Green and the missionaries seemed to rankle very deeply in their minds.

The return of the Damara caravan, nevertheless, enabled Anderson to procure one of the chiefs as a guide. Pereira returned from the mission with new supplies, and on the 5th of January, 1859, the party set out in search of the Ovampo River. When the missionaries, Hahn and Rath, first discovered this stream, it contained a considerable amount of water, and from the direction in which it flowed, they felt sure that it was a branch of the Kunene. There had been frequent rains, and Anderson kept watch, day after day, for the waters of the river. But the sky now remained clear, and evaporation went on so rapidly that pools, several feet deep, became dry ground in a week. After eleven days' travel, they came upon something like a river-bed, stretching to the northward, but without any running water. They used this as a road, and pushed onward, still hoping to reach the Ovampo, never suspecting that they were actually travelling in its bed. After a time its direction changed, and they then took to the northern bank. At the end of two days more, the calcareous soil changed to dry sand, the thorny jungles were again encountered, and a new plague came upon them in the shape of a fierce horse-fly, which drew blood at every bite. This does not appear to have been the *tsetse*, since the oxen did not die, but the hides of the poor beasts were encrusted with blood.

Having at last reached a spot which swarmed with game, especially elephants, Anderson made a halt of several days, to rest the cattle and supply his caravan with food. The flesh of the elephants was cut into strips and dried in the sun; a heavy rain fell, and then, provided with food and water for a short time, they pressed forwards. Their progress through the thorns, up and down the steep ridges, was only a few miles a day, and Anderson at last determined to choose one of the most promising of the dry water-courses and follow it to the westward. This soon brought them upon the dry, waste table-land they had traversed the year before.

Here, however, they fell in with a Bushman chief, who had accompanied the German missionaries in their journey, and who eagerly offered to guide them, on the condition that he should have an entire elephant as pay. His name was Kaganda: he proved to be an active, intelligent fellow, who not only knew every little pool or marshy spot in the whole country, but imparted a secret which was of great service. He showed them that a large tree, with willow-like leaves, was generally hollow, and formed a natural cistern, wherein rain-water was preserved for a long time. They tried the experiment, and found good supplies of water, which was still tolerably fresh.

Kaganda conducted the caravan through a region which swarmed with elephants, until finally, the landmarks were unknown to him, and he confessed that he could act as guide no longer. Anderson, as in the former journey, sent out and captured a native and his wife, and learned from them that the river he hoped to reach was only distant a journey of two and a half days. He thereupon left his wagons and heavy baggage near a water-pool, took half of his men with him, and set out. It was still uncertain what the Bushmen meant by "a river." He hoped it might be the Kunene, yet it was possibly merely a dry water-course, where the stream had shrunk to detached pools. On the second day, in fact, he reached such a dry bed, or valley, running from south to north, with the usual muddy pools, but, in addition to them, fresh springs and wells, —a refreshment he had long missed. Following this channel until noon the next day, the Bushman guides began to prepare themselves for a meeting with the inhabitants of the region watered by the promised river, by hiding their best arrows in the trees. They declared that the people they were approaching were a race of scamps, who would attempt to plunder them of all they owned.

Anderson rode on in a state of great excitement and expectation, his eyes turned to the north. Finally, he perceived a mountain-chain, along the horizon, running east and west, and soon afterwards found himself on the bank of a river, 600 hundred feet in breadth. It did not seem to be any of the streams of which he had previously heard. The Ovampo had spoken to him of a large river which flowed westward towards the ocean; but this, upon whose banks he stood, flowed distinctly eastward, into the heart of the continent. He was, therefore, inclined to look upon it as a great affluent of the Zambesi. The natives called the river the *Okavango*. Anderson guessed that the point he reached was somewhere between 17° and 18° S. Lat. and 17° and 19° E. from Greenwich. It is rather difficult to understand that a considerable branch of the Zambesi should be met with here: the absence of an exact observation leaves the question still undecided. In spite of its eastern course the river may have been the Kunene.

On the right bank, upon which he found himself,

"BEHOLD! A WHITE MAN."

there were no settlements of the Okavangari, as the tribe is called. They saw some habitations on the opposite bank, and it required a calling back and forth, a negotiation which lasted more than two hours, before the suspicious natives consented to bring their boats. They finally came armed, but were gradually persuaded that the strangers were peaceful.

In order to avoid any difficulties in his further exploration of the river, Anderson sent a messenger to the principal chief of the tribe, Chikongo, and begged that he might be received as a friend. The village where the chief resided lay further to the south, and the messenger soon returned with an invitation from Chikongo that Anderson should visit him, with assurances of his friendship. In the meantime the traveller had been well entertained, the natives having furnished him with meal and fruit, and also a cow. He waited in vain, however, for the arrival of a boat, and could only, at last, obtain with great difficulty a miserable canoe and a single guide. He soon perceived that the power of a chief over his subjects was by no means absolute, each of them acting much as he pleased. The native who had taken him in his frail canoe, seemed to consider the voyage in the light of his own amusement and vanity; for, instead of keeping in the swifter current, he floated slowly along the banks, and stopped at every hut in order to show the people the strange white man. Anderson began to look upon himself as a curious animal; but these incidents at least enabled him to observe the natives very thoroughly. He found the men nearly all strong and well-built, while each woman seemed to him uglier than the others.

The river and the landscapes on either side were delightful. Here and there the current was interrupted by islands, on which crocodiles were sunning themselves; hippopotamus and water-fowl were also seen. Among the latter Anderson noticed a new variety of wild-goose, four feet high. The river-bottoms were covered with fields of grain, and fruit-trees, and ranges of wooded mountains on either hand enclosed the landscapes.

At noon on the second day of the voyage he reached the residence of the chief, Chikongo. The houses of the village had precisely the appearance of bee-hives, and stood close together: around all there was a strong stockade, as a defence against enemies. The chief was as naked and as thickly plastered with grease and ochre as any of his subjects; he only wore a few more beads and rings, and carried two or three daggers of native make in his girdle. One of the natives, who understood the Bechuana language, which Anderson also spoke, interpreted a hearty welcome to the latter. The chief excused himself for entertaining the stranger in such a rude manner, "like a Bushman," on the ground that the Makololo (Livingstone's friends, on the Zambesi) had, a short time before, carried away the most of his cattle. Anderson further learned that the negro traders from Benguela visit this region, and exchange beads, powder, guns and brandy, for ivory and slaves.

In the mountains to the northward there are rich mines of iron and copper, and the natives are skilled in smelting the ores and manufacturing the metals into various articles, partly for their own use, and partly for barter. They stated that the Ovampo land lay to the west of them, and the tribe of Bavickos to the east, whose capital was the town of Libebe, which Anderson had tried to reach on the Tioge River. To the south, they said, there was nothing but deserts.

After a stay of three days in Chikongo's village, Anderson returned to the spot where he had left his wagons, and brought the whole caravan safely to the Okavango River. All aspects now seemed favorable, and he projected plans for the exploration of the river, which were suddenly frustrated by the appearance of another deadly enemy of the African traveller—fever. It was the dry season, and the exhalations from the pools and marshes make the air pestilential. Scarcely had the party reached the river-bank, when Anderson and five or six others were prostrated. For a whole month he waited from day to day, hoping to grow better, but at last was compelled to turn back, as the only means of saving his life.

He returned upon his old trail, difficult and dangerous as he had found it. This time, also, the plains of dry grass were on fire in various places. It almost appeared as if the Bushmen had intended to check the march of the weakened caravan, and finally obtain through fire or starvation the plunder which they were too cowardly to fight for. Once, indeed, the danger was so near that only a sudden change of the wind saved the whole party from death.

About this time, Mr. Green, who was at the mission-station, learned that the Ovampo chief, Chipango, had sent out a body of his people to intercept Anderson's return, and cut him off. He hastily gathered together a small body of men, and pressed forward to meet and assist his friend. The latter, however, had kept such a strict guard that the natives found no opportunity of taking him by surprise, and they did not dare to venture an open attack.

Green and Anderson met at the Ovampo River, and all danger was over. But Anderson was in a state of great exhaustion, from the fever which still clung to him, and the privations and anxieties of the return march. This was his last journey.

In the winter of 1860, Green, accompanied by his brother, also reached the Okavango River. His main object was elephant-hunting, and he killed 42 animals in three months. He found the native tribe on the river to be peaceable, timid people, with whom he had no difficulties. They were then suffering from the raids of the Namaqua chief, Yonker Africaner, who had taken possession of the Ovampo country, and was sending out plundering expeditions in all directions.

Green relates that he could easily have reached the Kunene River. The chief Chikongo offered him guides thither; but it was now the hot and unhealthy season, and he feared that Anderson's experience might become his own. Many geographical details of the region lying between the central Zambesi valley and the Atlantic Ocean still remain to be cleared up; yet so much has been achieved by Anderson, Green, and Magyar, that all its most important features are now known.

CHAPTER VIII.

LIVINGSTONE'S JOURNEY ACROSS THE CONTINENT.

I.—TO THE MAKOLOLO COUNTRY.

LIVINGSTONE'S plan, after having sent his wife and children to England, was to return alone to the Makololo country, on the Zambesi River, and continue his explorations until he should discover a healthy region wherein to establish a new missionary station, with which communication might be kept up, either with the Cape, or the eastern or western coast. The opening of trade with the natives was, of course, an incidental advantage, and thus the selection of a practical route was included in his design. He was heartily supported by the London Missionary Society in his undertaking, and set out from Capetown in June, 1852, tolerably well provided for the journey, the extent and importance of which he was far from anticipating at the time.

The travel through the colony and the Griqua country, made in wagons drawn by oxen, was necessarily slow. Livingstone was obliged to remain some time at Kuruman, on account of the raid which the Boers of the Transvaal Republic had made upon Kolobeng and the Bechuanas, and the consequent insecurity of the country. He gives the following interesting account of the native language:

"During the period of my visit at Kuruman, Mr. Moffat, who has been a missionary in Africa during upward of forty years, and is well known by his interesting work, 'Scenes and Labors in South Africa,' was busily engaged in carrying through the press, with which his station is furnished, the Bible in the language of the Bechuanas, which is called Sichuana. This has been a work of immense labor; and as he was the first to reduce their speech to a written form, and has had his attention directed to the study for at least thirty years, he may be supposed to be better adapted for the task than any man living. Some idea of the copiousness of the language may be formed from the fact that even he never spends a week at his work without discovering new words; the phenomenon, therefore, of any man who, after a few months' or years' study of a native tongue, cackles forth a torrent of vocables, may well be wondered at, if it is meant to convey instruction. In my own case, though I have had as much intercourse with the purest idiom as most Englishmen, and have studied the language carefully, yet I can never utter an important statement without doing so very slowly, and repeating it too, lest the foreign accent, which is distinctly perceptible in all Europeans, should render the sense unintelligible. In this I follow the example of the Bechuana orators, who, on important matters, always speak slowly, deliberately, and with reiteration. The capabilities of this language may be inferred from the fact that the Pentateuch is fully expressed in Mr. Moffat's translation in fewer words than in the Greek Septuagint, and in a very considerably smaller number than in our own English version.

THE MAKOLOLO COUNTRY. 101

"Having been detained at Kuruman about a fortnight by the breaking of a wagon-wheel, I was thus providentially prevented from being present at the attack of the Boers on the Bakwains, news of which was brought about the end of that time, by Masebele, the wife of Sechele. She had herself been hidden in a cleft of a rock, over which a number of Boers were firing. Her infant began to cry, and, terrified lest this should attract the attention of the men, the muzzles of whose guns appeared at every discharge over her head, she took off her armlets as playthings to quiet the child. She brought Mr. Moffat a letter, which tells its own tale. Nearly literally translated, it was as follows:

"'Friend of my heart's love, and of all the confidence of my heart, I am Sechele. I am undone by the Boers, who attacked me, though I had no guilt with them. They demanded that I should be in their kingdom, and I refused. They demanded that I should prevent the English and Griquas from passing (northward). I replied, These are my friends, and I can prevent no one (of them). They came on Saturday, and I besought them not to fight on Sunday, and they assented. They began on Monday morning at twilight, and fired with all their might, and burned the town with fire, and scattered us. They killed sixty of my people, and captured women, and children, and men. And the mother of Baleriling (a former wife of Sechele) they also took prisoner. They took all the cattle and all the goods of the Bakwains; and the house of Livingstone they plundered, taking away all his goods. The number of wagons they had was eighty-five, and a cannon; and after they had stolen my own wagon and that of Macabe, then the number of their wagons (counting the cannon as one) was eighty-eight. All the goods of the hunters (certain English gentlemen hunting and exploring in the north) were burnt in the town; and of the Boers were killed twenty-eight. Yes, my beloved friend, my wife goes to see the children, and Kobus Hae will convey her to you.

"'I am, SECHELE,

"'The Son of Mochoasele.'"

It was some time before Livingstone found three servants who were willing to risk a journey to the north. He was finally successful, and also accepted the company of a colored man named Fleming, who was desirous of opening trade with the Makololos. On the 20th of November they left Kuruman, and soon afterwards met the chief Sechele, on his way to the Cape. He was determined to embark for England, and lay his grievances before the Queen. He succeeded in getting as far as Capetown, but there his means became exhausted, and he was obliged to return to his country.

"Having parted with Sechele," Livingstone continues, "we skirted along the Kalihari Desert, and sometimes within its borders, giving the Boers a wide berth. A larger fall of rain than usual had occurred in 1852, and that was the completion of a cycle of eleven or twelve years, at which the same phenomenon is reported to have happened on three occasions. An unusually large crop of melons had appeared in consequence. We had the pleasure of meeting with Mr. J. Macabe returning from Lake Ngami, which he had succeeded in reaching by going right across the desert from a point a little to the south of Kolobeng. The accounts of the abundance of water-melons were amply confirmed by this energetic traveller; for, having these in vast quantities, his cattle subsisted on the fluid contained in them for a period of no less than twenty-one days; and when at last they reached a supply of water, they did not seem to care much about it. Coming to the lake from the south-east, he crossed the Teoughe, and went round the northern part of it, and is the only European traveller who had actually seen it all. His estimate of the extent of the lake is higher than that given by Mr. Oswell and myself, or from about ninety to one hundred miles in circumference.

"On the 31st of December, 1852, we reached the town of Sechele, called, from the part of the range on which it is situated, Litubaruba. Near the village there exists a cave named Lepelole; it is an interesting evidence of the former existence of a gushing fountain. No one dared to enter the Lohaheng, or cave, for it was the common belief that it was the habitation of the Deity. As we never had a holiday from January to December, and our Sundays were the periods of our greatest exertions in teaching, I projected an excursion into the cave on a week-day to see the god of the Bakwains. The old men said that every one who went in there remained there forever, adding, 'If the teacher is so mad as to kill himself, let him do so alone, we shall not be to blame.' The declaration of Sechele, that he would follow where I led, produced the greatest consternation. It is curious that in all their pretended dreams or visions of their god, he has always a crooked leg, like the Egyptian Thau. Supposing that those who were reported to have perished in this cave had fallen over some precipice, we went well provided with lights, ladder, lines, etc.; but it turned out to be only an open cave, with an entrance about ten feet square, which contracts into two water-worn branches, ending in round orifices through which the water once flowed. The only inhabitants it seems ever to have had were baboons. I left at the end of the upper branch one of Father Mathew's leaden teetotal tickets.

"The Bechuanas are universally much attached to children. A little child toddling near a party of men while they are eating is sure to get a handful of the food. This love of children may arise, in a great measure, from the patriarchal system under which they dwell. Every little stranger forms an increase of property to the whole community, and is duly reported to the chief—boys being more welcome than girls. The parents take the name of the child, and often address their children as Ma (mother), or Ra (father). Our eldest boy being named Robert, Mrs. Livingstone was, after his birth, always addressed as Ma-Robert, instead of Mary, her Christian name.

"The whole of the country adjacent to the desert, from Kuruman to Kolobeng, or Litubaruba, and beyond up to the latitude of Lake Ngami, is remarkable for its great salubrity of climate. Not only the natives, but Europeans whose constitutions have been impaired by an Indian climate, find the tract of country indicated both healthy and restorative. The health and longevity of the missionaries have always been fair, though mission-work is not very conducive to either elsewhere. Cases have been known in which patients have come from the coast with complaints closely resembling, if they were not actually, those of consumption; and they have recovered by the influence of the climate alone. It must always be borne in mind that the climate near the coast, from which we received such very favorable reports of the health of the British troops, is actually inferior for persons suffering from pulmonary complaints to that of any part not subjected to the influence of sea-air. I have never seen the beneficial effects of the inland climate on persons of shattered constitutions, nor heard their high praises of the benefit they have derived from travelling, without wishing that its bracing effects should become more extensively known in England.

"Having remained five days with the wretched Bakwains, seeing the effects of war, of which only a very inadequate idea can ever be formed by those who have not been eye-witnesses of its miseries, we prepared to depart on the 15th of January, 1853. On the 21st we reached the wells of Boatlanama, and found them for the first time empty. Lopepe, which I had formerly seen, a stream running from a large reedy pool, was also dry. The hot salt springs of Serináne, east of Lopepe, being undrinkable, we pushed on to Mashüe for its delicious waters. In travelling through this country, the olfactory nerves are frequently excited by a strong disagreeable odor. This is caused by a large jet-black ant named

'Leshónya.' It is nearly an inch in length, and emits a pungent smell when alarmed, in the same manner as the skunk. The scent must be as volatile as ether, for, on irritating the insect with a stick six feet long, the odor is instantly perceptible.

"Occasionally we lighted upon land tortoises, which, with their unlaid eggs, make a very agreeable dish. We saw many of their trails leading to the salt fountain; they must have come great distances for this health-giving article. In lieu thereof they often devour wood-ashes. It is wonderful how this reptile holds its place in the country. When seen, it never escapes. The young are taken for the sake of their shells; these are made into boxes, which, filled with sweet-smelling roots, the women hang around their persons. When older it is used as food, and the shell converted into a rude basin to hold food or water. It owes its continuance neither to speed nor cunning. Its color, yellow and dark brown, is well adapted, by its similarity to the surrounding grass and brushwood, to render it indistinguishable; and, though it makes an awkward attempt to run on the approach of man, its trust is in its bony covering, from which even the teeth of a hyæna glance off foiled. When this long-lived creature is about to deposit her eggs, she lets herself into the ground by throwing the earth up round her shell, until only the top is visible; then covering up the eggs, she leaves them until the rains begin to fall and the fresh herbage appears; the young ones then come out, their shells still quite soft, and, unattended by their dam, begin the world for themselves. Their food is tender grass and a plant named thotona, and they frequently resort to heaps of ashes and places containing efflorescence of the nitrates for the salts these contain."

Livingstone also gives the following interesting account of the South African ostrich and its habits: " The ostrich is generally seen quietly feeding on some spot where no one can approach him without being detected by his wary eye. As the wagon moves along far to the windward he thinks it is intending to circumvent him, so he rushes up a mile or so from the leeward, and so near to the front oxen that one sometimes gets a shot at the silly bird. When he begins to run all the game in sight follow his example. I have seen this folly taken advantage of when he was feeding quietly in a valley open at both ends. A number of men would commence running, as if to cut off his retreat from the end through which the wind came; and although he had the whole country hundreds of miles before him by going to the other end, on he madly rushed to get past the men, and so was speared. He never swerves from the course he once adopts, but only increases his speed.

" When the ostrich is feeding, his pace is from twenty to twenty-two inches; when walking, but not feeding, it is twenty-six inches; and when terrified, as in the case noticed, it is from eleven and a half to thirteen and even fourteen feet in length. Only in one case was I at all satisfied of being able to count the rate of speed by a stop-watch, and, if I am not mistaken, there were thirty in ten seconds; generally one's eye can no more follow the legs than it can the spokes of a carriage-wheel in rapid motion. If we take the above number, and twelve feet stride as the average pace, we have a speed of twenty-six miles an hour. It cannot be very much above that, and is therefore slower than a railway locomotive. They are sometimes shot by the horseman making a cross cut to their undeviating course, but few Englishmen ever succeed in killing them.

The ostrich begins to lay her eggs before she has fixed on a spot for a nest, which is only a hollow a few inches deep in the sand, and about a yard in diameter. Solitary eggs, named by the Bechuanas "lesetla," are thus found lying forsaken all over the country, and become a prey to the jackal. She seems averse to risking a spot for a nest, and often lays her eggs in that of another ostrich, so that as many as forty-five have been found in one nest. Some eggs contain small concretions of the matter which forms the shell, as occurs also in the egg of the common fowl: this has given rise to the idea of stones in the eggs. Both male and female assist in the incubations; but the numbers of females being always greatest, it is probable that cases occur in which the females have the entire charge. Several eggs lie out of the nest, and are thought to be intended as food for the first of the newly-hatched brood till the rest come out and enable the whole to start in quest of food. I have several times seen newly-hatched young in charge of the cock, who made a very good attempt at appearing lame in the plover fashion, in order to draw off the attention of pursuers. The young squat down and remain immovable when too small to run far, but attain a wonderful degree of speed when about the size of common fowls. It cannot be asserted that ostriches are polygamous, though they often appear to be so. When caught they are easily tamed, but are of no use in their domesticated state.

"The egg is possessed of very great vital power. One kept in a room during more than three months, in a temperature about 60°, when broken, was found to have a partially-developed live chick in it. The Bushmen carefully avoid touching the eggs, or leaving marks of human feet near them, when they find a nest. They go up the wind to the spot, and with a long stick remove some of them occasionally, and, by preventing any suspicion, keep the hen laying on for months, as we do with fowls. The eggs have a strong, disagreeable flavor, which only the keen appetite of the desert can reconcile one to. The Hottentots use their trowsers to carry home the twenty or twenty-five eggs usually found in a nest; and it has happened that an Englishman intending to imitate this knowing dodge, comes to the wagons with blistered legs, and, after great toil, finds all the eggs uneatable, from having been some time sat upon."

When they reached the Bamangwato tribe, the chief Sekomi was particularly friendly, and collected the natives of his encampment to hear the religious services. Here the caravan rested for some days before advancing into the arid plains to the eastward of Lake Ngami, over which Livingstone had passed in his first journey to the Makololo country. He adds some curious particulars of the habits of the natives: "All the Bechuana and Kaffer tribes south of the Zambesi practice circumcision (*boguera*), but the rites observed are carefully concealed. The initiated alone can approach, but in this town I was once a spectator of the second part of the ceremony of the circumcision, called 'sechu.' Just at the dawn of day, a row of boys of nearly fourteen years of age stood naked in the kotla, each having a pair of sandals as a shield on his hands. Facing them stood the men of the town in a similar state of nudity, all armed with long thin wands, of a tough, strong, supple bush called moretloa (*Grewia flava*), and engaged in a dance named 'koha,' in which questions are put to the boys, as 'Will you guard the chief well?' 'Will you herd the cattle well?' and, while the latter give an affirmative response, the men rush forward to them, and each aims a full-weight blow at the back of one of the boys. Shielding himself with the sandals above his head, he causes the supple wand to descend and bend into his back, and every stroke inflicted thus makes the blood squirt out of a wound a foot or eighteen inches long. At the end of the dance, the boys' backs are seamed with wounds and weals, the scars of which remain through life. This is intended to harden the young soldiers, and prepare them for the rank of men. After this ceremony, and after killing a rhinoceros, they may marry a wife.

"No one of the natives knows how old he is. If asked his age, he answers by putting another question, 'Does a man remember when he was born?' Age is reckoned by the number of mepato they have seen pass through the formulæ of admission. When they see four or five mepato younger than themselves, they are no longer obliged to bear arms. The oldest individual I ever met boasted he had seen eleven sets of boys submit to the boguera. Supposing him to have been fifteen when he saw his own, and fresh bands were added every six or seven years, he must have been about forty when he saw the fifth, and may have attained seventy-five or eighty years, which is no great age; but it seemed so to them, for he had now doubled the age for superannuation among them. It is an ingenious plan for attaching the members of the tribe to the chief's family, and for imparting a discipline which renders the tribe easy of command. On their return to the town from attendance on the ceremonies of initiation, a prize is given to the lad who can run fastest, the article being placed where all may see the winner run up to snatch it. They are then considered men (banona, viri), and can sit among the elders in the kotla. Formerly they were only boys (basimane, pueri). The first missionaries set their faces against the boguera, on account of its connection with heathenism, and the fact that the youths learned much evil, and became disobedient to their parents. From the general success of these men, it is perhaps better that younger missionaries should tread in their footsteps; for so much evil may result from breaking down the authority on which, to those who cannot read, the whole system of our influence appears to rest, that innovators ought to be made to propose their new measures as the Locrians did new laws— with ropes around their necks."

For a few days after leaving the Bamangwato there were good supplies of water. Then followed a stretch of sixty miles over a desert streaked with deposits of salt; and for nearly a month the privations of the caravan were very great, some of the few wells being spoiled by rhinoceros, while in other places water could only be found by digging. The tropical rains had been delayed long after their usual time, and it was not until the end of February, at a place called Unku, that they found fresh vegetation and abundant pools. Here the forest trees were all in blossom, and full of birds, the plains were covered with grass, and game of all kinds was plenty.

On the first of March Livingstone writes: "The thermometer in the shade generally stood at 98° from 1 to 3 P. M., but it sank as low as 65° by night, so that the heat was by no means exhausting. At the surface of the ground, in the sun, the thermometer marked 125°, and three inches below it 138°. The hand cannot be held on the ground, and even the horny soles of the feet of the natives must be protected by sandals of hide; yet the ants were busy working on it. The water in the ponds was as high as 100°; but as water does not conduct heat readily downward, deliciously cool water may be obtained by any one walking into the middle and lifting up the water from the bottom to the surface with his hands.

"Proceeding to the north, from Kama-kama, we entered into dense Mohonono bush, which required the constant application of the axe by three of our party for two days. This bush has fine silvery leaves, and the bark has a sweet taste. The elephant, with his usual delicacy of taste, feeds much on it. On emerging into the plains beyond, we found a number of Bushmen, who afterward proved very serviceable.

The rains had been copious, but now great numbers of pools were drying up. Lotus-plants abounded in them, and a low, sweet-scented plant covered their banks.

"The grass here was so tall that the oxen became uneasy, and one night the sight of a hyena made them rush away into the forest to the east of us. On rising on the morning of the 19th, I found that my Bakwain lad had run away with them. This I have often seen with persons of this tribe, even when the cattle are startled by a lion. Away go the young men in company with them, and dash through bush and brake for miles, till they think the panic is a little subsided; they then commence whistling to the cattle in the manner they do when milking the cows: having calmed them, they remain as a guard till the morning. The men generally return with their shins well peeled by the thorns. Each comrade of the Mopato would expect his fellow to act thus, without looking for any other reward than the brief praise of the chief. Our lad, Kibopechoe, had gone after the oxen, but had lost them in the rush through the flat, trackless forest. He remained on their trail all the next day and all the next night. On Sunday morning, as I was setting off in search of him, I found him near the wagon. He had found the oxen late in the afternoon of Saturday, and had been obliged to stand by them all night. It was wonderful how he managed without a compass, and in such a country, to find his way home at all, bringing about forty oxen with him.

"We wished to avoid the *tsetse* of our former

path, so kept a course on the magnetic meridian from Lurilopepe. The necessity of making a new path much increased our toil. We were, however, rewarded in lat. 18° with a sight we had not enjoyed the year before, namely, large patches of grape-bearing vines. There they stood before my eyes; but the sight was so entirely unexpected that I stood some time gazing at the clusters of grapes with which they were loaded, with no more thought of plucking than if I had been beholding them in a dream. The Bushmen know and eat them; but they are not well-flavored on account of the great astringency of the seeds, which are in shape and size like split peas. The elephants are fond of the fruit, plant, and root alike.

"Fleming had until this time always assisted to drive his own wagon, but about the end of March he knocked up, as well as his people. As I could not drive two wagons, I shared with him the remaining water, half a caskful, and went on, with the intention of coming back for him as soon as we should reach the next pool. Heavy rain now commenced; I was employed the whole day cutting down trees, and every stroke of the axe brought down a thick shower on my back, which in the hard work was very refreshing, as the water found its way down into my shoes. In the evening we met some Bushmen, who volunteered to show us a pool; and having unyoked, I walked some miles in search of it. At it became dark they showed their politeness—a quality which is by no means confined entirely to the civilized—by walking in front, breaking the branches which hung across the path, and pointing out the fallen trees. On returning to the wagon, we found that being left alone had brought out some of Fleming's energy, for he had managed to come up.

"As the water in this pond dried up, we were soon obliged to move again. One of the Bushmen took out his dice, and, after throwing them, said that God told him to go home. He threw again in order to show me the command, but the opposite result followed; so he remained and was useful, for we lost the oxen again by a lion driving them off to a very great distance. The lions here are not often heard. They seem to have a wholesome dread of the Bushmen, who, when they observe evidence of a lion's having made a full meal, follow up his spoor so quietly that his slumbers are not disturbed. One discharges a poisoned arrow from a distance of only a few feet, while his companion simultaneously throws his skin cloak on the beast's head. The sudden surprise makes the lion lose his presence of mind, and he bounds away in the greatest confusion and terror. Our friends here showed me the poison which they use on these occasions. It is the entrails of a caterpillar called N'gwa, half an inch long. They squeeze out these, and place them all around the bottom of the barb, and allow the poison to dry in the sun. They are very careful in cleaning their nails after working with it, as a small portion introduced into a scratch acts like morbid matter in dissection wounds. The agony is so great that the person cuts himself, calls for his mother's breast as if he were returned in idea to his childhood again, or flies from human habitations a raging maniac. The effects on the lion are equally terrible. He is heard moaning in distress, and becomes furious, biting the trees and ground in rage.

"As we went north the country became very lovely; many new trees appeared; the grass was green, and often higher than the wagons; the vines festooned the trees, among which appeared the real banian (*Ficus Indica*) with its drop-shoots, and the wild date and palmyra, and several other trees which were new to me; the hollows contained large patches of water. Next came water-courses, now resembling small rivers, twenty yards broad and four feet deep. The further we went, the broader and deeper these became; their bottoms contained great numbers of deep holes, made by elephants wading in them; in these the oxen floundered desperately, so that our wagon-pole broke, compelling us to work up to the breast in water for three hours and a half; yet I suffered no harm.

"We at last came to the Sanshureh, which presented an impassable barrier, so we drew up under a magnificent baobab-tree, (lat. 18° 4′ S., long. 24° 6′ E.), and resolved to explore the river for a ford. The great quanity of water we had passed through was part of the annual inundation of the Chobe; and this, which appeared a large, deep river, filled in many parts with reeds, and having hippopotami in it, is only one of the branches by which it sends its superabundant water to the south-east. From the hill N'gwa a ridge of higher land runs to the north-east, and bounds its course in that direction. We, being ignorant of this, were in the valley, and the only gap in the whole country destitute of *tsetse*. In company with the Bushmen, I explored all the banks of the Sanshureh to the west, till we came into *tsetse* on that side. We waded a long way among the reeds in water breast deep, but always found a broad, deep space free from vegetation and unfordable. A peculiar kind of lichen, which grows on the surface of the soil, becomes detached and floats on the water, giving out a very disagreeable odor, like sulphureted hydrogen, in some of these stagnant waters.

"Next morning, by climbing the highest trees, we could see a fine, large sheet of water, but surrounded on all sides by the same impenetrable belt of reeds. This is the broad part of the River Chobe, and is called Zabesa. Two tree-covered islands seemed to be much nearer to the water than the shore on which we were, so we made an attempt to get to them first. It was not the reeds alone we had to pass through; a peculiar serrated grass, which at certain angles cut the hands like a razor, was mingled with the reed, and the climbing convolvulus, with stalks which felt as strong as whipcord, bound the mass together. We felt like pigmies in it, and often the only way we could get on was by both of us leaning against a part and bending it down till we could stand upon it. The perspiration streamed off our bodies, and as the sun rose high, there being no ventilation among the reeds, the heat was stifling, and the water, which was up to the knees, felt agreeably refreshing. After some hours' toil, we reached one of the islands. Here we met an old friend, the bramble-bush. My strong moleskins were quite worn through at the knees, and the leather trowsers of my companion were torn and his legs bleeding. Tearing my handkerchief in two, I tied the pieces around my knees, and then encountered another difficulty. We were still forty or fifty yards from the clear water, but now we were opposed by great masses of papyrus, which are like palms in miniature, eight or ten feet high, and an inch and a half in diameter. These were laced together by twining convolvulus, so strongly that the weight of both of us could not make way into the clear water. At last we fortunately found a passage prepared by a hippopotamus. Eager as soon as we reached the island to look along the vista to clear water, I stepped in and found it took me at once up to the neck.

"Returning nearly worn out, we proceeded up the bank of the Chobe till we came to the point of departure of the branch Sanshureh; we then went in the opposite direction, or down the Chobe, though from the highest trees we could see nothing but one vast expanse of reed, with here and there a tree on the islands."

Next morning they started again, embarking on a light pontoon boat, which they had brought with them. "We paddled on from midday till sunset. There was nothing but a wall of reed on each bank, and we saw every prospect of spending a supperless night in our float; but just as the short twilight of these parts was commencing, we perceived, on the north bank of the village of Moremi, one of the Makololo, whose acquaintance I had made on our former visit, and who was now located on the island Mahonta (lat. 17° 58′ S., long. 24° 6′ E.). The villagers looked as we may suppose people do who see a ghost, and in their figurative way of speaking said, 'He has dropped among us from the clouds, yet came riding on the back of a hippopotamus! We Makalolo thought no one could cross the Chobe without our knowledge, but here he drops among us like a bird.'

"Next day we returned in canoes across the flooded lands, and found that, in our absence, the men had allowed the cattle to wander into a very small patch of wood to the west containing the *tsetse;* this carelessness cost me ten fine large oxen. After remaining a few days, some of the head men of the Makololo came down from Linyanti, with a large party of Barotse, to take us across the river. This they did in fine style, swimming and diving among the oxen more like alligators than men, and taking the wagons to pieces, and carrying them across on a number of canoes lashed together. We were now among friends; so going about thirty miles to the north, in order to avoid the still flooded lands on the north of the Chobe, we turned westward toward Linyanti (lat. 18° 17′ S., long. 23° 50′ E.), where we arrived on the 23d of May, 1853. This is the capital town of the Makololo, and only a short distance from our wagon-stand of 1851.

"The whole population of Linyanti, numbering between six and seven thousand souls, turned out *en masse* to see the wagons in motion. They had never witnessed the phenomenon before, we having on the former occasion departed by night. Sekeletu, now in power, received us in what is considered royal style, setting before us a great number of pots of boyaloa, the beer of the country. These were brought by women, and each bearer takes a good draught of the beer when she sets it down, by way of 'tasting' to show that there is no poison.

"The court herald, an old man who occupied the post also in Sebituane's time, stood up, and after some antics, such as leaping and shouting at the top of his voice, roared out some adulatory sentences, as, 'Don't I see the white man? Don't I see the comrade of Sebituane? Don't I see the father of Sekeletu?'—'We want sleep.'—'Give your son sleep, my lord' etc., etc. The perquisites of this man are the heads of all the cattle slaughtered by the chief, and he even takes a share of the tribute before it is distributed and taken out of the kotla. He is expected to utter all the proclamations, call assemblies, keep the kotla clean, and the fire burning every evening, and when a person is executed in public he drags away the body.

"I found Sekeletu, a young man of eighteen years of age, of that dark yellow or coffee-and-milk color, of which the Makololo are so proud, because it distinguishes them considerably from the black tribes on the rivers. He is about five feet seven in height, and neither so good looking nor of so much ability as his father was, but is equally friendly to the English. Sebituane installed his daughter Mamochisáne into the chieftainship long before his death, but, with all his acuteness, the idea of her having a husband who should not be her lord did not seem to enter his mind. He wished to make her his successor, probably in imitation of some of the negro tribes with whom he had come in contact; but, being of the Bechuana race, he could not look upon the husband except as the woman's lord; so he told her all the men were hers—she

might take any one, but ought to keep none. In fact, he thought she might do with the men what he could do with the women; but these men had other wives; and, according to a saying in the country, 'the tongues of women cannot be governed,' they made her miserable by their remarks. One man whom she chose was even called her wife, and her son, the child of Mamochisane's wife; but the arrangement was so distasteful to Mamochisane herself that, as soon as Sebituane died, she said she never would consent to govern the Makololo so long as she had a brother living. Sekeletu, being afraid of another member of the family, Mpepe, who had pretensions to the chieftainship, urged his sister strongly to remain as she had always been, and allow him to support her authority by leading the Makololo when they went forth to war. Three days were spent in public discussion on the point. Mpepe insinuated that Sekeletu was not the lawful son of Sebituane, on account of his mother having been the wife of another chief before her marriage with Sebituane; Mamochisane however upheld Sekeletu's claims, and at last stood up in the assembly and addressed him with a womanly gush of tears: 'I have been a chief only because my father wished it. I always would have preferred to be married and have a family like other women. You, Sekeletu, must be chief, and build up your father's house.' This was a death-blow to the hopes of Mpepe."

CHAPTER IX.

LIVINGSTONE'S JOURNEY ACROSS THE CONTINENT.

II.—VOYAGE UP THE ZAMBESI RIVER.

"MY object," Livingstone continues, "being first of all to examine the country for a healthy locality, before attempting to make a path to either the east or west coast, I proposed to Sekeletu the plan of ascending the great river which we had discovered in 1851. He volunteered to accompany me, and, when we got about sixty miles away, on the road to Sesheke, we encountered Mpepe. The Makololo, though possessing abundance of cattle, had never attempted to ride oxen until I advised it in 1851. The Bechuanas generally were in the same condition, until Europeans came among them and imparted the idea of riding. All their journeys previously were performed on foot. Sekeletu and his companions were mounted on oxen, though, having neither saddle nor bridle, they were perpetually falling off. Mpepe, armed with his little axe, came along a path parallel to, but a quarter of a mile distant from, that of our party, and, when he saw Sekeletu, he ran with all his might toward us; but Sekeletu, being on his guard, galloped off to an adjacent village. He then withdrew somewhere till all our party came up. Mpepe had given his own party to understand that he would cut down Sekeletu, either on their first meeting, or at the breaking up of their first conference. The former intention having been thus frustrated, he then determined to effect his purpose after their first interview. I happened to sit down between the two in the hut where they met. Being tired with riding all day in the sun, I soon asked Sekeletu where I should sleep, and he replied, 'Come, I will show you.' As we rose together, I unconsciously covered Sekeletu's body with mine, and saved him from the blow of the assassin. I knew nothing of the plot, but remarked that all Mpepe's men kept hold of their arms, even after we had sat down—a thing quite unusual in the presence of a chief; and when Sekeletu showed me the hut in which I was to spend the night, he said to me, 'That man wishes to kill me.' I afterward learned that some of Mpepe's attendants had divulged the secret; and, bearing in mind his father's instructions, Sekeletu put Mpepe to death that night. It was managed so quietly, that, although I was sleeping within a few yards of the scene, I knew nothing of it till the next day. Nokuane went to the fire, at which Mpepe sat, with a handful of snuff, as if he were about to sit down and regale himself therewith. Mpepe said to him, 'Nsepísa' (cause me to take a pinch); and, as he held out his hand, Nokuane caught hold of it, while another man seized the other hand, and, leading him out a mile, speared him. This is the common mode of executing criminals. They are not allowed to speak; though on one occasion a man, feeling his wrist held too tightly, said, 'Hold me gently, can't you? you will soon be led out in the same way yourselves.' Mpepe's men fled to the Barotse, and, it being unadvisable for us to go thither during the commotion which followed on Mpepe's death, we returned to Linyanti.

"Soon after our arrival, Sekeletu took me aside, and pressed me to mention those things I liked best and hoped to get from him. Anything, either in or out of his town, should be freely given if I would only mention it. I explained to him that my object was to elevate him and his people to be Christians; but he replied he did not wish to learn to read the Book, for he was afraid 'it might change his heart, and make him content with only one wife, like Sechele.' It was of little use to urge that the change of heart implied a contentment with one wife equal to his present complacency in polygamy. Such a preference after the change of mind could not now be understood by him any more than the real, unmistakable pleasure of religious services can by those who have not experienced what is known by the term the 'new heart.' I assured him that nothing was expected but by his own voluntary decision. 'No, no; he wanted always to have five wives at least.' I liked the frankness of Sekeletu, for nothing is so wearying to the spirit as talking to those who agree with everything advanced.

As I had declined to name anything as a present from Skeleletu, except a canoe to take me up the river, he brought ten fine elephants' tusks and laid them down beside my wagon. He would take no denial, though I told him I should prefer to see him trading with Fleming, a man of color from the West

Indies, who had come for the purpose. I had, during the eleven years of my previous course, invariably abstained from taking presents of ivory from an idea that a religious instructor degraded himself by accepting gifts from those whose spiritual welfare he professed to seek. My precedence of all traders in the line of discovery put me often in the way of very handsome offers, but I always advised the donors to sell their ivory to traders, who would be sure to follow.

"I had brought with me as presents an improved breed of goats, fowls, and a pair of cats. A superior bull was brought, also as a gift to Sekeletu, but I was compelled to leave it on account of its having become foot-sore. As the Makololo are very fond of improving the breed of their domestic animals, they were much pleased with my selection. I endeavored to bring the bull, in performance of a promise made to Sebituane before he died. Admiring a calf which we had with us, he proposed to give me a cow for it, which in the native estimation was offering three times its value. I presented it to him at once, and promised to bring him another and a better one. Sekeletu was much gratified by my attempt to keep my word given to his father.

"They have two breeds of cattle among them. One, called the Batoka, because captured from that tribe, is of diminutive size, but very beautiful, and closely resembles the short-horns of our own country. All are remarkably fond of their cattle, and spend much time in ornamenting and adorning them. Some are branded all over with a hot knife, so as to cause a permanent discoloration of the hair, in lines like the bands on the hide of a zebra. Pieces of skin two or three inches long and broad are detached, and allowed to heal in a dependent position around the head—a strange style of ornament; indeed, it is difficult to conceive in what their notion of beauty consists. The women have somewhat the same ideas with ourselves of what constitutes comeliness. They came frequently and asked for the looking-glass; and the remarks they made— while I was engaged in reading, and apparently not attending to them—on first seeing themselves therein, were amusingly ridiculous. 'Is that me?' 'What a big mouth I have!' 'My ears are as big as pumpkin-leaves.' 'I have no chin at all.' Or, 'I would have been pretty, but am spoiled by these high cheekbones.' 'See how my head shoots up in the middle!' laughing vociferously all the time at their own jokes. They readily perceived any defect in each other, and give nicknames accordingly. One man came alone to have a quiet gaze at his own features once, when he thought I was asleep; after twisting his mouth about in various directions, he remarked to himself, 'People say I am ugly, and how very ugly I am indeed!'

"The Makololo women work but little. Indeed, the families of that nation are spread over the country, one or two only in each village, as the lords of the land. They all have lordship over great numbers of subjected tribes, who pass by the general name Makalaka, and who are forced to render certain services, and to aid in tilling the soil; but each has his own land under cultivation, and otherwise lives nearly independent. They are proud to be called Makololo, but the other term is often used in reproach, as betokening inferiority. This species of servitude may be termed serfdom, as it has to be rendered in consequence of subjection by force of arms, but it is necessarily very mild. It is so easy for any one who is unkindly treated to make his escape to other tribes, that the Makololo are compelled to treat them, to a great extent, rather as children than slaves. Some masters, who fail from defect of temper or disposition to secure the affections of the conquered people, frequently find themselves left without a single servant, in consequence of the absence and impossibility of enforcing a fugitive-slave law, and the readiness with which those who are themselves subjected assist the fugitives across the rivers in canoes. The Makololo ladies are liberal in their presents of milk and other food, and seldom require to labor, except in the way of beautifying their own huts and court-yards. They drink large quantities of boyaloa or o-alo, the búza of the Arabs, which, being made of the grain called holcus sorghum or 'durasaifi,' in a minute state of subdivision, is very nutritious, and gives that plumpness of form which is considered beautiful. They dislike being seen at their potations by persons of the opposite sex. They cut their woolly hair quite short, and delight in having the whole person shining with butter. Their dress is a kilt reaching to the knees; its material is ox-hide, made as soft as cloth. It is not ungraceful. A soft skin mantle is thrown across the shoulders when the lady is unemployed, but when engaged in any sort of labor she throws this aside, and works in the kilt alone. The ornaments most coveted are large brass anklets as thick as the little finger, and armlets of both brass and ivory, the latter often an inch broad. The rings are so heavy that the ankles are often blistered by the weight pressing down; but it is the fashion, and is borne as magnanimously as tight lacing and tight shoes among ourselves. Strings of beads are hung around the neck, and the fashionable colors being light green and pink, a trader could get almost anything he chose for beads of these colors.

"At our public religious services in the kotla, the Makololo women always behaved with decorum from the first, except at the conclusion of the prayer. When all knelt down, many of those who had children, in following the example of the rest, bent over their little ones; the children, in terror of being crushed to death, set up a simultaneous yell, which so tickled the whole assembly that there was often a subdued titter, to be turned into a hearty laugh as soon as they heard Amen. This was not so difficult to overcome in them as similar peccadilloes were in the case of the women farther south. Long after we had settled at Mabotsa, when preaching on the most solemn subjects, a woman might be observed to look round, and, seeing a neighbor seated on her dress, give her a hunch with the elbow to make her move off; the other would return it with interest, and perhaps the remark, 'Take the nasty thing away, will you?' Then three or four would begin to hustle the first offenders, and the men to swear at them all, by way of enforcing silence."

On the 30th of May, Livingstone was attacked with fever at Linyanti, and more than three weeks elapsed before he was in a condition to travel. By the use of the hydropathic "wet sheet," and doses of quinine, he was finally restored to a tolerable condition, and set out on a voyage up the Zambesi, from the town of Sesheke (in Lat. 17° 31′ S.), to Naliele, the capital of the Barotse country (in Lat. 15° 24′ S.), at that time subject to the Makololo chief.

"I went," he says, "in company with Sekeletu and about one hundred and sixty attendants. We had most of the young men with us, and many of the under-chiefs besides. The country between Linyanti and Sesheke is perfectly flat, except patches elevated only a few feet above the surrounding level. There are also many mounds where the gigantic ant-hills of the country have been situated or still appear; these mounds are evidently the work of termites. No one who has not seen their gigantic structures can fancy the industry of these little laborers; they seem to impart fertility to the soil which has once passed through their mouths, for the Makololo find the sides of ant-hills the choice spots for rearing early maize, tobacco, or anything on which they wish to bestow especial care. In the parts through which we passed the mounds are generally covered with masses of wild date trees; the fruit is small, and no tree is allowed to stand long, for, having abundance of food, the Makololo have no inclination to preserve wild fruit trees; accordingly, when a date shoots up to seed, as soon as the fruit is ripe they cut down the tree rather than be at the trouble of climbing it. The other parts of the more elevated land have the camel-thorn, white-thorned mimosa, and baobabs.

"When we arrived at any village the women all

turned out to lulliloo their chief. Their shrill voices, to which they give a tremulous sound by a quick motion of the tongue, peal forth, 'Great lion!' 'Great chief!' 'Sleep, my lord!' etc. The men utter similar salutations; and Sekeletu receives all with becoming indifference. After a few minutes' conversation and telling the news, the head man of the village, who is almost always a Makololo, rises, and brings forth a number of large pots of beer. Calabashes, being used as drinking cups, are handed round, and as many as can partake of the beverage do so, grasping the vessels so eagerly that they are in danger of being broken.

"They bring forth also large pots and bowls of thick milk; some contain six or eight gallons; and each of these, as well as of the beer, is given to a particular person, who has the power to divide it with whom he pleases. The head man of any section of the tribe is generally selected for this office. Spoons not being generally in fashion, the milk is conveyed to the mouth with the hand. I often presented my friends with iron spoons, and it was curious to observe how the habit of hand-eating prevailed, though they were delighted with the spoons. They lifted out a little with the utensil, then put it on the left hand, and ate it out of that.

"Sekeletu and I had each a little gipsy-tent in which to sleep. The Makololo huts are generally clean, while those of the Makalaka are infested with vermin. The cleanliness of the former is owing to the habit of frequently smearing the floors with a plaster composed of cow-dung and earth. If we slept in the tent in some villages, the mice ran over our faces and disturbed our sleep, or hungry prowling dogs would eat our shoes and leave only the soles. When they were guilty of this and other misdemeanors, we got the loan of a hut. The best sort of Makololo huts consist of three circular walls; with small holes as doors, each similar to that in a dog-house; and it is necessary to bend down the body to get in, even when on all-fours. The roof is formed of reeds or straight sticks, in shape like a Chinaman's hat, bound firmly together with circular bands, which are lashed with the strong inner bark of the mimosa-tree. When all prepared except the thatch, it is lifted on to the circular wall, the rim resting on a circle of poles, between each of which the third wall is built. The roof is thatched with fine grass, and sewed with the same material as the lashings; and, as it projects far beyond the walls, and reaches within four feet of the ground, the shade is the best to be found in the country. These huts are very cool in the hottest day, but are close and deficient in ventilation by night.

"Our course at this time led us to a part above Sesheke, called Katonga, where there is a village belonging to a Bashubia man named Sekhosi. The river here is somewhat broader than at Sesheke, and certainly not less than six hundred yards. It flows somewhat slowly in the first part of its eastern course. When the canoes came from Sekhosi to take us over, one of the comrades of Sebituane rose, and, looking to Sekeletu, called out, 'The elders of a host always take the lead in an attack.' This was understood at once; and Sekeletu, with all the young men, were obliged to give the elders the precedence, and remain on the southern bank and see that all went orderly into the canoes. It took a considerable time to ferry over the whole of our large party, as, even with quick paddling, from six to eight minutes were spent in the mere passage from bank to bank.

"Several days were spent in collecting canoes from different villages on the river, which we now learned is called by the whole of the Barotse the Liambai or Leeambye. This we could not ascertain on our first visit, and, consequently, called the river after the town 'Sesheke.' This term Sesheke means 'white sand-banks,' many of which exist at this part. There is another village in the valley of the Barotse likewise called Sesheke, and for the same reason; but the term Leeambye means 'the large river,' or the river *par excellence*. Luambéji, Luambési, Ambézi, Ojimbési, and Zambési, etc., are names applied to it at different parts of its course, according to the dialect spoken, and all possess a similar signification, and express the native idea of this magnificent stream being the main drain of the country.

"In order to assist in the support of our large party, and at the same time to see the adjacent country, I went several times during our stay to the north of the village for game. The country is covered with clumps of beautiful trees, among which fine open glades stretch away in every direction; when the river is in flood these are inundated, but the tree-covered elevated spots are much more numerous here than in the country between the Chobe and the Leeambye. The soil is dark loam, as it is everywhere on spots reached by the inundation, while among the trees it is sandy, and not covered so densely with grass as elsewhere.

"Having at last procured a sufficient number of canoes, we began to ascend the river. I had the choice of the whole fleet, and selected the best, though not the largest; it was thirty-four feet long by twenty inches wide. I had six paddlers, and the larger canoe of Sekeletu had ten. They stand upright, and keep the stroke with great precision, though they change from side to side as the course demands. The men at the head and stern are selected from the strongest and most expert of the whole. The canoes, being flat-bottomed, can go into very shallow water; and whenever the men can feel the bottom, they use the paddles, which are about eight feet long, as poles to punt with. Our fleet consisted of thirty-three canoes, and about one hundred and sixty men. It was beautiful to see them skimming along so quickly, and keeping the time so well. On land the Makalaka fear the Makololo; on water the Makololo fear them, and cannot prevent them from racing with each other, dashing along at the top of their speed, and placing their masters' lives in danger. In the event of a capsize, many of the Makololo would sink like stones. A case of this kind happened on the first day of our voyage up. The wind, blowing generally from the east, raises very large waves on the Leeambye. An old doctor of the Makololo had his canoe filled by one of these waves, and, being unable to swim, was lost. The Barotse who were in the canoe with him saved themselves by swimming, and were afraid of being punished with death in the evening for not saving the doctor as well. Had he been a man of more influence, they certainly would have suffered death.

"We proceeded rapidly up the river, and I felt the pleasure of looking on lands which had never been seen by a European before. The river is, indeed, a magnificent one, often more than a mile broad, and adorned with many islands of from three to five miles in length. Both islands and banks are covered with forest, and most of the trees on the brink of the water send down roots from their branches like the banian, or *Ficus Indica*. The islands at a little distance seem great rounded masses of sylvan vegetation reclining on the bosom of the glorious stream. The beauty of the scenery of some of the islands is greatly increased by the date-palm, with its gracefully curved fronds and refreshing light green color, near the bottom of the picture, and the lofty palmyra towering far above, and casting its feathery foliage against a cloudless sky. It being winter, we had the strange coloring on the banks which many parts of the African landscape assume. The country adjacent to the river is rocky and undulating, abounding in elephants and all other large game, except leches and nakongs, which seem generally to avoid stony ground. The soil is of a reddish color, and very fertile, as is attested by the great quantity of grain raised annually by the Banyeti. A great many villages of this poor and very industrious people are situated on both banks of the river: they are expert hunters of the hippopotami and other animals, and very proficient in the manufacture of articles of wood and iron. The whole of this part of the country being infested with the *tsetse*, they are unable to rear domestic animals. This may have led to their skill in handicraft works. Some make large wooden vessels with very neat lids, and wooden bowls of all sizes; and since the idea of sitting on stools has entered the Makololo mind, they have shown great taste in the different forms given to the legs of these pieces of furniture.

"From the bend up to the north, called Katima-molelo (I quenched fire), the bed of the river is rocky, and the stream runs fast, forming a succession of rapids and cataracts, which prevent continuous navigation when the water is low. The rapids are not visible when the river is full, but the cataracts of Nambwe, Bombwe, and Kale must always be dangerous. The fall at each of these is between four and six feet. But the falls of Gonye present a much more serious obstacle. There we were obliged to take the canoes out of the water, and carry them more than a mile by land. The fall is about thirty feet. The main body of water, which comes over the ledge of rock when the river is low, is collected into a space seventy or eighty yards wide before it takes the leap, and, a mass of rock being thrust forward against the roaring torrent, a loud sound is produced. Tradition reports the destruction in this place of two hippopotamus-hunters, who, over-eager in the pursuit of a wounded animal, were, with their intended prey, drawn down into the frightful gulf.

"As we passed up the river, the different villages of Banyeti turned out to present Sekeletu with food and skins, as their tribute. One large village is placed at

Gonye, the inhabitants of which are required to assist the Makololo to carry their canoes past the falls. The *tsetse* here lighted on us even in the middle of the stream. This we crossed repeatedly, in order to make short cuts at bends of the river. The course is, however, remarkably straight among the rocks; and here the river is shallow, on account of the great breadth of surface which it covers. When we came to about 16° 16′ S. latitude, the high wooded banks seemed to leave the river, and no more *tsetse* appeared. Viewed from the flat, reedy basin in which the river then flowed, the banks seemed prolonged into ridges, of the same wooded character, two or three hundred feet high, and stretched away to the N.N.E. and N.N.W. until they were twenty or thirty miles apart. The intervening space, nearly one hundred miles in length, with the Leeambye winding gently near the middle, is the true Barotse valley. It bears a close resemblance to the valley of the Nile, and is inundated annually, not by rains but by the Leeambye, exactly as Lower Egypt is flooded by the Nile. The villages of the Barotse are built on mounds, some of which are said to have been raised artifically by Santuru, a former chief of the Barotse, and during the inundation the whole valley assumes the appearance of a large lake, with the villages on the mounds like islands, just as occurs in Egypt with the villages of the Egyptians.

"This visit was the first Sekeletu had made to these parts since he attained the chieftainship. Those who had taken part with Mpepe were consequently in great terror. When we came to the town of Mpepe's father, as he and another man had counseled Mamochisanc to put Sekeletu to death and marry Mpepe, the two were led forth and tossed into the river. Nokuane was again one of the executioners. When I remonstrated against human blood being shed in the offhand way in which they were proceeding, the counselors justified their acts by the evidence given by Mamochisane, and calmly added, 'You see we are still Boers; we are not yet taught.'

"Mpepe had given full permission to the Mambari slave-dealers to trade in all the Batoka and Bashukulompo villages to the east of this. He had given them cattle, ivory, and children, and had received in return a large blunderbuss to be mounted as a cannon. When the slight circumstance of my having covered the body of the chief with my own deranged the whole conspiracy, the Mambari, in their stockade, were placed in very awkward circumstances. It was proposed to attack them and drive them out of the country at once; but, dreading a commencement of hostilities, I urged the difficulties of that course, and showed that a stockade defended by perhaps forty muskets would be a very serious affair. 'Hunger is strong enough for that,' said an under-chief; 'a very great fellow is he.' They thought of attacking them by starvation. As the chief sufferers in case of such an attack would have been the poor slaves chained in gangs, I interceded for them, and the result of an intercession of which they were ignorant was that they were allowed to depart in peace.

"Naliele, the capital of the Barotse, is built on a mound which was constructed artificially by Santuru, and was his store-house for grain. His own capital stood about five hundred yards to the south of that, in what is now the bed of the river. All that remains of the largest mound in the valley are a few cubic yards of earth, to erect which cost the whole of the people of Santuru the labor of many years. The same thing has happened to another ancient site of a town, Linangelo, also on the left bank. It would seem, therefore, that the river in this part of the valley must be wearing eastward. No great rise of the river is required to submerge the whole valley; a rise of ten feet above the present low-water mark would reach the highest point it ever attains, as seen in the markings of the bank on which stood Santuru's ancient capital, and two or three feet more would deluge all the villages. This never happens, though the water sometimes comes so near the foundations of the huts that the people cannot move outside the walls of reeds which encircle their villages. When the river is compressed among the high rocky banks near Gonye, it rises sixty feet."

From the town of Naliele Livingstone walked to Katonga, a village to the eastward, on a ridge which seems to bound the valley of the Zambesi. But it was only the commencement of the inundated lands, which gradually rise from the dead level of the river-bottoms, like the edge of the desert in the valley of the Nile. The situation was not exempt from fever; so he returned to Naliele and continued his voyage up the river to the town of Libonta. Beyond this point, dense forests came to the water's edge, and the *tsetse* reappeared. Hearing that he was not far from a great river called Leeba, which came down from the country of Londa (reports of which had been received through the Portuguese), he pushed on, and in Lat. 14° 11′ S. reached the confluence of the Leeba with the Zambesi. The latter river here changes its course, and appears to come from the east; it is still a full, deep stream, about 300 yards wide, while the Leeba has a breadth of 250. There was no tradition of any white man having previously visited the region.

"It was now," says Livingstone, "quite evident that no healthy location could be obtained in which the Makololo would be allowed to live in peace. I had thus a fair excuse, if I had chosen to avail myself of it, of coming home and saying that the 'door was shut,' because the Lord's time had not yet come. But believing that it was my duty to devote some portion of my life to these (to me at least) very confiding and affectionate Makololo, I resolved to follow out the second part of my plan, though I had failed in accomplishing the first. The Leeba seemed to come from the N. and by W., or N.N.W.; so, having an old Portuguese map, which pointed out the Coanza as rising from the middle of the continent in 9° S. lat., I thought it probable that, when we had ascended the Leeba (from 14° 11′) two or three degrees, we should then be within one hundred and twenty miles of the Coanza, and find no difficulty in following it down to the coast near Loanda. This was the logical deduction; but, as is the case with many a plausible theory, one of the premises was decidedly defective. The Coanza, as we afterward found, does not come from anywhere near the centre of the country.

"A party of Arabs from Zanzibar were in the country at this time. Sekeletu had gone from Naliele to the town of his mother before we arrived from the north, but left an ox for our use, and instructions for us to follow him thither. We came down a branch of the Leeambye called Marile, which departs from the main river, and is a fine deep stream about sixty yards wide. It makes the whole of the country around Naliele an island. When sleeping at a village in the same latitude as Naliele town, two of the Arabs mentioned made their appearance. They were quite as dark as the Makololo, but, having their heads shaved, I could not compare their hair with that of the inhabitants of the country. When we were about to leave they came to bid adieu, but I asked them to stay and help us eat our ox. As they had scruples about eating an animal not blooded in their own way, I gained their good-will by saying I was quite of their opinion as to getting quit of the blood, and gave them two legs of an animal slaughtered by themselves.

"As this was the first visit which Sekeletu had paid to this part of his dominions, it was to many a season of great joy. The head men of each village presented oxen, milk, and beer, more than the horde which accompanied him could devour, though their abilities in that line are something wonderful. The people usually show their joy and work off their excitement in dances and songs. The dance consists of the men standing nearly naked in a circle, with clubs or small battle-axes in their hands, and each roaring at the loudest pitch of his voice, while they simultaneously lift one leg, stamp heavily twice with it, then lift the other and

MOONLIGHT DANCE.

give one stamp with that; this is the only movement in common. The arms and head are often thrown about also in every direction; and all this time the roaring is kept up with the utmost possible vigor; the continued stamping makes a cloud of dust ascend, and they leave a deep ring in the ground where they stood. If the scene were witnessed in a lunatic asylum it would be nothing out of the way, and quite appropriate even, as a means of letting off the excessive excitement of the brain; but here gray-headed men joined in the performance with as much zest as others whose youth might be an excuse for making the perspiration stream off their bodies with the exertion. Motibe asked what I thought of the Makololo dance. I replied, 'It is very hard work, and brings but small profit.' 'It is,' replied he, 'but it is very nice, and Sekeletu will give us an ox for dancing for him.' He usually does slaughter an ox for the dancers when the work is over.

"The women stand by, clapping their hands, and occasionally one advances into the circle, composed of a hundred men, makes a few movements, and then retires. As I never tried it, and am unable to enter into the spirit of the thing, I cannot recommend the Makololo polka to the dancing world, but I have the authority of no less a person than Motibe, Sekeletu's father-in-law, for saying 'it is very nice.' They often asked if white people ever danced. I thought of the disease called St. Vitus's dance, but could not say that all our dancers were affected by it, and gave an answer which, I ought to be ashamed to own, did not raise some of our young countrywomen in the estimation of the Makololo.

"As Sekeletu had been waiting for me at his mother's, we left the town as soon as I arrived, and proceeded down the river. Our speed with the stream was very great, for in one day we went from Litofe to Gonye, a distance of forty-four miles of latitude; and if we add to this the windings of the river, in longitude the distance will not be much less than sixty geographical miles. At this rate we soon reached Sesheke, and then the town of Linyanti.

"I had been, during a nine weeks' tour, in closer contact with heathenism than I had ever been before; and though all, including the chief, were as kind and attentive to me as possible, and there was no want of food (oxen being slaughtered daily, sometimes ten at a time, more than sufficient for the wants of all), yet to endure the dancing, roaring, and singing, the jesting, anecdotes, grumbling, quarreling, and murdering of these children of nature, seemed more like a severe penance than anything I had before met with in the course of my missionary duties. I took thence a more intense disgust at heathenism than I had before, and formed a greatly elevated opinion of the latent effects of missions, in the south, among tribes which are reported to have been as savage as the Makololo. The indirect benefits which, to a casual observer, lie beneath the surface and are inappreciable, in reference to the probable wide diffusion of Christianity at some future time, are worth all the money and labor that have been expended to produce them."

CHAPTER X.

LIVINGSTONE'S JOURNEY ACROSS THE CONTINENT.

III.—UP THE LEEBA RIVER.

THE Makololo were so quick to perceive the advantages of a regular trade with white men, that the greatest difficulties in the way of Livingstone's further exploration were removed. He decided to wait at Linyanti until the rains should have moderated the tropical heats, and then set out to find a way to St. Paul de Loanda. His observation of the latitude of Linyanti showed that the port of St. Philip de Benguela was much nearer, and he could have made arrangements with the Mambari tribe to pass through their territory; but he wisely preferred not to follow in the wake of slave-traders. Parties sent out to the westward, to discover a belt of territory free from the *tsetse* fly, returned unsuccessful, and the best prospect seemed to be to ascend the Zambesi and the Leeba as far as possible, and then strike westwards for the coast. Livingstone's account of the discussion of the matter among the natives, and his preparations for the further journey, must be given in his own words:

"A 'picho' was called to deliberate on the steps proposed. In these assemblies great freedom of speech is allowed; and on this occasion one of the old diviners said, 'Where is he taking you to? This white man is throwing you away. Your garments already smell of blood.' It is curious to observe how much identity of character appears all over the world. This man was a noted croaker. He always dreamed something dreadful in every expedition, and was certain that an eclipse or comet betokened the propriety of flight. But Sebituane formerly set his visions down to cowardice, and Sekeletu only laughed at him now. The general voice was in my favor; so a band of twenty-seven were appointed to accompany me to the west. These men were not hired, but sent to enable me to accomplish an object as much desired by the chief and most of his people as by me. They were eager to obtain free and profitable trade with white men. The prices which the Cape merchants could give, after defraying the great expenses of a long journey hither, being very small, made it scarce worth while for the natives to collect produce for that market; and the Mambari, giving only a few bits of print and baize for elephants' tusks worth more pounds than they gave yards of cloth, had produced the belief that trade with them was throwing ivory away. The desire of the Makololo for direct trade with the sea-coast coincided exactly with my own conviction that no permanent elevation of a people can be effected without commerce.

"The Makololo now put the question, 'In the event of your death, will not the white people blame us for having allowed you to go away into an unhealthy, unknown country of enemies?' I replied that none of my friends would blame them, because I would leave a book with Sekeletu, to be sent to Mr.

Moffat in case I did not return, which would explain to him all that had happened until the time of my departure. The book was a volume of my Journal; and, as I was detained longer than I expected at Loanda, this book, with a letter, was delivered by Sekeletu to a trader, and I have been unable to trace it. I regret this now, as it contained valuable notes on the habits of wild animals, and the request was made in the letter to convey the volume to my family. The prospect of passing away from this fair and beautiful world thus came before me in a pretty plain, matter-of-fact form, and it did seem a serious thing to leave wife and children—to break up all connection with earth, and enter on an untried state of existence; and I find myself in my Journal pondering over that fearful migration which lands us in eternity, wondering whether an angel will soothe the fluttering soul, sadly flurried as it must be on entering the spirit world, and hoping that Jesus might speak but one word of peace, for that would establish in the bosom an everlasting calm.

"I had three muskets for my people, a rifle and double-barreled smooth-bore for myself; and, having seen such great abundance of game in my visit to the Leeba, I imagined that I could easily supply the wants of my party. Wishing also to avoid the discouragement which would naturally be felt on meeting any obstacles if my companions were obliged to carry heavy loads, I took only a few biscuits, a few pounds of tea and sugar, and about twenty of coffee, which, as the Arabs find, though used without either milk or sugar, is a most refreshing beverage after fatigue or exposure to the sun. We carried one small tin canister, about fifteen inches square, filled with spare shirting, trowsers, and shoes, to be used when we reached civilized life, and others in a bag, which were expected to wear out on the way; another of the same size for medicines; and a third for books, my stock being a Nautical Almanac, Thomson's Logarithm Tables, and a Bible; a fourth box contained a magic lantern, which we found of much use. The sextant and artificial horizon, thermometer, and compasses were carried apart. My ammunition was distributed in portions through the whole luggage, so that, if an accident should befall one part, we could still have others to fall back upon. Our chief hopes for food were upon that; but in case of failure, I took about 20lbs. of beads, worth 40s., which still remained of the stock I brought from Capetown, a small gipsy-tent, just sufficient to sleep in, a sheep-skin mantle as a blanket, and a horse-rug as a bed. As I had always found that the art of successful travel consisted in taking as few 'impedimenta' as possible, and not forgetting to carry my wits about me, the outfit was rather spare, and intended to be still more so when we should come to leave the canoes. Some would consider it injudicious to adopt this plan, but I had a secret conviction that if I did not succeed, it would not be for want of the 'knick-knacks' advertised as indispensable for travellers, but from want of 'pluck,' or because a large array of baggage excited the cupidity of the tribes through whose country we wished to pass.

"The course of the Chobe River, after starting, we found to be extremely tortuous; so much so, indeed, as to carry us to all points of the compass every dozen miles. Some of us walked from a bend at the village of Moremi, to another nearly due east of that point, in six hours, while the canoes, going at more than double our speed, took twelve to accomplish the voyage between the same two places. And though the river is from thirteen to fifteen feet in depth at its lowest ebb, and broad enough to allow a steamer to ply upon it, the suddenness of the bendings would prevent navigation; but, should the country ever become civilized, the Chobe would be a convenient natural canal.

"After spending one night at the Makololo village on Mparia, we left the Chobe, and turning round, began to ascend the Leeambye; on the 19th of November we again reached the town of Sesheke. It stands on the north bank of the river, and contains a large population of Makalaka, under Moriantsane, brother-in-law of Sebituane. There are parties of various tribes here, assembled under their respective head men, but a few Makololo rule over all. Their sway, though essentially despotic, is considerably mollified by certain customs and laws.

"The following circumstance, which happened here when I was present with Sekeletu, shows that the simple mode of punishment, by forcing a criminal to work out a fine, did not strike the Makololo mind until now. A stranger having visited Sesheke for the purpose of barter, was robbed by one of the Makalaka of most of his goods. The thief, when caught, confessed the theft, and that he had given the articles to a person who had removed to a distance. The Makololo were much enraged at the idea of their good name being compromised by this treatment of a stranger. Their customary mode of punishing a crime which causes much indignation is to throw the criminal into the river; but, as this would not restore the lost property, they were sorely puzzled how to act. The case was referred to me, and I solved the difficulty by paying for the loss myself, and sentencing the thief to work out an equivalent with his hoe in a garden. This system was immediately introduced, and thieves are now sentenced to raise an amount of corn proportioned to their offences.

"On recovering partially from a severe attack of fever which remained upon me ever since our passing the village of Moremi on the Chobe, we made ready for our departure up the river by sending messages before us to the villages to prepare food. We took four elephants' tusks, belonging to Sekeletu, with us, as a means of testing the difference of prices between the Portuguese, whom we expected to reach, and the white traders from the south. Moriantsane supplied us well with honey, milk, and meal. The rains were just commencing in this district; but, though showers sufficient to lay the dust had fallen, they had no influence whatever on the amount of water in the river, yet never was there less in any part than three hundred yards of a deep flowing stream.

"Our progress up the river was rather slow; this was caused by waiting opposite different villages for supplies of food. We might have done with much less than we got; but my Makololo man, Pitsane, knew of the generous orders of Sekeletu, and was not at all disposed to allow them to remain a dead letter. The villages of the Banyeti contributed large quantities of mosibe, a bright red bean yielded by a large tree. The pulp inclosing the seed is not much thicker than a red wafer, and is the portion used. It requires the addition of honey to render it at all palatable. To these were added great numbers of the fruit which yields a variety of the nux vomica, from which we derive that virulent poison strychnia. The pulp between the nuts is the part eaten, and it is of a pleasant juicy nature, having a sweet acidulous taste. The fruit itself resembles a large yellow orange.

"When under way our usual procedure is this: We get up a little before five in the morning; it is then beginning to dawn. While I am dressing, coffee is made; and, having filled my pannikin, the remainder is handed to my companions, who eagerly partake of the refreshing beverage. The servants are busy loading the canoes, while the principal men are sipping the coffee, and, that being soon over, we embark. The next two hours are the most pleasant part of the day's sail. The men paddle away most vigorously; the Barotse, being a tribe of boatmen, have large, deeply-developed chests and shoulders, with indifferent lower extremities. They often engage in loud scolding of each other in order to relieve the tedium of their work. About eleven we land, and eat any meat which may have remained from the previous evening meal, or a biscuit with honey, and drink water.

"After an hour's rest we again embark and cower under an umbrella. The heat is oppressive, and, being weak from the last attack of fever, I cannot land and keep the camp supplied with flesh. The men, being quite uncovered in the sun, perspire profusely, and in the afternoon begin to stop, as if waiting for the canoes which have been left behind. Sometimes we reach a sleeping-place two hours before sunset, and, all being troubled with languor, we gladly remain for the night. Coffee again, and a biscuit, or a piece of course bread made of maize meal, or that of the native corn, make up the bill of fare for the evening, unless we have been fortunate enough to kill something, when we boil a potful of flesh. This is done by cutting it up into long strips and pouring in water till it is covered. When that is boiled dry, the meat is considered ready.

"The people of every village treated us most liberally, presenting besides oxen, butter, milk, and meal, more than we could stow away in our canoes. The cows in this valley are now yielding, as they frequently do, more milk than the people can use, and both men and women present butter in such quantity that I shall be able to refresh my men as we move along. Anointing the skin prevents the excessive evaporation of the fluids of the body, and acts as clothing in both sun and shade. They always made their presents gracefully. When an ox was given the owner would say, 'Here is a little bit of bread for you.' This was pleasing, for I had been accustomed to the Bechuanas presenting a miserable goat, with the pompous exclamation, 'Behold an ox!' The women persisted in giving me copious supplies of shrill praises, or 'lullilooing;' but though I frequently told them to modify their 'great lords' and 'great lions' to more humble expressions, they so evidently intended to do me honor that I could not help being pleased with the poor creatures' wishes for our success.

"The rains began while we were at Naliele; this is much later than usual; though the Barotse valley has been in need of rain, the people never lack abundance of food. The showers are refreshing, but the air feels hot and close; the thermometer, however, in a cool hut, stands only at 84°. The access of the external air to any spot at once raises its temperature above 90°. A new attack of fever here caused excessive languor; but, as I am already getting tired of quoting my fevers, and never liked to read travels myself where much was said about the illness of the traveller, I shall henceforth endeavor to say little about them.

"Leaving Naliele, amid abundance of good wishes for the success of our expedition, and hopes that we might return accompanied with white traders, we began again our ascent of the river. It was now beginning to rise, though the rains had but just commenced in the valley. The banks are low, but cleanly cut, and seldom sloping. At low water they are from four to eight feet high, and make the river always assume very much the aspect of a canal. They are in some parts of whitish, tenacious clay, with strata of black clay intermixed, and black loam in sand, or pure sand stratified. As the river rises it is always wearing to one side or the other, and is known to have cut across from one bend to another, and to form new channels. As we coast along the shore, pieces which are undermined often fall in with a splash like that caused by the plunge of an alligator, and endanger the canoe.

"Before leaving the villages entirely, we may

glance at our way of spending the nights. As soon as we land, some of the men cut a little grass for my bed, while Mashuána plants the poles of the little tent. These are used by day for carrying burdens, for the Barotse fashion is exactly like that of the natives of India, only the burden is fastened near the ends of the pole, and not suspended by long cords. The bed is made, and boxes ranged on each side of it, and then the tent pitched over all. Four or five feet in front of my tent is placed the principal or kotla fire, the wood for which must be collected by the man who occupies the post of herald, and takes as his perquisite the heads of all the oxen slaughtered, and of all the game too. Each person knows the station he is to occupy, in reference to the post of honor at the fire in front of the door of the tent. The two Makololo occupy my right and left, both in eating and sleeping, as long as the journey lasts. But Mashauana, my head boatman, makes his bed at the door of the tent as soon as I retire. The rest, divided into small companies according to their tribes, make sheds all round the fire, leaving a horseshoe-shaped space in front sufficient for the cattle to stand in. The fire gives confidence to the oxen, so the men are always careful to keep them in sight of it. The sheds are formed by planting two stout forked poles in an inclined direction, and placing another over these in a horizontal position. A number of branches are then stuck in the ground in the direction to which the poles are inclined, the twigs drawn down to the horizontal pole and tied with strips of bark. Long grass is then laid over the branches in sufficient quantity to draw off the rain, and we have sheds open to the fire in front, but secure from beasts behind. In less than an hour we were usually all under cover. We never lacked abundance of grass during the whole journey. It is a picturesque sight at night, when the clear bright moon of these climates glances on the sleeping forms around, to look out upon the attitudes of profound repose both men and beasts assume. There being no danger from wild animals in such a night, the fires are allowed almost to go out; and as there is no fear of hungry dogs coming over sleepers and devouring the food, or quietly eating up the poor fellows' blankets, which at best were but greasy skins, which sometimes happened in the villages, the picture was one of perfect peace.

"Part of our company marched along the banks with the oxen, and part went in the canoes, but our pace was regulated by the speed of the men on shore. Their course was rather difficult, on account of the numbers of departing and re-entering branches of the Leeambye, which they had to avoid or wait at till we ferried them over. The number of alligators is prodigious, and in this river they are more savage than in some others. Many children are carried off annually at Sesheke and other towns; for, notwithstanding the danger, when they go down for water they almost always must play a while. This reptile is said by the natives to strike the victim with its tail, then drag him in and drown him. When lying in the water watching for prey, the body never appears. Many calves are lost also, and it is seldom that a number of cows can swim over at Sesheke without some loss. I never could avoid shuddering on seeing my men swimming across these branches, after one of them had been caught by the thigh and taken below. He, however, retained, as nearly all of them in the most trying circumstances do, his full presence of mind, and, having a small, square, ragged-edged javelin with him, when dragged to the bottom, gave the alligator a stab behind the shoulder. The alligator, writhing in pain, left him, and he came out with the deep marks of the reptile's teeth on his thigh. Here the people have no antipathy to persons who have met with such an adventure, but, in the Bamangwato and Bakwain tribes, if a man is either bitten, or even has had water splashed over him by the reptile's tail, he is expelled his tribe. When on the Zouga we saw one of the Bamangwato living among the Bayeiye, who had the misfortune to have been bitten and driven out of his tribe in consequence. Fearing that I would regard him with the same disgust which his countrymen profess to feel, he would not tell me the cause of his exile, but the Bayeiye informed me of it, and the scars of the teeth were visible on his thigh. If the Bakwains happened to go near an alligator they would spit on the ground, and indicate its presence by saying, 'Boleo ki bo'—'There is sin.' They imagine the mere sight of it would give inflammation of the eyes; and though they eat the zebra without hesitation, yet if one bites a man he is expelled the tribe, and obliged to take his wife and family away to the Kalahari. These curious relics of the animal worship of former times scarcely exist among the Makololo. Sebituane acted on the principle, 'Whatever is food for men is food for me;' so no man is here considered unclean. The

Barotse appear inclined to pray to alligators and eat them too, for when I wounded a water-antelope, called mochose, it took to the water; when near the other side of the river an alligator appeared at its tail, and then both sank together. Mashauanu, who was nearer to it than I, told me that, 'though he had called to it to let his meat alone, it refused to listen.' One day we passed some Barotse lads who had speared an alligator, and were waiting in expectation of its floating soon after. The meat has a strong musky odor, not at all inviting for any one except the very hungry.

"On the 27th of December we were at the confluence of the Leeba and Leeambye (lat. 14° 10′ S., long. 23° 35′ E.). Masiko, the Barotse chief, for whom we had some captives, lived nearly due east of this point. They were two little boys, a little girl, a young man, and two middle-aged women. One of these was a member of a Babímpe tribe, who knock out both upper and lower front teeth as a distinction. As we had been informed by the captives on the previous Sunday that Masiko was in the habit of seizing all orphans, and those who have no powerful friend in the tribe whose protection they can claim, and selling them for clothing to the Mambari, we thought the objection of the women to go first to his town before seeing their friends quite reasonable, and resolved to send a party of our own people to see them safely among their relatives. I told the captive young man to inform Masiko that he was very unlike his father Santuru, who had refused to sell his people to Mambari. He will probably be afraid to deliver such a message himself, but it is meant for his people, and they will circulate it pretty widely, and Masiko may may yet feel a little pressure from without.

"We now began to ascend the Leeba. The water is black in color as compared with the main stream, which here assumes the name Kabompo. The Leeba flows placidly, and, unlike the parent river, receives numbers of little rivulets from both sides. It winds slowly through the most charming meadows, each of which has either a soft, sedgy centre, large pond, or trickling rill down the middle. The trees are now covered with a profusion of the freshest foliage, and seem planted in groups of such pleasant, graceful outline that art could give no additional charm. The grass, which had been burned off and was growing again after the rains, was short and green, and all the scenery so like that of a carefully-tended gentleman's park, that one is scarcely reminded that the surrounding region is in the hands of simple nature alone. I suspect that the level meadows are inundated annually, for the spots on which the trees stand are elevated three or four feet above them, and these elevations, being of different shapes, give the strange variety of outline of the park-like woods. Numbers of a fresh-water shell are scattered all over these valleys. The elevations, as I have observed elsewhere, are of a soft, sandy soil, and the meadows of black, rich alluvial loam. There are many beautiful flowers, and many bees to sip their nectar.

"When we reached the part of the river opposite to the village of Manenko, the first female chief whom we encountered, two of the people called Balunda, or Balŏnda, came to us in their little canoe. From them we learned that Kolimbóta, one of our party, who had been in the habit of visiting these parts, was believed by the Balŏnda to have acted as a guide to the marauders, whose captives we were now returning. They very naturally suspected this, from the facility with which their villages had been found, and, as they had since removed them to some distance from the river, they were unwilling to lead us to their places of concealment. We were in bad repute, but, having a captive boy and girl to show in evidence of Sekeletu and ourselves not being partakers in the guilt of inferior men, I could freely express my desire that all should live in peace.

"As it would have been impolitic to pass Manenko, or any chief, without at least showing so much respect as to call and explain the objects of our passing through the country, we waited two entire days for the return of the messengers to Manenko; and as I could not hurry matters, I went into the adjacent country to search for meat for the camp.

"The country is furnished largely with forest, having occasionally open lawns covered with grass, not in tufts as in the south, but so closely planted that one cannot see the soil. We came upon a man and his two wives and children, burning coarse rushes and the stalks of tsitla, growing in a brackish marsh, in order to extract a kind of salt from the ashes. They make a funnel of branches of trees, and line it with grass rope, twisted round until it is, as it were, a beehive-roof inverted. The ashes are put into water, in a calabash, and then it is allowed to percolate through the small hole in the bottom and through the grass.

When this water is evaporated in the sun, it yields sufficient salt to form a relish with food. The women and children fled with precipitation, but we sat down at a distance, and allowed the man time to gain courage enough to speak. He, however, trembled excessively at the apparition before him; but when we explained that our object was to hunt game, and not men, he became calm, and called back his wives. We soon afterward came to another party on the same errand with ourselves. The man had a bow about six feet long, and iron-headed arrows about thirty inches in length; he had also wooden arrows neatly barbed, to shoot in cases where he might not be quite certain of recovering them again. We soon afterward got a zebra, and gave our hunting acquaintances such a liberal share that we soon became friends.

"On the 6th of January 1854, we reached the village of another female chief, named Nyamoána, who is said to be the mother of Manenko, and sister of Shinté or Kabómpo, the greatest Balonda chief in this part of the country. Her people had but recently come to the present locality, and had erected only twenty huts. Her husband, Samoana, was clothed in a kilt of green and red baize, and was armed with a spear and a broadsword of antique form, about eighteen inches long and three broad. The chief and her husband were sitting on skins placed in the middle of a circle thirty paces in diameter, a little raised above the ordinary level of the ground, and having a trench round it. Outside the trench sat about a hundred persons of all ages and both sexes. The men were well armed with bows, arrows, spears, and broadswords. Beside the husband sat a rather aged woman, having a bad outward squint in the left eye. We put down our arms about forty yards off, and I walked up to the centre of the circular bench, and saluted him in the usual way by clapping the hands together in their fashion. He pointed to his wife, as much as to say the honor belongs to her. I saluted her in the same way, and a mat having been brought, I squatted down in front of them.

"The talker was then called, and I was asked who was my spokesman. Having pointed to Kolimbota, who knew their dialect best, the palaver began in due form. I explained the real objects I had in view, without any attempt to mystify or appear in any other character than my own, for I have always been satisfied that, even though there were no other considerations, the truthful way of dealing with the uncivilized is unquestionably the best. Kolimbota repeated to Nyamoana's talker what I had said to him. He delivered it all verbatim to her husband, who repeated it again to her. It was thus all rehearsed four times over, in a tone loud enough to be heard by the whole party of auditors. The response came back by the same roundabout route, beginning at the lady to her husband, etc.

"By way of gaining their confidence, I showed them my hair, which is considered a curiosity in all this region. They said, 'Is that hair? It is the mane of a lion, and not hair at all.' Some thought that I had made a wig of lion's mane, as they sometimes do with fibres of the 'ife,' and dye it black, and twist it so as to resemble a mass of their own wool.

I could not return the joke by telling them that theirs was not hair, but the wool of sheep, for they have none of these in the country; and even though they had, as Herodotus remarked, 'the African sheep are clothed with hair, and men's heads with wool.' So I had to be content with asserting that mine was the real original hair, such as theirs would have been had it not been scorched and frizzled by the sun. In proof of what the sun could do, I compared my own bronzed face and hands, then about the same in complexion as the lighter-colored Makololo, with the white skin of my chest. They readily believed that, as they go nearly naked and fully exposed to that influence, we might be of common origin after all. Here, as everywhere, when heat and moisture are combined, the people are very dark, but not quite black. There is always a shade of brown in the most deeply colored. I showed my watch and pocket compass, which are considered great curiosities; but, though the lady was called on by her husband to look, she would not be persuaded to approach near enough.

"As the Leeba seemed still to come from the direction in which we wished to go, I was desirous of proceeding farther up with the canoes; but Nyamoana was anxious that we should allow her people to conduct us to her brother Shinte; and when I explained the advantage of water-carriage, she represented that her brother did not live near the river, and, moreover, there was a cataract in front, over which it would be difficult to convey the canoes. She was afraid, too, that the Balobále, whose country lies to the west of the river, not knowing the objects for which we had come, would kill us. To my reply that I had been so often threatened with death if I visited a new tribe that I was now more afraid of killing any one than of being killed, she rejoined that the Balobale would not kill me, but the Makololo would all be sacrificed as their enemies. This produced considerable effect on my companions, and inclined them to the plan of Nyamoana, of going to the town of her brother rather than ascending the Leeba. The arrival of Manenko herself on the scene threw so much weight into the scale on their side that I was forced to yield the point.

"Manenko was a tall, strapping woman about twenty, distinguished by a profusion of ornaments and medicines hung round her person; the latter are supposed to act as charms. Her body was smeared all over with a mixture of fat and red ochre, as a protection against the weather; a necessary precaution, for, like most of the Balonda ladies, she was otherwise in a state of frightful nudity. This was not from want of clothing, for, being a chief, she might have been as well clad as any of her subjects, but from her peculiar ideas of elegance in dress. When she arrived with her husband, Sambanza, they listened for some time to the statements I was making to the people of Nyamoana, after which the husband, acting as spokesman, commenced an oration, stating the reasons for their coming, and, during every two or three seconds of the delivery, he picked up a little sand, and rubbed it on the upper part of his arms and chest. This is a common mode of salutation in Londa; and when they wish to be excessively polite, they bring a quantity of ashes or pipe-clay in a piece of skin, and, taking up handfuls, rub it on the chest and upper front part of each arm; others, in saluting, drum their ribs with their elbows; while others still touch the ground with one cheek after the other, and clap their hands. The chiefs go through the manœuvre of rubbing the sand on the arms, but only make a feint at picking up some. When Sambanza had finished his oration, he rose up, and showed his ankles ornamented with a bundle of copper rings; had they been very heavy, they would have made him adopt a straggling walk. Some chiefs have really so many as to be forced, by the weight and size, to keep one foot apart from the other, the weight being a serious inconvenience in walking.

"Manenko gave us some manioc roots in the morning, and had determined to carry our baggage to her uncle's, Kabompo or Shinte. We had heard a sample of what she could do with her tongue; and as neither my men nor myself had much inclination to encounter a scolding from this black Mrs. Caudle, we made ready the packages; but she came and said the men whom she had ordered for the service had not yet come; they would arrive to-morrow. Being on low and disagreeable diet, I felt annoyed at this further delay, and ordered the packages to be put into the canoes to proceed up the river without her servants; but Manenko was not to be circumvented in this way; she came forward with her people, and said her uncle would be angry if she did not carry forward the tusks and goods of Sekeletu, seized the luggage, and declared that she would carry it in spite of me. My men succumbed sooner to this petticoat government than I felt inclined to do, and left me no power; and, being unwilling to encounter her tongue, I was moving off to the canoes, when she gave me a kind explanation, and, with her hand on my shoulder, put on a motherly look, saying, 'Now, my little man, just do as the rest have done.' My feelings of annoyance of course vanished, and I went out to try and get some meat.

"On starting, the morning of the 11th, Samoana (or rather Myamoana, for the ladies are the chiefs here) presented a string of beads, and a shell highly valued among them, as an atonement for having assisted Manenko, as they thought to vex me the day before. They seemed anxious to avert any evil which might arise from my displeasure; but having replied that I never kept my anger up all night, they were much pleased to see me satisfied. We had to cross, in a canoe, a stream which flows past the village of Nyamoana. Manenko's doctor waved some charms over her, and she took some in her hand and on her body before she ventured upon the water. One of my men spoke rather loudly when near the doctor's basket of medicines. The doctor reproved him, and always spoke in a whisper himself, glancing back to the basket as if afraid of being heard by something therein. So much superstition is quite unknown in the south, and is mentioned here to show the difference in the feelings of this new people, and the comparative want of reverence on these points among Kaffers and Bechuanas.

"Manenko was accompanied by her husband and her drummer; the latter continued to thump most vigorously until a heavy, drizzling mist set in and compelled him to desist. Her husband used various incantations and vociferations to drive away the rain, but down it poured incessantly, and on our Amazon went, in the very lightest marching order, and at a pace that few of the men could keep up with. Being on oxback, I kept pretty close to our leader, and asked her why she did not clothe herself during the rain, and learned that it is not considered proper for a chief to appear effeminate. He or she must always wear the appearance of robust youth, and bear vicissitudes without wincing. My men, in admiration of her pedestrian powers, every now and then remarked, 'Manenko is a soldier;' and thoroughly wet and cold, we were all glad when she proposed a halt to prepare our night's lodging on the banks of a stream.

"The forests became more dense as we went north. We travelled much more in the deep gloom of the forest than in open sunlight. No passage existed on either side of the narrow path made by the axe. Large climbing plants entwined themselves around the trunks and branches of gigantic trees like boa constrictors, and they often do constrict the trees by which they rise, and, killing them, stand erect themselves. The bark of a fine tree found in abundance here, and called 'motuia,' is used by the Barotse for making fishlines and nets, and the 'molompi,' so well adapted for paddles by its lightness and flexibility, was abundant. There were other trees quite new to my companions; many of them ran up to a height of fifty feet of one thickness, and without branches.

"The number of little villages seemed about equal to the number of valleys. At some we stopped and rested, the people becoming more liberal as we advanced. Others we found deserted, a sudden panic having seized the inhabitants, though the drum of Manenko was kept beaten pretty constantly, in order to give notice of the approach of great people. When we had decided to remain for the night at any village, the inhabitants lent us the roofs of their huts, which in form resemble those of the Makololo, or a Chinaman's hat, and can be taken off the walls at pleasure. They lifted them off, and brought them to the spot we had selected as our lodging, and, when my men had propped them up with stakes, they were then safely housed for the night. Every one who comes to salute either Manenko or ourselves rubs the upper parts of the arms and chest with ashes; those who wish to show profounder reverence put some also on the face.

"We found that every village had its idols near it. This is the case all through the country of the Balonda, so that, when we came to an idol in the woods, we always knew that we were within a quarter of an hour of human habitations. One very ugly idol we passed rested on a horizontal beam placed on two upright posts. This beam was furnished with two loops of cord, as of a chain, to suspend offerings before it. On remarking to my companions that these idols had ears, but that they heard not, etc., I learned that the Balonda, and even the Barotse, believe that divination may be performed by means of these blocks of wood and clay! and though the wood itself could not hear, the owners had medicines by which it could be made to hear and give responses, so that if an enemy were approaching they would have full information.

"While delayed, by Manenko's management, among the Balonda villages, a little to the south of the town of Shinte, we were well supplied by the villagers with sweet potatoes and green maize; Sambanza went to his mother's village for supplies of other food. I was laboring under fever, and did not find it very difficult to exercise patience with her whims; but it being Saturday, I thought we might as well go to the town for Sunday (15th). 'No; her messenger must return from her uncle first.' Being sure that the answer of the uncle would be favorable, I thought we might go on at once, and not lose two days in the same spot. 'No, it is our custom;' and everything else I could urge was answered in the genuine pertinacious lady style. She ground some meal for me with her own hands, and when she brought it told me she had actually gone to a village and begged corn for the purpose. She said this with an air as if the inference must be drawn by even a stupid white man: 'I know how to manage, don't I?' It was refreshing to get food which could be eaten without producing the unpleasantness described by the Rev. John Newton, of St. Mary's, Woolnoth, London, when obliged to eat the same roots while a slave in the West Indies. The day (January 14), for a wonder, was fair, and the sun shone, so as to allow us to dry our clothing and other goods, many of which were mouldy and rotten from the long-continued damp. The guns rusted, in spite of being oiled every evening.

"During the night we were all awakened by a terrific shriek from one of Manenko's ladies. She piped out so loud and long that we all imagined she had been seized by a lion, and my men snatched up their arms, which they always place so as to be ready at a moment's notice, and ran to the rescue; but we found the alarm had been caused by one of the oxen thrusting his head into her hut and smelling her: she had put her hand on his cold, wet nose, and thought it was all over with her.

"On Sunday afternoon messengers arrived from Shinte, expressing his approbation of the objects we had in view in our journey through the country, and that he was glad of the prospect of a way being opened by which white men might visit him, and allow him to purchase ornaments at pleasure. Manenko now threatened in sport to go on, and I soon afterward perceived that what now seemed to me the dilly-dallying way of this lady was the proper mode of making acquaintance with the Balonda; and much of the favor with which I was received in different places was owing to my sending forward messengers to state the object of our coming before entering each town and village. When we came in sight of a village we sat down under the shade of a tree and sent forward a man to give notice who we were and what were our objects. The head man of the village then sent out his principal men, as Shinte now did, to bid us welcome and show us a tree under which we might sleep. Before I had profited by the rather tedious teaching of Manenko, I sometimes entered a village and created unintentional alarm.

"Our friends informed us that Shinte would be highly honored by the presence of three white men in his town at once. Two others had sent forward notice of their approach from another quarter (the west); could it be Barth or Krapf? How pleasant to meet with Europeans in such an out-of-the-way region! The rush of thoughts made me almost forget my fever. Are they of the same color as I am? 'Yes; exactly so.' And have the same hair? 'Is that hair? we thought it was a wig; we never saw the like before; this white man must be of the sort that lives in the sea.' Henceforth my men took the hint, and always sounded my praises as a true specimen of the variety of white men who live in the sea. 'Only look at his hair; it is made quite straight by the sea-water!'

" As the strangers had woolly hair like themselves, I had to give up the idea of meeting anything more European than two half-caste Portuguese, engaged in trading for slaves, ivory and bees'-wax.

"After a short march on the 16th, we came to a most lovely valley about a mile and a half wide, and stretching away eastward up to a low prolongation of Monakadzi. A small stream meanders down the centre of this pleasant green glen: and on a little rill, which flows into it from the western side, stands the town of Kabompo, or, as he likes best to be called, Shinte. (Lat. 12° 37' S., Long. 22° 47' E.) When Manenko thought the sun was high enough for us to make a lucky entrance, we found the town embowered in banana and other tropical trees having great expansion of leaf; the streets are straight, and present a complete contrast to those of the Bechuanas, which are all very tortuous. Here, too, we first saw native huts with square walls and round roofs. The fences or walls of the courts which surround the huts are wonderfully straight, and made of upright poles a few inches apart, with strong grass or leafy bushes neatly woven between. In the courts were small plantations of tobacco, and a little solanaceous plant which the Balonda use as a relish; also sugar-cane and bananas.

"We were honored next day with a grand reception by Shinte about eleven o'clock. Sambanza claimed the honor of presenting us, Manenko being slightly indisposed. The kotla, or place of audience, was about a hundred yards square, and two graceful specimens of a species of banian stood near one end; under one of these sat Shinte, on a sort of throne covered with a leopard's skin. He had on a checked jacket, and a kilt of scarlet baize edged with green; many strings of large beads hung from his neck, and his limbs were covered with iron and copper armlets and bracelets; on his head he wore a helmet made of beads woven neatly together, and crowned with a great bunch of goose-feathers. Close to him sat three lads with large sheaves of arrows over their shoulders.

"When we entered the kotla, the whole of Manenko's party saluted Shinte by clapping their hands, and Sambanza did obeisance by rubbing his chest and arms with ashes. One of the trees being unoccupied, I retreated to it for the sake of the shade, and my whole party did the same. We were now about forty yards from the chief, and could see the whole ceremony. The different sections of the tribe came forward in the same way that we did, the head man of each making obeisance with ashes which he carried with him for the purpose; then came the soldiers, all armed to the teeth, running and shouting toward us, with their swords drawn, and their faces screwed up so as to appear as savage as possible, for the purpose, I thought, of trying whether they could not make us take to our heels. As we did not, they turned round toward Shinte and saluted him, then retired. When all had come and were seated, then began the curious capering usually seen in pichos. A man starts up, and imitates the most approved attitudes observed in actual fight, as throwing one javelin, receiving another on the shield, springing to one side to avoid a third, running backward, or forward, leaping, etc. This over, Sambanza and the spokesman of Nyamoana stalked backward and forward in front of Shinte, and gave forth, in a loud voice, all they had been able to learn, either from myself or people, of my past history and connection with the Makololo; the return of the captives; the wish to open the country to trade; the Bible as a word from heaven; the white man's desire for the tribes to live in peace: he ought to have taught the Makololo that first, for the Balonda never attacked them, yet they had assailed the Balonda: perhaps he is fibbing, perhaps not; they rather thought he was; but as the Balonda had good hearts, and Shinte had never done harm to any one, he had better receive the white man well, and send him on his way.

"When nine speakers had concluded their orations, Shinte stood up, and so did all the people. He had maintained true African dignity of manner all the while, but my people remarked that he scarcely ever took his eyes off me for a moment. About a thousand people were present, according to my calculation, and three hundred soldiers. The sun had now become hot; and the scene ended by the Mambari discharging their guns.

"We were awakened the following night by a message from Shinte, requesting a visit at a very unseasonable hour. As I was just in the sweating stage of an intermittent, and the path to the town lay through a wet valley, I declined going. Kolimbota, who knows their customs best, urged me to go; but, independent of sickness, I hated words of the night and deeds of darkness. 'I was neither a hyena nor a witch.' Kolimbota thought that we ought to conform to their wishes in everything: I thought we ought to have some choice in the matter as well, which put him into high dudgeon. However, at ten next morning we went, and were led into the courts of Shinte, the walls of which were woven rods, all very neat and high. Many trees stood within the inclosure, and afforded a grateful shade. These had been planted, for we saw some recently put in, with grass wound round the trunk to protect them from the sun. The otherwise waste corners of the streets were planted with sugar-cane and bananas, which spread their large light leaves over the walls.

"The Ficus Indica tree, under which we now sat, had very large leaves, but showed its relationship to the Indian banian by sending down shoots toward the ground. Shinte soon came, and appeared a man of upward of fifty-five years of age, of frank and open countenance, and about the middle height. He seemed in good humor, and said he had expected yesterday 'that a man who came from the gods would have approached and talked to him.' That had been my own intention in going to the reception; but when we came and saw the formidable preparations, and all his own men keeping at least forty yards off from him, I yielded to the solicitations of my men, and remained by the tree opposite to that under which he sat. His remark confirmed my previous belief that a frank, open, fearless, manner is the most winning with all these Africans. I stated the object of my journey and mission, and to all I advanced the old gentleman clapped his hands in approbation. He replied through a spokesman; then all the company joined in the response by clapping of hands, too.

"After the more serious business was over, I asked if he had ever seen a white man before. He replied, 'Never; you are the very first I have seen with a white skin and straight hair; your clothing, too, is different from any we have ever seen.' They had been visited by native Portuguese and Mambari only.

"On learning from some of the people that 'Shinte's mouth was bitter for want of tasting ox-flesh,' I presented him with an ox, to his great delight; and, as his country is so well adapted for cattle, I advised him to begin a trade in cows with the Makololo. He was pleased with the idea, and when we returned from Loanda, we found that he had profited by the hint, for he had got three, and one of them justified my opinion of the country, for it was more like a prize heifer for fatness than any we had seen in Africa. He soon afterward sent us a basket of green maize boiled, another of manioc-meal, and a small fowl.

"I was awakened at an early hour by a messenger from Shinte; but the thirst of a raging fever being just assuaged by the bursting forth of a copious perspiration, I declined going for a few hours. Violent action of the heart all the way to the town did not predispose me to be patient with the delay which then occurred, probably on account of the divination being unfavorable: 'They could not find Shinte.' When I returned to bed, another message was received, 'Shinte wished to say all he had to tell me at once.' This was too tempting an offer, so we went, and he had a fowl ready in his hand to present, also a basket of manioc-meal, and a calabash of mead. Referring to the constantly-recurring attacks of fever, he remarked that it was the only thing which would prevent a successful issue to my journey, for he had men to guide me who knew all the paths which led to the white men. He had himself travelled far when a young man. On asking what he would recommend for the fever, 'Drink plenty of the mead, and as it gets in, it will drive the fever out.' It was rather strong, and I suspect he liked the remedy pretty well, even though he had no fever.

"Shinte was most anxious to see the pictures of the magic lantern; but fever had so weakening an effect, and I had such violent action of the heart, with buzzing in the ears, that I could not go for several days; when I did go for the purpose, he had his principal men and the same crowd of court-beauties near him as at the reception. The first picture exhibited was Abraham about to slaughter his son Isaac; it was shown as large as life, and the uplifted knife was in the act of striking the lad; the Balonda men remarked that the picture was much more like a god than the things of wood or clay they worshipped. I explained that this man was the first of a race to whom God had given the Bible we now held, and that among his children our Saviour appeared. The ladies listened with silent awe; but, when I moved the slide, the uplifted dagger moving toward them, they thought it was to be sheathed in their bodies instead of Isaac's. 'Mother! mother!' all shouted at once, and off they rushed helter-skelter, tumbling pellmell over each other, and over the little idol-huts and tobacco-bushes: we could not get one of them back again. Shinte, however, sat bravely through the whole, and afterward examined the instrument with interest. An explanation was always added after each time of showing its powers, so that no one should imagine there was aught supernatural in it; and had Mr. Murray, who kindly brought it from England, seen its popularity among both Makololo and Balonda, he would have been gratified with the direction his generosity then took. It was the only mode of instruction I was ever pressed to repeat. The people came long distances for the express purpose of seeing the objects and hearing the explanations."

Livingstone remained ten days in the town of Shinte, resting his party, and making preparations for the journey westward towards the Portuguese territory. This was likely to be the most hazardous part of the trip, since the natives themselves were not acquainted with the regions beyond those they inhabited. The chief interposed no obstacle, for half-breed traders from Loando sometimes reached his town; but he could only furnish guides for a short distance.

"As the last proof of friendship," Livingstone says, "Shinte came into my tent, though it could scarcely contain more than one person, looked at all the curiosities, the quicksilver, the looking-glass, books, hair-brushes, comb, watch, etc., etc., with the greatest interest; then closing the tent, so that none of his own people might see the extravagance of which he was about to be guilty, he drew out from his clothing a string of beads, and the end of a conical shell, which is considered, in regions far from the sea, of as great value as the Lord Mayor's badge is in London. He hung it round my neck, and said, 'There, now you *have* a proof of my friendship.'

"My men informed me that these shells are so highly valued in this quarter, as evidences of distinction, that for two of them a slave might be bought, and five would be considered a handsome price for an elephant's tusk worth ten pounds. At our last interview old Shinte pointed out our principal guide, Intemese, a man about fifty, who was, he said, ordered to remain by us till we should reach the sea; that I had now left Sekeletu far behind, and must henceforth look to Shinte alone for aid, and that it would always be most cheerfully rendered. This was only a polite way of expressing his wishes for my success. It was the good words only of the guides which were to aid me from the next chief, Katema, on to the sea; they were to turn back on reaching him; but he gave a good supply of food for the journey before us, and, after mentioning as a reason for letting us go even now that no one could say we had been driven away from the town, since we had been several days with him, he gave a most hearty salutation, and we parted with the wish that God might bless him."

HALT UNDER THE BAOBAB.

CHAPTER XI.

LIVINGSTONE'S JOURNEY ACROSS THE CONTINENT.

IV.—FROM SHINTE TO LOANDA.

THE party left the town of Shinte on the 26th of January, with eight of the chief's men to assist in carrying their luggage. We continue the narrative in Livingstone's words:

"We passed, in a northerly direction, down the lovely valley on which the town stands, then went a little to the west through pretty open forest, and slept at a village of Balonda. In the morning we had a fine range of green hills, called Saloisho, on our right, and were informed that they were rather thickly inhabited by the people of Shinte, who worked in iron, the ore of which abounds in these hills.

"The country through which we passed possessed the same general character of flatness and forest that we noticed before. The soil is dark, with a tinge of red—in some places it might be called red—and appeared very fertile. Every valley contained villages of twenty or thirty huts, with gardens of manioc, which here is looked upon as the staff of life. Very little labor is required for its cultivation.

"Our chief guide, Intemese, sent orders to all the villages around our route that Shinte's friends must have abundance of provisions. Our progress was impeded by the time requisite for communicating the chief's desire and consequent preparation of meal. We received far more food from Shinte's people than from himself. Kapende, for instance, presented two large baskets of meal, three of manioc roots steeped and dried in the sun and ready to be converted into flour, three fowls, and seven eggs, with three smoke-dried fishes; and others gave with similar liberality. I gave to the head men small bunches of my stock of beads, with an apology that we were now on our way to the market for these goods. The present was always politely received.

"We had an opportunity of observing that our guides had much more etiquette than any of the tribes farther south. They gave us food, but would not partake of it when we had cooked it, nor would they eat their own food in our presence. When it was cooked they retired into a thicket and ate their porridge; then all stood up, and clapped their hands, and praised Intemese for it. The Makololo, who are accustomed to the most free-and-easy manners, held out handfuls of what they had cooked to any of the Balonda near, but they refused to taste. They are very punctilious in their manners to each other. Each hut has its own fire, and when it goes out they make it afresh for themselves rather than take it from a neighbor. I believe much of this arises from superstitious fears. In the deep, dark forests near each village, as already mentioned, you see idols intended to represent the human head or a lion, or a crooked stick smeared with medicine, or simply a small pot of medicine in a little shed, or miniature huts with little mounds of earth in them. But in the darker recesses we meet with human faces cut in the bark of trees, the outlines of which, with the beards, closely resemble those seen on Egyptian monuments."

After a journey of five days they reached the Leeba river, which Livingstone found to be considerably smaller than at the point where he left it. A village on the bank lent his men two canoes for the crossing, which occupied four hours, although the stream was only about a hundred yards wide. The latitude of the point was 12° 6′ S. Beyond the Leeba, they came upon a plain, twenty miles wide, and flooded with water. The heavy tropical rains continued, and the path for several days was such a succession of quagmires and pools that their progress was very slow. At night they were obliged to seek some little hillock or mound, above the general inundation, for an encampment.

This region is threaded by many branches of the Leeba, some of which, as there were no canoes, the party was obliged to ford, the water often covering all of the oxen except their lifted heads. Livingstone was obliged to carry his watch in his arm-pit, as the only place where it could be kept dry. The guides furnished by Shinte had orders to conduct him to the town of a chief named Katema, and on the 7th of February, he reached a village belonging to that chief's brother. The latter said that the white man was welcome, but was much disturbed by the presence of the Makololo. However, he seemed much more anxious to receive presents than to furnish provisions.

For five or six days longer the party were led,

through the tricks of Shinte's guide, who wished to derive some profit for himself from the journey, from one village to another. Fortunately, some of the chiefs were more generous than the first, and the men were at last tolerably well supplied with food. On the 13th of February they crossed the river Lotembwa, the last of the affluents of the Leeba, after which—to return to Livingstone's narrative—" we travelled about eight miles, and came to Katema's straggling town (lat. 11° 35′ S., long. 22° 27′ E.). It is more a collection of villages than a town. We were led out about half a mile from the houses, that we might make for ourselves the best lodging we could of the trees and grass, while Intemese was taken to Katema to undergo the usual process of pumping as to our past conduct and professions. Katema soon afterward sent a handsome present of food.

"Next morning we had a formal presentation, and found Katema seated on a sort of throne, with about three hundred men on the ground around, and thirty women, who were said to be his wives, close behind him. The main body of the people were seated in a semicircle, at a distance of fifty yards. Each party had its own head-man stationed at a little distance in front, and, when beckoned by the chief, came near him as councilors. Intemese gave our history, and Katema placed sixteen large baskets of meal before us, half-a-dozen fowls, and a dozen eggs, and expressed regret that we had slept hungry: he did not like any stranger to suffer want in his town; and added, 'Go home, and cook and eat, and you will then be in a fit state to speak to me at an audience I will give you to-morrow.' He was busily engaged in hearing the statements of a large body of fine young men who had fled from Kangénke, chief of Lobale, on account of his selling their relatives to the native Portuguese who frequent his country. Katema is a tall man, about forty years of age, and his head was ornamented with a helmet of beads and feathers. He had on a snuff-brown coat, with a broad band of tinsel down the arms, and carried in his hand a large tail made of the caudal extremities of a number of gnus. This has charms attached to it, and he continued waving it in front of himself all the time we were there. He seemed in good spirits, laughing heartily several times. This is a good sign, for a man who shakes his sides with mirth is seldom difficult to deal with. When we rose to take leave, all rose with us, as at Shinte's.

"Returning next morning, Katema addressed me thus: 'I am the great Moene (lord) Katema, the fellow of Matiamvo. There is no one in the country equal to Matiamvo and me. I have always lived here, and my forefathers too. There is the house in which my father lived. You found no human skulls near the place where you are encamped. I never killed any of the traders; they all come to me. I am the great Moene Katema, of whom you have heard.' He looked as if he had fallen asleep tipsy, and dreamed of his greatness. On explaining my objects to him, he promptly pointed out three men who would be our guides, and explained that the north-west path was the most direct, and that by which all traders came, but that the water at present standing on the plains would reach up to the loins; he would therefore send us by a more northerly route, which no trader had yet traversed. This was more suited to our wishes, for we never found a path safe that had been trodden by slave-traders.

"We presented a few articles, which pleased him highly: a small shawl, a razor, three bunches of beads, some buttons, and a powder-horn. Apologizing for the insignificance of the gift, I wished to know what I could bring him from Loanda, saying, not a large thing, but something small. He laughed heartily at the limitation, and replied, 'Everything of the white people would be acceptable, and he would receive any thing thankfully; but the coat he then had on was old, and he would like another.' I introduced the subject of the Bible, but one of the old councilors broke in, told all he had picked up from the Mambari, and glided off into several other subjects. It is a misery to speak through an interpreter, as I was now forced to do. With a body of men like mine, composed as they were of six different tribes, and all speaking the language of the Bechuanas, there was no difficulty in communicating on common subjects with any tribe we came to; but doling out a story in which they felt no interest, and which I understood only sufficiently well to perceive that a mere abridgement was given, was uncommonly slow work. Neither could Katema's attention be arrested, except by compliments, of which they have always plenty to bestow as well as receive. We were strangers, and knew that, as Makololo, we had not the best of characters, yet his treatment of us was wonderfully good and liberal.

"I complimented him on the possession of cattle, and pleased him by telling him how he might milk the cows. He has a herd of about thirty, really splendid animals, all reared from two which he bought from the Balobale when he was young. They are generally of a white color, and are quite wild, running off with graceful ease like a herd of elands on the approach of a stranger. They excited the unbounded admiration of the Makololo, and clearly proved that the country was well adapted for them. When Katema wishes to slaughter one, he is obliged to shoot it as if it were a buffalo.

"Katema promised us the aid of some of his people as carriers, but his rule is not very stringent or efficient, for they refused to turn out for the work. They were Balobale; and he remarked on their disobedience that, though he received them as fugitives, they did not feel grateful enough to obey, and if they continued rebellious he must drive them back whence they came; but there is little fear of that, as all the chiefs are excessively anxious to collect men in great numbers around them. These Balobale would not go, though our guide Shakatwala ran after some of them with a drawn sword.

"On Sunday, the 19th, both I and several of our party were seized with fever, and I could do nothing but toss about in my little tent, with the thermometer above 90°, though this was the beginning of winter, and my men made as much shade as possible by planting branches of trees all around and over it. We have, for the first time in my experience in Africa, had a cold wind from the north. All the winds from that quarter are hot, and those from the south are cold, but they seldom blow from either direction.

"We were glad to get away the next day, though not on account of any scarcity of food ; for my men, by giving small presents of meat as an earnest of their sincerity, formed many friendships with the people of Katema. We went about four or five miles in a N.N.W. direction, then two in a westerly one, and came round the small end of Lake Dilolo. It seemed, as far as we could at this time discern, to be like a river a quarter of a mile wide. It is abundantly supplied with fish and hippopotami; the broad part, which we did not this time see, is about three miles wide, and the lake is almost seven or eight long. If it be thought strange that I did not go a few miles to see the broad part, which, according to Katema, had never been visited by any of the traders, it must be remembered that in consequence of fever I had eaten nothing for two entire days, and, instead of sleep, the whole of the nights were employed in incessant drinking of water, and I was now so glad to get on in the journey and see some of my fellow fever-patients crawling along, that I could not brook the delay, which astronomical observations for accurately determining the geographical position of this most interesting spot would have occasioned."

Beyond this lake, they crossed a marshy plain, twenty miles in breadth. The heavy rains still continued, and the feet of the men became sore from wading in water and mud among the strong grass. The country which followed was under the rule of another chief, whom, however, Livingstone did not wait to see. From this point commenced the territories of small, scattered and often hostile tribes, which have been demoralized by the slave-trade.

"On reaching unflooded lands beyond the plain, we found the villages there acknowledged the authority of the chief named Katénde, and we discovered, also, to our surprise, that the almost level plain we had passed forms the water-shed between the southern and northern rivers, for we had now entered a district in which the rivers flowed in a northerly direction into the Kasai or Loké, near to which we now were, while the rivers we had hitherto crossed were all running southward. Having met with kind treatment and aid at the first village, Katema's guides returned, and we were led to the N.N.W. by the inhabitants, and descended into the very first really deep valley we had seen since leaving Kolobeng. A stream ran along the bottom of a slope of three or four hundred yards from the plains above." This was crossed by a bridge, and also many of the following streams, and at some of them the natives demanded toll.

"Reaching the village of Kabinje, in the evening he sent us a present of tobacco, Mutokuane or 'bang' (*Cannabis sativa*), and maize, by the man who went forward to announce our arrival, and a message expressing satisfaction at the prospect of having trade with the coast. The westing we were making brought us among people who are frequently visited by the Mambari as slave-dealers. This trade causes bloodshed; for when a poor family is selected as the victims, it is necessary to get rid of the older members of it, because they are supposed to be able to give annoyance to the chief afterward by means of enchantments. The belief in the power of charms for good or evil produces not only honesty, but a great amount of gentle dealing.

"When we wished to move on, Kabinje refused a guide to the next village because he was at war with it; but, after much persuasion he consented, provided that the guide should be allowed to return as soon as he came in sight of the enemy's village. This we felt to be a misfortune, as the people all suspect a man who comes telling his own tale; but there being no help for it, we went on and found the head man of a village on the rivulet Kalómba, called Kangénke, a very different man from what his enemy represented. We found, too, that the idea of buying and selling took the place of giving for friendship. As I had nothing with which to purchase food except a parcel of beads which were preserved for worse times, I began to fear that we should soon be compelled to suffer more from hunger than we had done. The people demanded gunpowder for everything. If we had possessed any quantity of that article, we should have got on well, for here it is of great value.

"Kangenke promptly furnished guides on the 27th of February, so we went briskly on a short distance, and came to a part of the Kasye, Kasai, or Loke, where he had appointed two canoes to convey us across. This is a most beautiful river, and very much like the Clyde in Scotland. The slope of the valley down to the stream is about five hundred yards, and finely wooded. It is, perhaps, one hundred yards broad, and was winding slowly from side to side in the beautiful green glen, in a course to the north and north-east. In both the directions from which it came and to which it went it seemed to be alternately embowered in sylvan vegetation, or rich meadows covered with tall grass. The men pointed out its course, and said, 'Though you sail along it for months, you will turn without seeing the end of it.'

"We were now in want of food, for, to the great surprise of my companions, the people of Kangenke gave nothing except by way of sale, and charged the most exorbitant prices for the little meal and manioc they brought. The only article of barter my men had was a little fat saved from the ox we slaughtered at Katema's, so I was obliged to give them a portion of the stock of beads. One day of westing brought us from the Kasai to near the village of Katende, and we saw that we were in a land where no hope could be entertained of getting supplies of animal food, for one of our guides caught a light-blue colored mole and two mice for his supper. The care with which he wrapped them up in a leaf and slung them on his spear told that we could not hope to enjoy any larger game. We saw no evidence of any animals besides; and, on coming to the villages beyond this, we often saw boys and girls engaged in digging up these tiny quadrupeds.

"Katende sent for me on the day following our arrival, and, being quite willing to visit him, I walked, for this purpose, about three miles from our encampment. When we approached the village we were desired to enter a hut, and, as it was raining at the time, we did so. After a long time spent in giving and receiving messages from the great man, we were told that he wanted either a man, a tusk, beads, copper rings, or a shell, as payment for leave to pass through his country. No one, we were assured, was allowed that liberty, or even to behold him, without something of the sort being presented. Having humbly explained our circumstances, and that he could not expect to 'catch a humble cow by the horns'—a proverb similar to ours that 'you can't draw milk out of a stone'—we were told to go home, and he would speak again to us next day. I could not avoid a hearty laugh at the cool impudence of the savage, and made the best of my way home in the still pouring rain. My men were rather nettled at this want of hospitality, but, after talking over the matter with one of Katende's servants, he proposed that some small article should be given, and an attempt made to please Katende. I turned out my shirts, and selected the worst one as a sop for him, and invited Katende to come and choose anything else I had."

It was with some difficulty that the party got away from this unfriendly and avaricious chief. When the villages were fairly behind them, the native guides declared that they did not know the country, and left Livingstone to push forward at random in the direction of Loanda. The first day they came to a valley, a mile wide, entirely covered with water to the depth of four or five feet,—an experience which was frequently renewed during the following days. One of these adventures is thus described:

"In the afternoon we came to another stream, ñuana Loke (or child of Loke), with a bridge over it. The men had to swim off to each end of the bridge, and when on it were breast deep; some preferred holding on by the tails of the oxen the whole way across. I intended to do this, too; but, riding to the deep part, before I could dismount and seize the helm the ox dashed off with his companions, and his body sank so deep that I failed in my attempt even to catch the blanket belt, and if I pulled the bridle the ox seemed as if he would come backward upon me, so I struck out for the opposite bank alone. My poor fellows were dreadfully alarmed when they saw me parted from the cattle, and about twenty of them made a simultaneous rush into the water for my rescue, and just as I reached the opposite bank one seized my arm, and another threw his around my body. When I stood up, it was most gratifying to see them all struggling toward me. Some had leaped off the bridge, and allowed their cloaks to float down the stream. Part of my goods, abandoned in the hurry, were brought up from the bottom after I was safe. Great was the pleasure expressed when they found that I could swim, like themselves, without the aid of a tail, and I did and do feel grateful to these poor heathens for the promptitude with which they dashed in to save, as they thought, my life. I found my clothes cumbersome in the water; they could swim quicker from being naked. They swim like dogs, not frog-fashion, as we do.

"The amount of population in the central parts of the country may be called large only as compared with the Cape Colony or the Bechuana country. The cultivated land is as nothing compared with what might be brought under the plough. There are flowing streams in abundance, which, were it necessary, could be turned to the purpose of irrigation with but little labor. Miles of fruitful country are now lying absolutely waste, for there is not even game to eat off the fine pasturage, and to recline under the evergreen, shady groves which we are ever passing in our progress. The people who inhabit the central region are not all quite black in color. Many incline to that of bronze, and others are as light in hue as the Bushmen, who, it may be remembered, afford a proof that heat alone does not cause blackness, but that heat and moisture combined do very materially deepen the color."

On the 4th of March they reached the country of the Chiboque, a fierce, plundering tribe, who would have attacked them but for Livingstone's courage and self-possession. He finally succeeded in making a temporary truce by the present of one of his few remaining oxen. The supplies were growing small, and the insolent demands of the natives increased, so that it became a question whether he could succeed in crossing the comparatively narrow strip of territory which separated him from the Portuguese outposts.

"We were informed," says Livingstone, " that the people on the west of the Chiboque were familiar with the visits of slave-traders; and it was the opinion of our guides that so many of my companions would be demanded from me, in the same manner as these people had done, that I should reach the coast without a single attendant; I therefore resolved to alter our course and strike away to the N.N.E., in the hope that at some point farther north I might find an exit to the Portuguese settlement of Cassange. We proceeded at first due north, with the Kasabi villages on our right, and the Kasau on our left. During the first twenty miles we crossed many small, but now swollen streams, having the usual boggy banks, and wherever the water had stood for any length of time it was discolored with rust of iron. We saw a 'nakong' antelope one day, a rare sight in this quarter; and many new and pretty flowers adorned the valleys.

"In passing through the narrow paths of the forests I had an opportunity of observing the peculiarities of my ox 'Sinbad.' He had a softer back than the others, but a much more intractable temper. His horns were bent downward and hung loosely, so he could do no harm with them: but as we wended our way slowly along the narrow path, he would suddenly dart aside. A string tied to a stick put through the cartilage of the nose serves instead of a bridle: if you jerk this back, it makes him run faster on; if you pull it to one side, he allows the nose and head to go, but keeps the opposite eye directed to the forbidden spot, and goes in spite of you. The only way he can be brought to a stand is by a stroke with a wand across the nose. When Sinbad ran in below a climber stretched over the path so low that I could not stoop under it, I was dragged off and came down on the crown of my head; and he never allowed an opportunity of the kind to pass without trying to inflict a kick, as if I neither had nor deserved his love.

"On Friday, the 23d of March, we came to a village of civil people on the banks of a river called the Loajima, and we were wet all day in consequence of crossing it. The bridges over it, and another stream which we crossed at midday, were submerged, as we have hitherto invariably found, by a flood of perfectly clear water. At the second ford we were met by a hostile party who refused us further passage. I ordered my men to proceed in the same direction we had been pursuing, but our enemies spread themselves out in front of us with loud cries. Our numbers were about equal to theirs this time, so I moved on at the head of my men. Some ran off to other villages, or back to their own village, on pretense of getting ammunition; others called out that all traders came to them, and that we must do the same. As these people had plenty of iron-headed arrows and some guns, when we came to the edge of the forest I ordered my men to put the luggage in our centre; and, if our enemies did not fire, to cut down some young trees and make a screen as quickly as possible, but do nothing to them except in case of actual attack. I then dismounted, and, advancing a little toward our principal opponent, showed him how easily I could kill him, but pointed upward, saying, 'I fear God.' He did the same, placing his hand on his heart, pointing upward, and saying, 'I fear to kill; but come to our village; come—do come.' At this juncture, the old head man, Ionga Panza, a venerable negro, came up, and I invited him and all to be seated, that we might talk the matter over. Ionga Panza soon let us know that he thought himself very ill-treated in being passed by. As most skirmishes arise from misunderstanding, this might have been a serious one; for, like all the tribes near the Portuguese settlements, people here imagine that they have a right to demand payment from every one who passes through the country; and now, though Ionga Panza was certainly no match for my men, yet they were determined not to forego their right without a struggle. I removed with my men to the vicinity of the village, thankful that no accident had as yet brought us into actual collision.

"Ionga Panza's sons agreed to act as guides into the territory of the Portuguese if I would give them the shell given by Shinte. I was strongly averse to this, and especially to give it beforehand, but yielded to the entreaty of my people to appear as if showing confidence in these hopeful youths. They urged that they wished to leave the shell with their wives, as a sort of payment to them for enduring their husband's absence so long. Having delivered the precious shell, we went west-by-north to the river Chikapa, which here (lat. 10° 22′ S.) is forty or fifty yards wide, and at present was deep; it was seen flowing over a rocky, broken cataract with great noise about half a mile above our ford. We were ferried over in a canoe, made out of a single piece of bark sewed together at the ends, and having sticks placed in it at different parts to act as ribs.

"Next morning our guides went only about a mile, and then told us they would return home. I expected this when paying them beforehand, in accordance with the entreaties of the Makololo, who are rather ignorant of the world. Very energetic remonstrances were addressed to the guides, but they slipped off one by one in the thick forest through which we were passing, and I was glad to hear my companions coming to the conclusion that, as we were now in parts visited by traders, we did not require the guides, whose chief use had been to prevent misapprehension of our objects in the minds of the villagers. The country was somewhat more undulating now than it had been, and several fine small streams flowed in deep woody dells. The trees are very tall and straight, and the forests gloomy and damp; the ground in these solitudes is quite covered with yellow and brown mosses, and light-colored lichens clothe all the trees.

"The village on the river Kweelo, at which we spent Sunday, was that of a civil, lively old man, called Sakandala, who offered no objections to our progress. We found we should soon enter on the territory of the Bashinjé (Chinge of the Portuguese). Rains and fever, as usual, helped to impede our progress until we were put on the path which leads from Cassange and Bihe to Matiamvo, by a head man named Kamboéla. This was a well-beaten footpath, and soon after entering upon it we met a party of half-caste traders from Bihe, who confirmed the information we had already got of this path leading straight to Cassange. They kindly presented my men with some tobacco, and marveled greatly when they found that I had never been able to teach myself to smoke.

"As we were now alone, and sure of being on the way to the abodes of civilization, we went on briskly.

"On the 30th we came to a sudden descent from the high land, indented by deep, narrow valleys, over which we had lately been travelling. It is generally so steep that it can only be descended at particular points, and even there I was obliged to dismount, though so weak that I had to be led by my companions to prevent my toppling over in walking down. It was annoying to feel myself so helpless, for I never liked to see a man, either sick or well, giving in effeminately. Below us lay the valley of the Quango. If you sit on the spot where Mary Queen of Scots viewed the battle of Langside, and look down on the vale of Clyde, you may see in miniature the glorious sight which a much greater and richer valley presented to our view. It is about a hundred miles broad, clothed with dark forest, except where the light green grass covers meadow-lands on the Quango, which here and there glances out in the sun as it wends its way to the north. The opposite side of this great valley appears like a range of lofty mountains, and the descent into it about a mile, which, measured perpendicularly, may be from a thousand to twelve hundred feet. Emerging from the gloomy forests of Londa, this magnificent prospect made us all feel as if a weight had been lifted off our eyelids. A cloud was passing across the middle of the valley, from which rolling thunder pealed, while above all was glorious sunlight; and when we went down to the part where we saw it passing, we found that a very heavy thunder-shower had fallen under the path of the cloud; and the bottom of the valley, which from above seemed quite smooth, we discovered to be intersected and furrowed by great numbers of deep-cut streams.

They now entered the territory of the Bashinge, the chief of whom sent a demand for a man, an ox, or an elephant's tusk. This was refused, and of course no food could be expected. The chief afterwards came himself, and after a long conversation threatened to prevent the further progress of the party. The next morning they started very early, in a heavy rain, passing the village without molestation, and kept on, in a half-famished condition.

"Hunger," Livingstone remarks, "has a powerful effect on the temper. When we had got a good meal of meat, we could all bear the petty annoyances of these borderers on the more civilized region in front with equanimity: but having suffered considerably of late, we were all rather soured in our feelings, and not unfrequently I overheard my companions remark in their own tongue, in answer to threats of attack, 'That's what we want: only begin them;' or with clenched teeth they would exclaim to each other, 'These things have never travelled, and they do not know what men are.' The worrying, of which I give only a slight sketch, had considerable influence on my own mind, and more especially as it was impossible to make any allowance for the Bashinje, such as I was willing to award to the Chiboque. They saw that we had nothing to give, nor would they be benefited in the least by enforcing the impudent order to return whence we had come. They were adding insult to injury, and this put us all into a fighting spirit, and, as nearly as we could judge, we expected to be obliged to cut our way through the Bashinje."

On reaching the river before them, which the natives called the Quango (Congo?), on the 4th of April, they were met by the same natives with the usual fierce demand for presents. After the Makololo had stripped themselves of their copper rings, but in vain, Livingstone determined to cross the river in spite of their opposition. He fell in with a Portuguese half-caste, Cypriano by name, who assisted him across the stream. On the opposite bank the tribes were subjects of the Portuguese, and all difficulties and dangers were over.

"We were detained by rains and a desire to ascertain our geographical position till Monday, the 10th," he continues, "and only got the latitude 9° 50′ S.; and, after three days' pretty hard travelling through the long grass, reached Cassange, the farthest inland station of the Portuguese in Western Africa. We crossed several fine little streams running into the Quango; and as the grass continued to tower about two feet over our heads, it generally obstructed our view of the adjacent country, and sometimes hung over the path, making one side of the body wet with the dew every morning, or, when it rained, kept me wet during the whole day. I made my entrance in a somewhat forlorn state as to clothing among our Portuguese allies. The first gentleman I met in the village asked if I had a passport, and said it was necessary to take me before the authorities. As I was in the same state of mind in which individuals are who commit a petty depredation in order to obtain the shelter and food of a prison, I gladly accompanied him to the house of the commandant or Chefe, Senhor de Silva Rego. Having shown my passport to this gentleman, he politely asked me to supper, and, as we had eaten nothing except the farina of Cypriano from the Quango to this, I suspect I appeared particularly ravenous to the other gentlemen around the table. They seemed, however, to understand my position pretty well, from having all travelled extensively themselves; had they not been present, I might have put some in my pocket to eat by night; for, after fever, the appetite is excessively keen, and manioc is one of the most unsatisfying kinds of food. Captain Antonio Rodrigues Neves then kindly invited me to take up my abode in his house. Next morning this generous man arrayed me in decent clothing, and continued during the whole period of my stay to treat me as if I had been his brother. He not only attended to my wants, but also furnished food for my famishing party free of charge.

"The village of Cassange (pronounced Kassanjé) is composed of thirty or forty traders' houses, scattered about without any regularity, on an elevated flat spot in the great Quango or Cassange valley. They are built of wattle and daub, and surrounded by plantations of manioc, maize, etc. Behind them there are usually kitchen gardens, in which the common European vegetables, as potatoes, peas, cabbages, onions, tomatoes, etc., etc., grow. Guavas and bananas appear, from the size and abundance of the trees, to have been introduced many years ago, while the land was still in the possession of the natives; but pine-apples, orange, fig, and cashew trees have but lately been tried. There are about forty Portuguese traders in this district, all of whom are officers in the militia, and many of them have become rich from adopting the plan of sending out pombeiros, or native traders, with large quantities of goods, to trade in the more remote parts of the country.

"The latitude and longitude of Cassange, the most

easterly station of the Portuguese in Western Africa, is lat. 9° 37′ S., and long. 17° 49′ E; consequently we had still about 300 miles to traverse before we could reach the coast. We had a black militia corporal as a guide. He was a native of Ambaca, and, like nearly all the inhabitants of that district, known by the name of Ambakistas, could both read and write. He had three slaves with him, and was carried by them in a 'tipoia,' or hammock slung to a pole. His slaves were young, and unable to convey him far at a time, but he was considerate enough to walk except when we came near to a village. He then mounted his tipoia and entered the village in state; his departure was made in the same manner, and he continued in the hammock till the village was out of sight. It was interesting to observe the manners of our soldier-guide. Two slaves were always employed in carrying his tipoia, and the third carried a wooden box, about three feet long, containing his writing materials, dishes, and clothing. He was cleanly in all his ways, and, though quite black himself, when he scolded any one of his own color, abused him as a 'negro.' When he wanted to purchase any article from a village, he would sit down, mix a little gunpowder as ink, and write a note in a neat hand to ask the price, addressing it to the shopkeeper with the rather pompous title, 'Illustrissimo Senhor' (Most Illustrious Sir). This is the invariable mode of address throughout Angola.

"Having left Cassange on the 21st of April, we passed across the remaining portion of the excessively fertile valley to the foot of Tala Mungongo. We crossed a fine little stream called the Lui on the 22d, and another named the Luare on the 24th, then slept at the bottom of the height, which is from a thousand to fifteen hundred feet. The clouds came floating along the valley, and broke against the sides of the ascent, and the dripping rain on the tall grass made the slaps in the face it gave, when the hand or a stick was not held up before it, anything but agreeable. This edge of the valley is exactly like the other; jutting spurs and defiles give the red ascent the same serrated appearance as that which we descended from the highlands of Londa.

"It would have afforded me pleasure to have cultivated a more intimate acquaintance with the inhabitants of this part of the country, but the vertigo produced by frequent fevers made it as much as I could do to stick on the ox and crawl along in misery. In crossing the Lombe, my ox Sinbad, in the indulgence of his propensity to strike out a new path for himself, plunged overhead into a deep hole, and so soused me that I was obliged to move on to dry my clothing, without calling on the Europeans who live on the bank. This I regretted, for all the Portuguese were very kind, and like the Boers placed in similar circumstances, feel it a slight to be passed without a word of salutation. But we went on to a spot where orange-trees had been planted by the natives themselves, and where abundance of that refreshing fruit was exposed for sale.

"On entering the district of Ambaca, we found the landscape enlivened by the appearance of lofty mountains in the distance, the grass comparatively short, and the whole country at this time looking gay and verdant.

PASS OF PUNGO ADONGO.

On our left we saw certain rocks of the same nature with those of Pungo Andongo, and which closely resemble the Stonehenge group on Salisbury Plain, only the stone pillars here are of gigantic size. This region is all wonderfully fertile, famed for raising cattle, and all kinds of agricultural produce, at a cheap rate.

"We were most kindly received by the commandant of Ambaca, Arsenio de Carpo, who spoke a little English. He recommended wine for my debility, and here I took the first glass of that beverage I had taken in Africa. I felt much refreshed, and could then realize and meditate on the weakening effects of the fever. They were curious even to myself; for, though I had tried several times since we left Ngio to take lunar observations, I could not avoid confusion of time and distance, neither could I hold the instrument steady, nor perform a simple calculation; hence many of the positions of this part of the route were left till my return from Loanda. Often, on getting up in the mornings, I found my clothing as wet from perspiration as if it had been dipped in water."

The journey was slow, on account of Livingstone's condition, which the kindness of the Portuguese officials in the interior could not relieve. It was nearly a month before he reached the station of Golungo Alto, among the last mountains. Here he rested a few days, and then somewhat refreshed, started for Loanda on the 24th of May.

"Farther on we left the mountainous country, and, as we descended toward the west coast, saw the lands assuming a more sterile, uninviting aspect. On our right ran the river Senza, which nearer the sea takes the name of Bengo. It is about fifty yards broad, and navigable for canoes. The low plains adjacent to its banks are protected from inundation by embankments, and the population is entirely occupied in raising food and fruits for exportation to Loanda by means of canoes. The banks are infested by myriads of the most ferocious musquitos I ever met. Not one of our party could get a snatch of sleep. I was taken into the house of a Portuguese, but was soon glad to make my escape and lie across the path on the lee side of the fire, where the smoke blew over my body. My host wondered at my want of taste, and I at his want of feeling; for, to our astonishment, he and the other inhabitants had actually become used to what was at least equal to a nail through the heel of one's boot, or the tooth-ache.

"As we were now drawing near to the sea, my companions were looking at everything in a serious light. One of them asked me if we should all have an opportunity of watching each other at Loanda. 'Suppose one went for water, would the others see if he were kidnapped?' I replied, 'I see what you are driving at; and if you suspect me, you may return, for I am as ignorant of Loanda as you are; but nothing will happen to you but what happens to myself. We have stood by each other hitherto, and will do so to the last.' The plains adjacent to Loanda are somewhat elevated and comparatively sterile. On coming across these we first beheld the sea: my companions looked upon the boundless ocean with awe. On describing their feelings afterward, they remarked that 'we marched along with our father, believing that what the ancients had always told us was true, that the world has no end; but all at once the world said to us, *I am finished; there is no more of me!*' They had always imagined that the world was one extended plain without limit.

"They were now somewhat apprehensive of suffering want, and I was unable to allay their fears with any promise of supply, for my own mind was depressed by disease and care. The fever had induced a state of chronic dysentery, so troublesome that I could not remain on the ox more than ten minutes at a time; and as we came down the declivity above the city of Loanda on the 31st of May, I was laboring under great depression of spirits, as I understood that, in a population of twelve thousand souls, there was but one genuine English gentleman. I naturally felt anxious to know whether he were possessed of good-nature, or was one of those crusty mortals one would rather not meet at all.

"This gentleman, Mr. Gabriel, our commissioner for the suppression of the slave-trade, had kindly forwarded an invitation to meet me on the way from Cassange, but, unfortunately, it crossed me on the road. When we entered his porch, I was delighted to see a number of flowers cultivated carefully, and inferred from this circumstance that he was, what I soon discovered him to be, a real, whole-hearted Englishman.

"Seeing me ill, he benevolently offered me his bed. Never shall I forget the luxurious pleasure I enjoyed in feeling myself again on a good English couch, after six months' sleeping on the ground. I was soon asleep; and Mr. Gabriel, coming in almost immediately, rejoiced at the soundness of my repose."

CHAPTER XII.

LIVINGSTONE'S JOURNEY ACROSS THE CONTINENT.

V.—RETURN TO THE MAKOLOLO COUNTRY.

CONTINUED attacks of fever, and the necessity of providing himself thoroughly for the return journey, obliged Livingstone to remain nearly four months in Loanda. During this time he was treated with great kindness by the Portuguese authorities and the officers of the English vessels in port, all of whom contributed liberally to make up his supplies. The Makololo who accompanied him soon found employment sufficient to support them, and enabled them to buy muslin and trinkets. Livingstone gives an interesting picture of their behavior, in the midst of scenes so new and strange to them:

"Every one remarked the serious deportment of the Makololo. They viewed the large stone houses and churches in the vicinity of the great ocean with awe. A house with two stories was, until now, beyond their comprehension. In explanation of this strange thing, I had always been obliged to use the word for hut; and as huts are constructed by the poles being let into the earth, they never could comprehend how the poles of one hut could be founded upon the roof of another, or how men could live in the upper story, with the conical roof of the lower one in the middle. Some Makololo, who had visited my little house at Kolobeng, in trying to describe it to their countrymen at Linyanti, said, 'It is not a hut: it is a mountain with several caves in it.'

"Commander Bedingfeld and Captain Skene invited them to visit their vessels, the 'Pluto' and 'Philomel.' Knowing their fears, I told them that no one need go if he entertained the least suspicion of foul play. Nearly the whole party went; and when on deck, I pointed to the sailors, and said, 'Now these are all my countrymen, sent by our Queen for the purpose of putting down the trade of those that buy and sell black men.' They replied, 'Truly! they are just like you!' and all their fears seemed to vanish at once, for they went forward among the men, and the jolly tars, acting much as the Makololo would have done in similar circumstances, handed them a share of the bread and beef which they had for dinner. The commander allowed them to fire off a cannon; and, having the most exalted ideas of its power, they were greatly pleased when I told them, 'That is what they put down the slave-trade with.' The size of the brig-of-war amazed them. 'It is not a canoe at all; it is a town!' The sailors' deck they named 'the kotla;' and then, as a climax to their description of this great ark, added, 'And what sort of a town is it that you must climb up into with a rope?'

"The objects which I had in view in opening up the country, as stated in a few notes of my journey, published in the newspapers of Angola, so commended themselves to the general government and merchants of Loanda, that, at the instance of his excellency the bishop, a handsome present for Sekeletu was granted by the Board of Public Works. It consisted of a colonel's complete uniform and a horse for the chief, and suits of clothing for all the men who accompanied me. The merchants also made a present, by public subscription, of handsome specimens of all their articles of trade, and two donkeys, for the purpose of introducing the breed into his country, as *tsetse* cannot kill this beast of burden. These presents were accompanied by letters from the bishop and merchants; and I was kindly favored with letters of recommendation to the Portuguese authorities in Eastern Africa.

"I took with me a good stock of cotton cloth, fresh supplies of ammunition and beads, and gave each of my men a musket. As my companions had amassed considerable quantities of goods, they were unable to carry mine, but the bishop furnished me with twenty carriers, and sent forward orders to all the commandants of the districts through which we were to pass to render me every assistance in their power. Being now supplied with a good new tent made by my friends on board the Philomel, we left Loanda on the 20th of September, 1854, and passed round by sea to the mouth of the river Bengo.

"On returning to Golungo Alto, after a canoe voyage down the Lucalla to its junction with the large Coanza River, I found several of my men laid up with fever. One of the reasons for my leaving them there was that they might recover from the fatigue of the journey from Loanda, which had much more effect upon their feet than hundreds of miles had on our way westward. They had always been accustomed to moisture in their own well-watered land, and we certainly had a superabundance of that in Loanda. The roads, however, from Loanda to Golungo Alto were both hard and dry, and they suffered severely in consequence; yet they were composing songs to be sung when they should reach home. The Argonauts were nothing to them; and they remarked very impressively to me, 'It was well you came with Makololo, for no tribe could have done what we have accomplished in coming to the white man's country; we are the true ancients, who can tell wonderful things.' Two of them now had fever in the continued form, and became jaundiced, the whites or conjunctival membrane of their eyes becoming as yellow as saffron; and a third suffered from an attack of mania. He came to his companions one day, and said, 'Remain well. I am called away by the gods!' and set off at the top of his speed. The young men caught him before he had gone a mile, and bound him. By gentle treatment and watching for a few days, he recovered. I have observed several instances of this kind in the country, but very few cases of idiocy, and I believe that continued insanity is rare.

"Both myself and men having recovered from severe attacks of fever, we left the hospitable residence of Mr. Canto on the 14th of December, with a deep sense of his kindness to us all, and proceeded on our way to Ambaca.

"On crossing the Lucalla we a made détour to the south, in order to visit the famous rocks of Pungo Andongo. As soon as we crossed the rivulet Lotete, a change in the vegetation of the country was apparent. We found the trees identical with those to be seen south of the Chobe. The grass, too, stands in tufts, and is of that kind which the natives consider to be best adapted for cattle. Two species of grape-bearing vines abound everywhere in this district, and the influence of the good pasturage is seen in the plump condition of the cattle. In all my previous inquiries respecting the vegetable products of Angola, I was invariably directed to Pungo Andongo. Do you grow wheat? 'Oh, yes, in Pungo Andongo.'—Grapes, figs, or peaches? 'Oh, yes, in Pungo Andongo.'—Do you make butter, cheese, etc.? The uniform answer was, 'Oh, yes, there is abundance of all these in Pungo Andongo.' But when we arrived here, we found that the answers all referred to the activity of one man, Colonel Manuel Antonio Pires. The presence of the wild grape shows that vineyards might be cultivated with success; the wheat grows well without irrigation; and any one who tasted the butter and cheese at the table of Colonel Pires would prefer them to the stale produce of the Irish dairy, in general use throughout that province.

"While enjoying the hospitality of this merchant-prince in his commodious residence, which is outside the rocks, and commands a beautiful view of all the adjacent country, I learned that all my dispatches, maps, and journal had gone to the bottom of the sea in the mail-packet 'Forerunner.' I felt so glad that my friend Lieutenant Bedingfeld, to whose care I had committed them, though in the most imminent danger, had not shared a similar fate, that I was at once reconciled to the labor of rewriting. I availed myself of the kindness of Colonel Pires, and remained till the end of the year reproducing my lost papers.

"The fort of Pungo Andongo (lat. 9° 42′ S., long. 15° 30′ E.) is situated in the midst of a group of curious columnar-shaped rocks, each of which is upward of three hundred feet in height. They are composed of conglomerate, made up of a great variety of rounded pieces in a matrix of dark red sandstone. They rest on a thick stratum of this last rock, with very few of the pebbles in its substance. On this a fossil palm has been found, and if of the same age as those on the eastern side of the continent, on which similar palms now lie, there may be coal underneath this, as well as under that at Tete.

"*January* 1, 1855. Having, through the kindness of Colonel Pires, reproduced some of my lost papers, I left Pungo Andongo the first day of this year, and at Candumba slept in one of the dairy establishments of my friend, who had sent forward orders for an ample supply of butter, cheese, and milk. Our path lay along the right bank of the Coanza. This is composed of the same sandstone rock, with pebbles, which forms the flooring of the country. The land is level, has much open forest, and is well adapted for pasturage.

"Before we reached Cassange we were overtaken by the Commandant, Senhor Carvalho, who was returning, with a detachment of fifty men and a field-piece, from an unsuccessful search after some rebels. The rebels had fled, and all he could do was to burn their huts. He kindly invited me to take up my residence with him; but, not wishing to pass by the gentleman (Captain Neves) who had so kindly received me on my first arrival in the Portuguese possessions, I declined." Livingstone remained some time at Cassange, resting his men, and waiting for some Portuguese *pombeiros*, or half-breed traders, who were about to start for the interior, and whose company would greatly strengthen his party. They finally left Cassange on the 20th of February.

"On the day of starting the westerly wind blew strongly, and on the day following we were brought to a stand by several of our party being laid up with fever. This complaint is the only serious drawback Angola possesses. It is in every other respect an agreeable land, and admirably adapted for yielding a rich abundance of tropical produce for the rest of the world. Indeed, I have no hesitation in asserting that, had it been in the possession of England, it would now have been yielding as much or more of the raw material for her manufactures as an equal extent of territory in the cotton-growing States of America. A railway from Loanda to this valley would secure the trade of most of the interior of South Central Africa.

"On coming back to Cypriano's village on the 28th, we found that his step-father had died after we had passed, and according to the custom of the country, he had spent more than his patrimony in funeral orgies. He acted with his wonted kindness, though, unfortunately, drinking has got him so deeply in debt that he now keeps out of the way of his creditors. He informed us that the source of the Quango is eight days, or one hundred miles, to the south of this, and in a range called Mosamba, in the country of the Basongo. We can see from this a sort of break in the high land which stretches away round to Tala Mongongo, through which the river comes.

"The ferrymen demanded thirty yards of calico, but received six thankfully. The canoes were wretched, carrying only two persons at a time; but my men being well acquainted with the water, we all got over in about two hours and a half. They excited the admiration of the inhabitants by the manner in which they managed the cattle and donkeys in crossing. The most stubborn of beasts found himself powerless in their hands. Five or six, seizing hold on one, bundled him at once into the stream, and, in this predicament, he always thought it best policy to give in and swim. The men sometimes swam along with the cattle, and forced them to go on by dashing water at their heads. The difference between my men and those of the native traders who accompanied us was never more apparent than now; for, while my men felt an interest in everything we possessed in common, theirs were rather glad when the oxen refused to cross, for, being obliged to slaughter them on such occasions, the loss to their masters was a welcome feast to themselves."

After crossing the Quango, where he was not molested, as on the westward journey, Livingstone decided to accompany the traders as far as the town of Cabongo, in the Londa country, in order to avoid the territories of the Chiboque and the great swampy regions lying between him and the distant Leeba River. This route took him further to the eastward, but did not increase the distance to be traversed. Moreover, he would have the company of the Portuguese traders as far as Cabongo, and the indications were that between the latter place and the town of his friend Shinte, few difficulties would be encountered from the native tribes.

"On proceeding to our former station near Sansawe's village," the narrative continues, "he ran to meet us with wonderful urbanity, asking if we had seen Moene Put, king of the white men (or Portuguese); and added, on parting, that he would come to receive his dues in the evening. I replied that, as he had treated us so scurvily, even forbidding his people to sell us any food, if he did not bring us a fowl and some eggs as part of his duty as a chief, he should receive no present from me. When he came, it was in the usual Londa way of showing the exalted position he occupies, mounted on the shoulders of his spokesman, as school-boys sometimes do in England, and as was represented to have been the case in the southern islands when Captain Cook visited them. My companions, amused at his idea of dignity, greeted him with a hearty laugh. He visited the native traders first, and then came to me with two cocks as a present. I spoke to him about the impolicy of treatment we had received at his hands, and quoted the example of the Bangalas, who had been conquered by the Portuguese, for their extortionate demands of payment for firewood, grass, water, etc., and concluded by denying his right to any payment for simply passing through uncultivated land. To all this he agreed; and then I gave him, as a token of friendship, a pannikin of coarse powder, two iron spoons, and two yards of coarse printed calico.

"Finding the progress of Senhor Pascoal and the other pombeiros excessively slow, I resolved to forego his company to Cabango after I had delivered to him some letters to be sent back to Cassange. I went forward with the intention of finishing my writing, and leaving a packet for him at some village. We ascended the eastern acclivity that bounds the Cassange valley, which has rather a gradual ascent up from the Quango, and we found that the last ascent, though apparently not quite so high as that at Tala Mungongo, is actually much higher. The top is about 5,000 feet above the level of the sea, and the bottom 3,500 feet. We had now gained the summit of the western subtending ridge, and began to descend toward the centre of the country, hoping soon to get out of the Chiboque territory, which when we ascended from the Cassange valley, we had entered; but, on the 19th of April, the intermittent, which had begun on the 16th of March, was changed into an extremely severe attack of rheumatic fever. This was brought on by being obliged to sleep on an extensive plain covered with water. The rain poured down incessantly, but we formed our beds by dragging up the earth into oblong mounds, somewhat like graves in a country church-yard, and then placing grass upon them. The rain continuing to deluge us, we were unable to leave for two days, but as soon as it became fair we continued our march. The heavy dew upon the high grass was so cold as to cause shivering, and I was forced to lie by for eight days, tossing and groaning with violent pain in the head. This was the most severe attack I had endured. It made me quite unfit to move, or even know what was passing outside my little tent. Senhor Pascoal, who had been detained by the severe rain at a better spot, at last came up, and, knowing that leeches abounded in the rivulets, procured a number, and applied some dozens to the nape of the neck and the loins. This partially relieved the pain. He was then obliged to move forward, in order to purchase food for his large party. After many days I began to recover, and wished to move on, but my men at first objected to the attempt on account of my weakness.

"The country was generally covered with forest, and we slept every night at some village. I was so weak, and had become so deaf from the effects of the fever, that I was glad to avail myself of the company of Senhor Pascoal and the other native traders. Our rate of travelling was only two geographical miles per hour, and the average number of hours three and a half per day, or seven miles. Two-thirds of the month was spent in stoppages, there being only ten travelling days in each month. The stoppages were caused by sickness, and the necessity of remaining in different parts to purchase food; and also because, when one carrier was sick, the rest refused to carry his load.

"We crossed the Loange, a deep but narrow stream, by a bridge. It becomes much larger, and contains hippopotami, lower down. It is the boundary of Londa on the west. We slept also on the banks of the Pezo, now flooded, and could not but admire their capabilities for easy irrigation. On reaching the river Chikapa, the 25th of March, we found it fifty or sixty yards wide, and flowing E.N.E. into the Kasai. The adjacent country is of the same level nature as that part of Londa formerly described; but, having come farther to the eastward than our previous course, we found that all the rivers had worn for themselves much

HEADDRESSES IN LONDA.

deeper valleys than at the points we had formerly crossed them.

"Surrounded on all sides by large gloomy forests, the people of these parts have a much more indistinct idea of the geography of their country than those who live in hilly regions. It was only after long and patient inquiry that I became fully persuaded that the Quilo runs into the Chikapa. As we now crossed them both considerably farther down, and were greatly to the eastward of our first route, there can be no doubt that these rivers take the same course as the others, into the Kasai, and that I had been led into a mistake in saying that any of them flowed to the westward.

"The people seemed more slender in form, and their color a lighter olive, than any we had hitherto met. The mode of dressing the great masses of woolly hair which lay upon their shoulders, together with their general features, again reminded me of the ancient Egyptians. Several were seen with the upward inclination of the outer angles of the eye, but this was not general. A few of the ladies adopt a curious custom of attaching the hair to a hoop which encircles the head, giving it somewhat the appearance of the glory round the head of the Virgin. Some have a small hoop behind that represented in the wood-cut. Others wear an ornament of woven hair and hide adorned with beads. The hair of the tails of buffaloes, which are to be found farther east, is sometimes added; while others weave their own hair on pieces of hide into the form of buffalo horns, or make a single horn in front. The features given are frequently met with, but they are by no means universal. Many tattoo their bodies by inserting some black substance beneath the skin, which leaves an elevated cicatrix about half an inch long: these are made in the form of stars, and other figures of no particular beauty.

"We made a little détour to the southward in order to get provisions in a cheaper market. This led us along the rivulet called Tamba, where we found the people, who had not been visited so frequently by the slave-traders as the rest, rather timid and very civil. It was agreeable to get again among the uncontaminated, and to see the natives look at us without that air of superciliousness which is so unpleasant and common in the beaten track. The same olive color prevailed. They file their teeth to a point, which makes the smile of the women frightful, as it reminds one of the grin of an alligator. The inhabitants throughout this country exhibit as great a variety of taste as appears on the surface of society among ourselves. Many of the men are dandies; their shoulders are always wet with the oil dropping from their lubricated hair, and everything about them is ornamented in one way or another. Some thrum a musical instrument the livelong day, and, when they wake at night, proceed at once to their musical performance. Many of these musicians are too poor to have iron keys to their instrument, but make them of bamboo, and persevere, though no one hears the music but themselves. Others try to appear warlike by never going out of their huts except with a load of bows and arrows, or a gun ornamented with a strip of hide for every animal they have shot; and others never go anywhere without a canary in a cage. Ladies may be seen carefully tending little lap-dogs, which are intended to be eaten. Their villages are generally in forests, and composed of groups of irregularly-planted brown huts, with banana and cotton trees, and tobacco growing around. There is also at every hut a high stage erected for drying manioc roots and meal, and elevated cages to hold domestic fowls. Round baskets are laid on the thatch of the huts for the hens to lay in, and on the arrival of strangers, men, women, and children ply their calling as hucksters with a great deal of noisy haggling; all their transactions are conducted with civil banter and good temper.

"We passed on through forests abounding in climbing-plants, many of which are so extremely tough that a man is required to go in front with a hatchet; and when the burdens of the carriers are caught, they are obliged to cut the climbers with their teeth, for no amount of tugging will make them break. The paths in all these forests are so zigzag that a person may imagine he has travelled a distance of thirty miles, which, when reckoned as the crow flies, may not be fifteen.

"We crossed two small streams, the Kanesi and Fombeji, before reaching Cabango, a village situated on the banks of the Chihombo. The country was becoming more densely peopled as we proceeded, but it bears no population compared to what it might easily sustain. Provisions were to be had in great abundance; a fowl and basket of meal weighing 20 lbs. were sold for a yard and a half of very inferior cotton cloth, worth not more than three-pence."

The progress of the party was so slow, on account of Livingstone's illness, and the many streams to be crossed, that it was the 10th of

May when they reached Cabango. Here they remained until the 21st. It would have been quite easy for Livingstone to have gone on to the town of Matiamvo, the great chief of the powerful Londa tribe, reports of which have been given to the world by the Portuguese; but his duty to his Makololo followers compelled him to renounce the chances of exploration.

"Cabango (lat. 9° 31′ S., long. 20° 31′ E.) is the dwelling-place of Muanzánza, one of Matiamvo's subordinate chiefs. His village consists of about two hundred huts and ten or twelve square houses, constructed of poles with grass interwoven. The latter are occupied by half-caste Portuguese from Ambaca, agents for the Cassange traders. The cold in the mornings was now severe to the feelings, the thermometer ranging from 58° to 60°, though, when protected, sometimes standing as high as 64° at six A. M. When the sun is well up, the thermometer in the shade rises to 80°, and in the evenings it is about 78°.

"A person having died in this village, we could transact no business with the chief until the funeral obsequies were finished. These occupy about four days, during which there is a constant succession of dancing, wailing, and feasting. Guns are fired by day, and drums beaten by night, and all the relatives, dressed in fantastic caps, keep up the ceremonies with spirit proportionate to the amount of beer and beef expended. When there is a large expenditure, the remark is often made afterward, 'What a fine funeral that was!' A figure, consisting chiefly of feathers and beads, is paraded on these occasions, and seems to be regarded as an idol.

"As we thought it best to strike away to the S. E. from Cabango to our old friend Katema, I asked a guide from Muanzanza as soon as the funeral proceedings were over. He agreed to furnish one, and also accepted a smaller present from me than usual, when it was represented to him by Pascoal and Faria that I was not a trader. We were forced to prepay our guide and his father too, and he went but one day, although he promised to go with us to Katema. He was not in the least ashamed at breaking his engagements, and probably no disgrace will be attached to the deed by Muanzanza. Among the Bakwains he would have been punished. My men would have stripped him of the wages which he wore on his person, but thought that, as we had always acted on the mildest principles, they would let him move off with his unearned gains.

"On the 28th we reached the village of the chief Bango who brought us a handsome present of meal, and the meat of an entire pallah. We here slaughtered the last of the cows presented to us in Loanda, which I had kept milked until it gave only a teaspoonful at a time. My men enjoyed a hearty laugh when they found that I had given up all hope of more, for they had been talking among themselves about my perseverance. We offered a leg of the cow to Bango, but he informed us that neither he nor his people ever partook of beef, as they looked upon cattle as human, and living at home like men.

"We left Bango on the 30th of May, and proceeded to the river Loembwe, which abounds in hippopotami. It is about sixty yards wide, and four feet deep, but usually contains much less water than this, for there are fishing-weirs placed right across it. Like all the African rivers in this quarter, it has morasses on each bank, yet the valley in which it winds, when seen from the high lands above, is extremely beautiful. This valley is about the fourth of a mile wide, and it was easy to fancy the similarity of many spots on it to the goodly manors in our country, and feel assured that there was still ample territory left for an indefinite increase of the world's population. The villages are widely apart and difficult of access, from the paths being so covered with tall grass, that even an ox can scarcely follow the tract. The grass cuts the feet of the men; yet we met a woman with a little child, and a girl, wending their way home with loads of manioc. The sight of a white man always infuses a tremor into their dark bosoms, and in every case of the kind they appeared immensely relieved when I had fairly passed without having sprung upon them. In the villages the dogs run away with their tails between their legs, as if they had seen a lion. The women peer from behind the walls till he comes near them, and then hastily dash into the house. When a little child, unconscious of danger, meets you in the street, he sets up a scream at the apparition, and conveys the impression that he is not far from going into fits. Among the Bechuanas I have been obliged to reprove the women for making a hobgoblin of the white man, and telling their children that they would send for him to bite them.

"At every village attempts were made to induce us to remain a night. Sometimes large pots of beer were offered to us as a temptation. Occasionally the head man would peremptorily order us to halt under a tree which he pointed out. At other times young men volunteered to guide us to the impassable part of the next bog, in the hope of bringing us to a stand, for all are excessively eager to trade; but food was so very cheap that we sometimes preferred paying them to keep it, and let us part in good humor. A good-sized fowl could be had for a single charge of gunpowder."

The only difficulty which Livingstone encountered was with a chief named Kawawa, who, after receiving him in a friendly manner, demanded tribute, and, when it was refused, threatened to prevent the party from crossing the great Kasai River, which they were approaching. After an altercation which came near resulting in bloodshed, Livingstone marched away from the village with his men.

"But Kawawa," he says, "was not to be balked of his supposed rights by the unceremonious way in which we had left him; for, when we had reached the ford of the Kasai, about ten miles distant, we found that he had sent four of his men, with orders to the ferrymen to refuse us passage. We were here duly informed that we must deliver up all the articles mentioned, and one of our men besides. This demand for one of our number always nettled every heart. The canoes were taken away before our eyes, and we were supposed to be quite helpless without them, at a river a good hundred yards broad, and very deep. Pitsane stood on the bank, gazing with apparent indifference on the stream, and made an accurate observation of where the canoes were hidden among the reeds. The ferrymen casually asked one of my Batoka if they had rivers in his country, and he answered with truth, 'No, we have none.' Kawawa's people then felt sure we could not cross. I thought of swimming when they were gone; but after it was dark, by the unasked loan of one of the hidden canoes, we soon were snug in our bivouac on the southern bank of the Kasai. I left some beads as payment for some meal which had been presented by the ferrymen; and, the canoe having been left on their own side of the river, Pitsane and his companions laughed uproariously at the disgust our enemies would feel, and their perplexity as to who had been our paddler across. They were quite sure that Kawawa would imagine that we had been ferried over by his own people, and would be divining to find out who had done the deed. When ready to depart in the morning, Kawawa's people appeared on the opposite heights, and could scarcely believe their eyes when they saw us prepared to start away to the south. At last one of them called out, ' Ah! ye are bad,' to which Pitsane and his companions retorted, 'Ah! ye are good, and we thank you for the loan of your canoe.' We were careful to explain the whole of the circumstances to Katema and the other chiefs, and they all agreed that we were perfectly justifiable under the circumstances, and that Matiamvo would approve our conduct.

"After leaving the Kasai, we entered upon the extensive level plains which we had formerly found in a flooded condition. The water on them was not yet dried up, as it still remained in certain hollow spots. Vultures were seen floating in the air, showing that carrion was to be found; and, indeed, we saw several of the large game, but so exceedingly wild as to be unapproachable. Numbers of caterpillars mounted the stalks of grass, and many dragonflies and butterflies appeared, though this was winter.

"During our second day on this extensive plain I suffered from my twenty-seventh attack of fever, at a part where no surface-water was to be found. We never thought it necessary to carry water with us in this region; and now, when I was quite unable to move on, my men soon found water to allay my burning thirst by digging with sticks a few feet beneath the surface. We had thus an opportunity of observing the state of these remarkable plains at different seasons of the year. Next day we pursued our way, and on the 8th of June we forded the Lotembwa to the N.W. of Dilolo, and regained our former path."

Nothing further occurred to interrupt the progress of the party. The chief Katema received them kindly, and, after a short rest at his village, they proceeded onward across the many tributaries of the Leeba, then that river itself, and finally reached the town of the friendly Shinte, on the 24th of June.

"We received a hearty welcome from this friendly old man, and abundant provisions of the best he had. On hearing the report of the journey given by my companions, and receiving a piece of cotton cloth about two yards square, he said, 'These Mambari cheat us by bringing little pieces only; but the next time you pass I shall send men with you to trade for me in Loanda.' When I explained the use made of the slaves he sold, and that he was just destroying his own tribe by selling his people, and enlarging that of the Mambari for the sake of these small pieces of cloth, it seemed to him quite a new idea. He entered into a long detail of his troubles with Masiko, who had prevented him from cultivating that friendship with the Makololo which I had inculcated, and had even plundered the messengers he had sent with Kolimbota to the Barotse valley.

"As I had been desirous of introducing some of the fruit-trees of Angola, both for my own sake and that of the inhabitants, we had carried a pot containing a little plantation of orange, cashew-trees, custard-apple-trees, and a fig-tree, with coffee, araças, and papaws. Fearing that if we took them farther south at present they might be killed by the cold, we planted them out in an inclosure of one of Shinte's principal men, and, at his request, promised to give Shinte a share when grown. They know the value of fruits, but at present have none except wild ones. A wild fruit we frequently met with in Londa is eatable, and, when boiled, yields a large quantity of oil, which is much used in anointing both head and body. He eagerly accepted some of the seeds of the palm-oil-tree when told that this would produce oil in much greater quantity than their native tree, which is not a palm.

"We parted on the best possible terms with our friend Shinte, and proceeded by our former path to the village of his sister Nyamoana, who is now a widow. She received us with much apparent feeling, and said, 'We had removed from our former abode to the place where you found us, and had no idea then that it was the spot where my husband was to die.' She had come to the river Lofujé, as they never remain in a place where death has once visited them. We received the loan of five small canoes from her, and also one of those we had left here before, to proceed down the Leeba. After viewing the Coanza at Massangano, I thought the Leeba at least a third larger, and upward of two hundred yards wide. We saw evidence of its rise during its last flood having been upward of forty feet in perpendicular height; but this is probably more than usual, as the amount of rain was above the average. My companions purchased also a number of canoes from the Balonda. These are very small, and can carry only two persons. They are made quite thin and light, and as sharp as racing-skiffs, because they are used in hunting animals in the water. The price paid was a string of beads equal to the length of the canoe. We advised them to bring canoes for sale to the Makololo, as they would gladly give them cows in exchange."

Livingstone waited a day or two to see the chieftainess Manenko, and while there, became a blood-relation to her husband Maneako, each drinking a few drops of the other's blood, in a pot of beer. "On one occasion," he says, "I became blood-relation to a young woman by accident. She had a large cartilaginous tumor between the bones of the fore-arm, which, as it gradually enlarged, so distended the muscles as to render her unable to work. She applied to me to excise it. I requested her to bring her husband, if he were willing to have the operation performed, and, while removing the tumor, one of the small arteries squirted some blood into my eye. She remarked, when I was wiping the blood out of it, 'You were a friend before, now you are a blood-relation; and when you pass this way, always send me word, that I may cook food for you.' In creating these friendships, my men had the full intention of returning; each one had his *molekane* (friend) in every village of the friendly Balonda.

"We reached the town of Libonta on the 27th of July, and were received with demonstrations of joy such as I had never witnessed before. The women came forth to meet us, making their curious dancing gestures and loud lulliloos. Some carried a mat and stick, in imitation of a spear and shield. Others rushed forward and kissed the hands and cheeks of the different persons of their acquaintance among us, raising such a dust that it was quite a relief to get to the men assembled and sitting with proper African decorum in the kotla. We were looked upon as men risen from the dead, for the most skillful of their diviners had pronounced us to have perished long ago. After many expressions of joy at meeting, I arose, and, thanking them, explained the causes of our long delay, but left the report to be made by their own countrymen. Formerly I had been the chief speaker, now I would leave the task of speaking to them. Pitsane then delivered a speech of upward of an hour in length, giving a highly flattering picture of the whole journey, of the kindness of the white men in general, and of Mr. Gabriel in particular. He concluded by saying that I had done more for them than they expected; that I had not only opened up a path for them to the other white men, but conciliated all the chiefs along the route.

"My men decked themselves out in their best, and I found that, although their goods were finished, they had managed to save suits of European clothing, which, being white, with their red caps, gave them rather a dashing appearance. They tried to walk like the soldiers they had seen in Loanda, and called themselves my 'braves' (batlabani). During the service they all sat with their guns over their shoulders, and excited the unbounded admiration of the women and children. I addressed them all on the goodness of God in preserving us from all the dangers of strange tribes and disease. We had a similar service in the afternoon. The men gave us two fine oxen for slaughter, and the women supplied us abundantly with milk, meal, and butter. It was all quite gratuitous, and I felt ashamed that I could make no return. My men explained the total expenditure of our means, and the Libontese answered gracefully, 'It does not matter; you have opened a path for us, and we shall have sleep.' Strangers came flocking from a distance, and seldom empty-handed. Their presents I distributed among my men.

"Our progress down the Barotse valley was just like this. Every village gave us an ox, and sometimes two. The people were wonderfully kind. I felt, and still feel, most deeply grateful, and tried to benefit them in the only way I could, by imparting the knowledge of that Saviour who can comfort and supply them in the time of need, and my prayer is that he may send his good Spirit to instruct them and lead them into his kingdom. Even now I earnestly long to return, and make some recompense to them for their kindness.

"On reaching Naliele on the 1st of August we found Mpololo in great affliction on account of the death of his daughter and her child. She had been lately confined; and her father naturally remembered her when an ox was slaughtered, or when the tribute of other food, which he receives in lieu of Sekeletu, came in his way, and sent frequent presents to her. This moved the envy of one of the Makololo who hated Mpololo, and wishing to vex him, he entered the daughter's hut by night, and strangled both her and her child. He then tried to make fire in the hut and burn it, so that the murder might not be known; but the squeaking noise of rubbing the sticks awakened a servant, and the murderer was detected. Both he and his wife were thrown into the river; the latter having 'known of her husband's intentions, and not revealing them.' She declared she had dissuaded him from the crime, and, had any one interposed a word, she might have been spared.

"I left Naliele on the 13th of August, and, when proceeding along the shore at midday, a hippopotamus struck the canoe with her forehead, lifting one half of it quite out of the water, so as nearly to overturn it. The force of the butt she gave tilted Mashauana out into the river; the rest of us sprang to the shore, which was only about ten yards off. Glancing back, I saw her come to the surface a short way off, and look to the canoe, as if to see if she had done much mischief. It was a female, whose young one had been speared the day before. No damage was done except wetting person and goods. This is so unusual an occurrence, when the precaution is taken to coast along

HIPPOPOTAMUS UPSETTING A BOAT.

the shore, that my men exclaimed, 'Is the beast mad?' There were eight of us in the canoe at the time, and the shake it received shows the immense power of this animal in the water.

"Having got the loan of other canoes from Mpololo, and three oxen as provision for the way, which made the number we had been presented with in the Barotse valley amount to thirteen, we proceeded down the river toward Sesheke, and were as much struck as formerly with the noble river. The whole scenery is lovely, though the atmosphere is murky in consequence of the continuance of the smoky tinge of winter.

"Long before reaching Sesheke we had been informed that a party of Matebele, the people of Mosilikatse, had brought some packages of goods for me to the south bank of the river, near the Victoria Falls, and, though they declared that they had been sent by Mr. Moffat, the Makololo had refused to credit the statement of their sworn enemies. They imagined that the parcels were directed to me as a mere trick, whereby to place witchcraft-medicine into the hands of the Makololo. When the Matebele on the south bank called to the Makololo on the north to come over in canoes and receive the goods sent by Moffat to 'Nake,' the Makololo replied, 'Go along with you, we know better than that; how could he tell Moffat to send his things here, he having gone away to the north?' The Matebele answered, 'Here are the goods; we place them now before you, and if you leave them to perish the guilt will be yours.' When they had departed the Makololo thought better of it, and, after much divination, went over with fear and trembling, and carried the packages carefully to an island in the middle of the stream; then, building a hut over them to protect them from the weather, they left them; and there I found they had remained from September, 1854, till September, 1855, in perfect safety. Here, as I had often experienced before, I found the news was very old, and had lost much of its interest by keeping, but there were some good eatables from Mrs. Moffat.

"Having waited a few days at Sesheke till the horses which we had left at Linyanti should arrive, we proceeded to that town, and found the wagon, and everything we had left in November, 1853, perfectly safe. A grand meeting of all the people was called to receive our report, and the articles which had been sent by the governor and merchants of Loanda. I explained that none of these were my property, but that they were sent to show the friendly feelings of the white men, and their eagerness to enter into commercial relations with the Makololo. I then requested my companions to give a true account of what they had seen. The wonderful things lost nothing in the telling, the climax always being that they had finished the whole world, and had turned only when there was no more land. One glib old gentleman asked, 'Then you reached Ma Robert (Mrs. L.)?' They were obliged to confess that she lived a little beyond the world. The presents were received with expressions of great satisfaction and delight; and on Sunday, when Sekeletu made his appearance at church in his uniform, it attracted more attention than the sermon; and the kind expressions they made use of respecting

THE VILLAGE OF SKULLS.

myself were so very flattering that I felt inclined to shut my eyes. Their private opinion must have tallied with their public report, for I very soon received offers from volunteers to accompany me to the east coast."

[In his narrative Livingstone omits the relation of the manner in which the goods had been forwarded by Mr. Moffat to the island on the Zambesi.

His father-in-law, still full of energy in spite of his age, had determined that no chance should be lost of forwarding supplies; and undertook the task himself, since it involved a journey into the Matebele country, which (as the reader will see by referring to Chapter III.) he had first visited in 1829. The famous chief, Mosilikatse, was still living, though very old, and Moffat believed that—although the Matebele and Makololo were hostile—he could prevail upon the chief to forward supplies to Livingstone through his country.

Starting from Kuruman, in the spring of 1854, Moffat travelled about 400 miles, in a north-eastern direction, before reaching the frontiers of the Matabele tribe. After a journey of several weeks, he arrived at the Village of Skulls, the town of Mosilikatse. Each hut is surrounded with high poles, every one of which is crowned with the skulls of those slain by the owner of the hut. The surrounding country was mountainous, but very beautiful and fertile, and the people were becoming agricultural in their habits.

The first interview which Moffat had with the old chief was an evidence that the latter possessed some native goodness of heart, in spite of the savage acts of which he had been guilty during all his long life.

Mosilikatse was carried in a kind of chair to meet the missionary. The hero of so many battles was hardly to be recognized. His body and his legs were so swollen by dropsy that he could neither walk nor sit erect. When he saw Moffat, he grasped his hand silently, then threw his garment over his face and wept.

Many times he repeated the words: "Surely, I am only dreaming that you are Moffat," and then said: "Matshobane (the name of my father) I will call you, because you have been a father to me. You have made my heart as soft as milk. I cannot cease to wonder at the affection of a stranger. You have never seen me before, and yet you love me more than any one of my own people. You have fed me, when I was hungry; you have clothed me, when I was naked; you have held me in your bosom, and your arm has protected me from my enemies."

When Moffat answered that he was not conscious of having rendered him any of these services, the chief pointed to two native messengers who had seated themselves at the missionary's feet, and answered: "These two are very important men; Umbate is my right hand. When I send them where the white men live, I send my ears, my eyes, and my mouth with them. What they have heard, I hear; what they have seen, I see; and what they have said, was said by Mosilikatse. You have fed and clothed them, and when their lives were in danger, you were their shield. What you did to them, that you did to me."

Pointing to his dropsical legs, which he declared would soon bring him to death, he added: "Your God has sent you to me, to give me help and healing." Moffat undertook the treatment of his case, and was fortunate enough to enable him to walk a little; but he was always obliged to administer the medicine himself, as the chief was in constant fear of being poisoned by his wives.

The journey was entirely successful. The Matebele, as we have seen, took charge of the supplies for Livingstone, carried them to the Zambesi, and there conscientiously deposited them, leaving the further responsibility of their care to the Makololo. Moffat returned in safety to Kuruman.]

CHAPTER XIII.

LIVINGSTONE'S JOURNEY ACROSS THE CONTINENT.

VI.—DOWN THE ZAMBESI TO THE EASTERN COAST.

HAVING found it impracticable to open a wagon-road to the western coast, it was now necessary that Livingstone should make choice of route by which the Indian Ocean might be reached. The Arab traders to be transported from Zanzibar to the Makololo country assured him that he could return upon their track with safety, by way of the great lake Tanganyika, which had not then been reached by any white man; but he was anxious to ascertain whether the Zambesi River might not be a navigable stream for some distance into the interior. His first desire, of course, was to follow the river. The Makololo, however, who were acquainted with the country as far eastward as the Kafue, a large tributary of the Zambesi, objected to this, declaring that the country was so broken and rocky as to render it almost impassable.

They proposed a direct course eastward, on the northern side of the Zambesi, to the Kafue, and then a journey along the former river to the first Portuguese station at Tete. As Livingstone was indebted to Sekeletu for much of his outfit, and his success, as on the westward journey, would depend entirely on the conduct of his followers, he felt obliged to accept their decision. So much of his great design had already been accomplished, that it scarcely seemed necessary to hazard the remaining portion without the certainty of some advantage in return. We will now let him resume his narrative:

"On the 3d of November we bade adieu to our friends at Linyanti, accompanied by Sekeletu and about 200 followers. We were all fed at his expense, and he took cattle for this purpose from every station we came to. The principal men of the Makololo, Lebeóle, Ntlarié, Nkwatléle, etc., were also of the party. We passed through the patch of the *tsetse*, which exists between Linyanti and Sesheke, by night. The majority of the company went on by daylight, in order to prepare our beds. Sekeletu and I, with about forty young men, waited outside the *tsetse* till dark. We then went forward, and about ten o'clock it became so pitchy dark that both horses and men were completely blinded. The lightning spread over the sky, forming eight or ten branches at a time, in shape exactly like those of a tree. This, with great volumes of sheet-lightning, enabled us at times to see the whole country. The intervals between the flashes were so densely dark as to convey the idea of stone-blindness. The horses trembled, cried out, and turned round, as if searching for each other, and every new flash revealed the men taking different directions, laughing, and stumbling against each other.

"While at Sesheke, Sekeletu supplied me with twelve oxen—three of which were accustomed to being ridden upon—hoes, and beads to purchase a canoe when we should strike the Leeambye beyond the falls.

He likewise presented abundance of good fresh butter and honey, and did everything in his power to make me comfortable for the journey. I was entirely dependent on his generosity, for the goods I originally brought from the Cape were all expended by the time I set off from Linyanti to the west coast. I there drew £70 of my salary, paid my men with it, and purchased goods for the return journey to Linyanti. These being now all expended, the Makololo again fitted me out, and sent me on to the east coast. I was thus dependent on their bounty, and that of other Africans, for the means of going from Linyanti to Loanda, and again from Linyanti to the east coast, and I feel deeply grateful to them. Coin would have been of no benefit, for gold and silver are quite unknown.

"As this was the point from which we intended to strike off to the north-east, I resolved on the following day to visit the Falls of Victoria, called by the natives Mosioatunya, or more anciently Shongwe. Of these we had often heard since we came into the country; indeed, one of the questions asked by Sebituane was, 'Have you smoke that sounds in your country?' They did not go near enough to examine them, but, viewing them with awe at a distance, said, in reference to the vapor and noise, 'Mosi oa tunya' (smoke does sound there). It was previously called Shongwe, the meaning of which I could not ascertain. The word for a 'pot' resembles this, and it may mean a seething caldron, but I am not certain of it. Being persuaded that Mr. Oswell and myself were the very first Europeans who ever visited the Zambesi in the centre of the country, and that this is the connecting link between the known and unknown portions of that river, I decided to use the same liberty as the Makololo did, and gave the only English name I have affixed to any part of the country.

"Sekeletu intended to accompany me, but one canoe only having come instead of the two he had ordered, he resigned it to me. After twenty minutes' sail from Kalai we came in sight, for the first time, of the columns of vapor appropriately called 'smoke,' rising at a distance of five or six miles, exactly as when large tracts of grass are burned in Africa. Five columns now arose, and, bending in the direction of the wind, they seemed placed against a low ridge covered with trees; the tops of the columns at this distance appeared to mingle with the clouds. They were white below, and higher up became dark, so as to simulate smoke very closely. The whole scene was extremely beautiful; the banks and islands dotted over the river are adorned with sylvan vegetation of great variety of color and form. At the period of our visit several trees were spangled over with blossoms. Some trees resemble the great spreading oak, others assume the character of our own elms and chestnuts; but no one can imagine the beauty of the view from anything witnessed in England. It had never been seen before by European eyes; but scenes so lovely must have been gazed upon by angels in their flight. The only want felt is that of mountains in the background. The falls are bounded on three sides by ridges 300 or 400 feet in height, which are covered with forest, with the red soil appearing among the trees. When about half a mile from the falls, I left the canoe by which we had come down thus far, and embarked in a lighter one, with men well acquainted with the rapids, who, by passing down the centre of the stream in the eddies and still places caused by many jutting rocks, brought me to an island situated in the middle of the river, and on the edge of the lip over which the water rolls. In coming hither there was danger of being swept down by the streams which rushed along on each side of the island; but the river was now low, and we sailed where it is totally impossible to go when the water is high. But, though we had reached the island, and were within a few yards of the spot, a view from which would solve the whole problem, I believe that no one could perceive where the vast body of water went; it seemed to lose itself in the earth, the opposite lip of the fissure into which it disappeared being only 80 feet distant. At least I did not comprehend it until, creeping with awe to the verge, I peered down into a large rent which had been made from bank to bank of the broad Zambesi, and saw that a stream of a thousand yards broad leaped down a hundred feet, and then became suddenly compressed into a space of fifteen or twenty yards. The entire falls are simply a crack made in a hard basaltic rock from the right to the left bank of the Zambesi, and then prolonged from the left bank away through thirty or forty miles of hills. If one imagines the Thames filled with low, tree-covered hills immediately beyond the tunnel, extending as far as Gravesend, the bed of black basaltic rock instead of London mud, and a fissure made therein from one end of the tunnel to the other down through the keystones of the arch, and

FALLS OF THE ZAMBESI.

prolonged from the left end of the tunnel through thirty miles of hills, the pathway being 100 feet down from the bed of the river instead of what it is, with the lips of the fissure from 80 to 100 feet apart, then fancy the Thames leaping bodily into the gulf, and forced there to change its direction, and flow from the right to the left bank, and then rush boiling and roaring through the hills, he may have some idea of what takes place at this, the most wonderful sight I had witnessed in Africa. In looking down into the fissure on the right of the island, one sees nothing but a dense white cloud, which, at the time we visited the spot, had two bright rainbows on it. (The sun was on the meridian, and the declination about equal to the latitude of the place). From this cloud rushed up a great jet of vapor exactly like steam, and it mounted 200 or 300 feet high; there condensing, it changed its hue to that of dark smoke, and came back in a constant shower, which soon wetted us to the skin. This shower falls chiefly on the opposite side of the fissure, and a few yards back from the lip there stands a straight hedge of evergreen trees, whose leaves are always wet. From their roots a number of little rills run back into the gulf, but, as they flow down the steep wall there, the column of vapor, in its ascent, licks them up clean off the rock, and away they mount again. They are constantly running down, but never reach the bottom.

"On the left of the island we see the water at the bottom, a white rolling mass moving away to the prolongation of the fissure, which branches off near the left bank of the river. A piece of the rock has fallen off a spot on the left of the island, and juts out from the water below, and from it I judged the distance which the water falls to be about 100 feet. The walls of this gigantic crack are perpendicular, and composed of one homogeneous mass of rock.

"On the left side of the island we have a good view of the mass of water which causes one of the columns of vapor to ascend, as it leaps quite clear of the rock, and forms a thick unbroken fleece all the way to the bottom. Its whiteness gave the idea of snow, a sight I had not seen for many a day. As it broke into (if I may use the term) pieces of water, all rushing on in the same direction, each gave off several rays of foam exactly as bits of steel, when burned in oxygen gas, give off rays of sparks. The snow-white sheet seemed like myriads of small comets rushing on in one direction, each of which left behind its nucleus rays of foam. I never saw the appearance referred to noticed elsewhere. It seemed to be the effect of the mass of water leaping at once clear of the rock, and but slowly breaking up into spray.

"I have mentioned that we saw five columns of vapor ascending from this strange abyss. They are evidently formed by the compression suffered by the force of the water's own fall into an unyielding wedge-shaped space. Of the five columns, two on the right and one on the left of the island were the largest, and the streams which formed them seemed each to exceed in size the falls of the Clyde at Stonebyres when that river is in flood. This was the period of low water in the Leeambye; but, as far as I could guess, there was a flow of five or six hundred yards of water, which, at the edge of the fall, seemed at least three feet deep.

"The fissure is said by the Makololo to be very much deeper farther to the eastward; there is one part at which the walls are so sloping that people accustomed to it can go down by descending in a sitting position. The Makololo on one occasion, pursuing some fugitive Batoka, saw them, unable to stop the impetus of their flight at the edge, literally dashed to pieces at the bottom. They beheld the stream like a 'white cord' at the bottom, and so far down (probably 300 feet) that they became giddy, and were faint to go away holding on to the ground.

"Sekeletu and his large party having conveyed me thus far, and furnished me with a company of 114 men to carry the tusks to the coast, we bade adieu to the Makololo on the 20th of November, and proceeded northward to the Lekone. The country around is very beautiful, and was once well peopled with Batoka, who possessed enormous herds of cattle. When Sebituane came in former times, with his small but warlike party of Makololo, to this spot, a general rising took place of the Batoka through the whole country, in order to 'eat him up;' but his usual success followed him, and, dispersing them, the Makololo obtained so many cattle that they could not take any note of the herds of sheep and goats. The *tsetse* has been brought by buffaloes into some districts where formerly cattle abounded. This obliged us to travel the first few stages by night. We could not well detect the nature of the country in the dim moonlight; the path, however, seemed to lead along the high bank of what may have been the ancient bed of the Zambesi before the fissure was made. The Lekone now winds in it in an opposite direction to that in which the ancient river must have flowed.

"For a few days we travelled over an uninhabited, gently undulating, and most beautiful district, the border territory between those who accept and those who reject the sway of the Makololo. The face of the country appears as if in long waves, running north and south. There are no rivers, though water stands in pools in the hollows. We were now come into the country which my people all magnify as a perfect paradise. Sebituane was driven from it by the Matebele. It suited him exactly for cattle, corn, and health. The soil is dry, and often a reddish sand; there are few trees, but fine large shady ones stand dotted here and there over the country where towns formerly stood. One of the fig family I measured, and found to be forty feet in circumference; the heart had been burned out, and some one had made a lodging in it, for we saw the remains of a bed and a fire. The sight of the open country, with the increased altitude we were attaining, was most refreshing to the spirits. Large game abound. We see in the distance buffaloes, elands, hartebeest, gnus, and elephants, all very tame, as no one disturbs them. Lions, which always accompany other large animals, roared about us, but, as it was moonlight, there was no danger. In the evening, while standing on a mass of granite, one began to roar at me, though it was still light.

"On the 3d of December we crossed the river Mozuma, or river of Dila, having travelled through a beautifully undulating pastoral country. To the south, and a little east of this, stands the hill Taba Cheu, or 'White Mountains,' from a mass of white rock, probably dolomite, on its top. But none of the hills are of any great altitude. The Mozuma, or river of Dila, was the first water-course which indicated that we were now on the slopes toward the eastern coast. It contained no flowing water, but revealed in its banks what gave me great pleasure at the time—pieces of lignite, possibly indicating the existence of a mineral, namely, coal, the want of which in the central country I had always deplored. Again and again we came to the ruins of large towns, containing the only hieroglyphics of this country, worn mill-stones, with the round ball of quartz with which the grinding was effected. Great numbers of these balls were lying about, showing that the depopulation had been the result of war; for, had the people removed in peace, they would have taken the balls with them.

"When we had passed the outskirting villages, which alone consider themselves in a state of war with the Makololo, we found the Batoka, or Batonga, as they here call themselves, quite friendly. Great numbers of them came from all the surrounding villages with presents of maize and masuka, and expressed great joy at the first appearance of a white man, and harbinger of peace. The women clothe themselves better than the Balonda, but the men go *in puris naturalibus*. They walk about without the smallest sense of shame.

"The further we advanced, the more we found the country swarming with inhabitants. Great numbers came to see the white man, a sight they had never beheld before. They always brought presents of maize and masuka. Their mode of salutation is quite singular. They throw themselves on their backs on the ground, and, rolling from side to side, slap the outside of their thighs as expressions of thankfulness and welcome, uttering the words 'Kina bomba.' This method of salutation was to me very disagreeable, and I never could get reconciled to it. I called out, 'Stop, stop; I don't want that;' but they, imagining I was dissatisfied, only tumbled about more furiously, and slapped their thighs with greater vigor."

For nearly a month the party pushed slowly on, varying the monotony of the journey by hunting elephants, or overcoming difficulties occasioned by the greed or suspicion of the natives. In the latter cases, one of the Makololo, Sekwebu by name, was of great service. The party reached the Kafue on the 18th of December, and finally the Zambesi about the close of the year.

"As we approached nearer the Zambesi," says Livingstone, "the country became covered with broad-leaved bushes, pretty thickly planted, and we had several times to shout to elephants to get out of our way. At an open space, a herd of buffaloes came trotting up to look at our oxen, and it was only by shooting one that I made them retreat. The meat is very much like that of an ox, and this one was very fine. The only danger we actually encountered was from a female elephant, with three young ones of different sizes. Charging through the centre of our extended line, and causing the men to throw down their burdens in a great hurry, she received a spear for her temerity. I never saw an elephant with more than one calf before. We knew that we were near our Zambesi again, even before the great river burst upon our sight, by the numbers of water-fowl we met. I killed four geese with two shots, and, had I followed the wishes of my men, could have secured a meal of water-fowl for the whole party. I never saw a river with so much animal life around and in it, and, as the Barotse say, 'Its fish and fowl are always fat.' When our eyes were gladdened by a view of its goodly broad waters, we found it very much larger than it is even above the falls. One might try to make his voice heard across it in vain. Its flow was more rapid than near Sesheke, being often four and a half miles an hour."

During January and February, 1856, the party moved slowly eastward, encountering great difficulties from the hostility of the natives. More than once they were on the point of fighting, and the trouble was scarcely avoided, before a similar one would arise at the next settlement. At the confluence of the Loangwe, a large stream which comes down from the north, with the Zambesi, Livingstone found some remains of the old Portuguese station of Zumbo. Below this, he was obliged to cross the Zambesi, and take a direct route across the rough and dangerous region to the south of the river, directly towards Tete. This narrative is full of exciting details, which, however, there is no space to reproduce here. We must pass on to the close of the eventful journey, and give his account of the approach to the semi-civilization of a Portuguese trading-port, on the eastern side of the continent:

"Being pretty well tired out in the evening of the 2d of March, I remained at about eight miles distance from Tete. My men asked me to go on; I felt too fatigued to proceed, but sent forward to the commandant the letters of recommendation with which I had been favored in Angola by the bishop and others, and lay down to rest. Our food having been exhausted, my men had been subsisting for some time on roots and honey. About two o'clock in the morning of the 3d we were aroused by two officers and a company of soldiers, who had been sent with the materials for a civilized breakfast and a 'masheela' to bring me to Tete. My companions thought that we were captured by the armed men, and called me in alarm. When I understood the errand on which they had come, and had partaken of a good breakfast, though I had just before been too tired to sleep, all my fatigue vanished. It was the most refreshing breakfast I ever partook of, and I walked the last eight miles without the least feeling of weariness, although the path was so rough that one of the officers remarked to me, 'This is enough to tear a man's life out of him.' The pleasure experienced in partaking of that breakfast was only equalled by the enjoyment of Mr. Gabriel's bed on my arrival at Loanda. It was also enhanced by the news that Sebastopol had fallen and the war was finished.

"The village of Tete is built on a long slope down to the river, the fort being close to the water. The rock beneath is gray sand-stone, and has the appearance of being crushed away from the river: the strata have thus a crumpled form. The hollow between each crease is a street, the houses being built upon the projecting fold. The rocks at the top of the slope are much higher than the fort, and of course completely command it. There is then a large valley, and beyond that anoblong hill called Karueira. The whole of the adjacent country is rocky and broken, but every available spot is under cultivation. The stone houses in Tete are cemented with mud instead of lime, and thatched with reeds and grass. The rains, having washed out the mud between the stones, give all the houses a rough, untidy appearance. No lime was known to be found nearer than Mozambique; some used in making seats in the verandas had actually been brought all that distance.

"There are about twelve hundred huts in all, which with European households would give a population of about four thousand five hundred souls. Only a small proportion of these, however, live on the spot; the majority are engaged in agricultural operations in the adjacent country. Generally there are not more than two thousand people resident, for, compared with what it was, Tete is now a ruin. The number of Portuguese is very small; if we exclude the military, it is under twenty.

"As it was necessary to leave most of my men at this place, Major Sicard gave them a portion of land on which to cultivate their own food, generously supplying them with corn in the meantime. He also said that my young men might go and hunt elephants in company with his servants, and purchase goods with both the ivory and dried meat, in order that they might have something to take with them on their return to Sekeletu. The men were delighted with his liberality, and soon sixty or seventy of them set off to engage in this enterprise. There was no calico to be had at this time in Tete, but the commandant handsomely furnished my men with clothing. I was in a state of want myself, and, though I pressed him to take payment in ivory for both myself and men, he refused all recompense. I shall ever remember his kindness with deep gratitude."

After a good rest at Tete, Livingstone, heartily assisted by the Portuguese authorities, commenced his voyage down the Zambesi. He had now reached territory which was known, and the interest of his narrative ceases. The toils and privations of the journey were also over: he floated comfortably on through the fever-haunted lowlands of Eastern Africa, and on the 20th of May reached the village of Kilimane. "It wanted," he says, "only a few days of being four years since I started from Capetown. Here I was received into the house of Colonel Galdino Jose Nunes, one of the best men in the country. I had been three years without hearing from my family; letters having frequently been sent, but somehow or other, with but a single exception, they never reached me. I received, however, a letter from Admiral Trotter, conveying information of their welfare, and some newspapers, which were a treat indeed. Her Majesty's brig the 'Frolic' had called to inquire for me in the November previous, and Captain Nolluth, of that ship, had most considerately left a case of wine; and his surgeon, Dr. James Walsh, divining what I should need most, left an ounce of quinine. These gifts made my heart overflow. I had not tasted any liquor whatever during the time I had been in Africa; but when reduced in Angola to extreme weakness, I found much benefit from a little wine, and took from Loanda one bottle of brandy in my medicine chest, intending to use it if it were again required; but the boy who carried it whirled the box upside down, and smashed the bottle, so I cannot give my testimony either in favor of or against the brandy.

"Eight of my men begged to be allowed to come as far as Kilimane, and, thinking that they would there see the ocean, I consented to their coming, though the food was so scarce in consequence of a dearth that they were compelled to suffer some hunger. They would fain have come farther; for when Sekeletu parted with them, his orders were that none of them should turn until they had reached Ma Robert and brought her back with them. On my explaining the difficulty of crossing the sea, he said, 'Wherever you lead, they must follow.' As I did not know well how I should get home myself, I advised them to go back to Tete, where food was abundant, and there await my return. I bought a quantity of calico and brass wire with ten of the smaller tusks which we had in our charge, and sent the former back as clothing to those who remained at Tete. As there were still twenty tusks left, I deposited them with Colonel Nunes, that, in the event of anything happening to prevent my return, the impression might not be produced in the country that I had made away with Sekeletu's ivory. I instructed Colonel Nunes, in case of my death, to sell the tusks and deliver the proceeds to my men; but I intended, if my life should be prolonged, to purchase the goods ordered by Sekeletu in England with my own money, and pay myself on my return out of the price of the ivory. This I explained to the men fully, and they, understanding the matter, replied, 'Nay, father, you will not die; you will return to take us back to Sekeletu.' They promised to wait till I came back, and, on my part, I assured them that nothing but death would prevent my return.

"After waiting about six weeks at this unhealthy spot, in which, however, by the kind attentions of Colonel Nunes and his nephew, I partially recovered from my tertian, H. M. brig 'Frolic' arrived off Kilimane. As the village is twelve miles from the bar, and the weather was rough, she was at anchor ten days before we knew of her presence about seven miles from the entrance to the port. She brought abundant supplies for all my need, and £150 to pay my passage home, from my kind friend Mr. Thompson, the Society's agent at the Cape. The admiral at the Cape kindly sent an offer of a passage to the Mauritius, which I thankfully accepted. Sekwebu and one attendant alone remained with me now. He was very intelligent, and had been of the greatest service to me, indeed, but for his good sense, tact, and command of the language of the tribes through which we passed, I believe we should scarcely have succeeded in reaching the coast. I naturally felt grateful to him; and as his chief wished *all* my companions to go to England with me, and would probably be disappointed if none went, I thought it would be beneficial for him to see the effects of civilization, and report them to his countrymen; I wished also to make some return for his very important services. Others had petitioned to come, but I explained the danger of a change of climate and food, and with difficulty restrained them. The only one who now remained begged so hard to come on board ship that I greatly regretted that the expense prevented my acceding to his wish to visit England. I said to him 'You will die if you go to such a cold country as mine.' 'That is nothing,' he reiterated; 'let me die at your feet.'

"We left Kilimane on the 12th of July, and reached the Mauritius on the 12th of August, 1856. Sekwebu was picking up English, and becoming a favorite with both men and officers. He seemed a little bewildered, everything on board a man-of-war being so new and strange; but he remarked to me several times, 'Your countrymen are very agreeable,' and, 'What a strange country this is—all water together!' He also said that he now understood why I used the sextant. When we reached the Mauritius a steamer came out to tow us into the harbor. The constant strain on his untutored mind seemed now to reach a climax, for during the night he became insane. I thought at first that he was intoxicated. He had descended into a boat, and, when I attempted to go down and bring him into the ship, he ran to the stern and said, 'No! no! it is enough that I die alone. You must not perish; if you come, I shall throw myself into the water.' Perceiving that his mind was affected, I said, 'Now, Sekwebu, we are going to Ma Robert.' This struck a chord in his bosom, and he said, 'Oh, yes; where is she, and where is Robert?' and he seemed to recover. The officers proposed to secure him by putting him in irons; but, being a gentleman in his own country, I objected, knowing that the insane often retain an impression of ill-treatment, and I could not bear to have it said in Sekeletu's country that I had chained one of his principal men as they had seen slaves treated. I tried to get him on shore by day, but he refused. In the evening a fresh accession of insanity occurred; he tried to spear one of the crew, then leaped overboard, and, though he could swim well, pulled himself down hand under hand by the chain cable. We never found the body of poor Sekwebu.

"At the Mauritius I was most hospitably received by Major-General C. M. Hay, and he generously constrained me to remain with him till, by the influence of the good climate and quiet English comfort, I got rid of an enlarged spleen from African fever. In November I came up the Red Sea; escaped the danger of shipwreck through the admirable management of Captain Powell, of the Peninsular and Oriental Steam Company's ship 'Candia,' and on the 12th of December was once more in dear old England."

CHAPTER XIV.

MAGYAR'S JOURNEY TO BIHE.

THE Hungarian traveller, Ládislaus Magyar, has succeeded in nearly supplying our knowledge of the district lying between the route of Livingstone from the upper valley of the Zambesi to the western coast, and the most northern points reached by Anderson and Green.

Magyar, as his name indicates, was a Hungarian, a native of Theresiopol. He entered the Austrian navy in 1840, and, after various voyages, left the service in South America, and was employed by the Argentine Republic. The fleet of the latter power having been destroyed by that of Uruguay, he went to Brazil for a time, and afterwards engaged in the African trade, which he followed for two or three years. Partly from a passion for exploration, and partly from a desire to recover his health, which had been shattered by the deadly coast fever, he finally went to Benguela, the most southern Portuguese port, in order to settle himself in the healthier inland regions.

The trading-town of Benguela, which contains a population of about 3,000, has a climate which seems to be fatal to the white race. "A man of twenty-five," says Magyar, "when he has finally become acclimated, after a residence of two years, and usually after much suffering, looks like a man of thirty-five. If he remains eight or nine years longer, he has the appearance of one aged in mind and body, with white hair, sunken face, and toothless mouth. In from ten to twelve years the European race disappears."

The inland region is inhabited by a number of negro tribes, who live in a state of continual war, yet, from their language and habits, appear to be of the same blood. They are called, collectively, the Kimbunda. The country is threaded by the affluents of the Coanza River, which rises in Lat. 13° and flows northward over a table-land, 6,000 feet above the sea, to about Lat. 9°, where it turns westward, and empties into the sea not far from St. Paul de Loanda. The land rises, from the coast, in successive terraces, each of which has its distinct climate and productions.

The coast region is sandy, arid, and intensely hot. The tribe nearest to Benguela, called the Mundombe, is a strong and rather handsome race, but repulsive in its habits. Instead of bathing, they rub their bodies, every third day, with fat or butter, and soak their single cotton garments in the same, so that they stick to their bodies. They live in huts but two or three feet high, built of sticks and mud, and always filled with smoke from the fires which they keep up, even in summer. They have herds of cattle, and also cultivate maize, beans, and manioc.

Magyar remained but a short time in Benguela, in order to complete his arrangement for the journey to the native kingdom of Bihe, which comprises the elevated table-land of the interior. The caravans are infrequent but large, on account of greater security. The

ST. PAUL DE LOANDA.

native or half-caste traders usually announce their intention beforehand, and the men who desire to join them as porters or assistants seek them of their own accord and offer their services. If the traders asked them to come, they would make themselves responsible for any loss or injury which the latter might suffer. Men of other tribes go to their prophet, taking a goat as an offering, and ask his advice concerning the result of the journey. The prophet anoints parts of their bodies with the blood of the animal, and then sends them to the chief, who makes the sign of the tribes on their foreheads, with white paint. This is an African passport, which is always respected, and, singularly enough, is never counterfeited.

Goods of all kinds are slung to poles, which are carried on the shoulders of the porters: travellers are obliged to lie in a hammock which is also suspended from a long pole, carried by two men, who are relieved by others from time to time. But the progress of the caravan, especially in marshes, forests, or the passes of the mountains, is exceedingly slow and toilsome, and the traveller is compelled to walk where the road is worst.

The leader of the caravan from Bihe was very ready to accept Magyar's application to join him, since the presence of a European is considered an additional protection. The traveller also obtained a *kissongo*, or body-guard,—a man whose office was to attend him, watch over his property, and defend him in case of danger. An interpreter, three slaves for personal service, and six hammock-bearers were also necessary. Provided with these, and with the proper goods for trade with the natives, Magyar left Benguela on the 15th of January, 1849—the middle of summer, and made his way across the burning lowlands towards the first range of mountains.

In this region there was no sign of vegetable life except some leafless thorn-bushes and tufts of dried grass. The vertical sun shone so powerfully upon the heads of the travellers that even the natives complained of the heat, and made use of the tails of quaggas as a sort of fan. As the elevation above the sea increased, trees began to appear, and the banks of the Katumbele River, beyond the first range of hills, were covered with a dense tropical vegetation. This stream was crossed by means of bamboo rafts, and the caravan was so large that many hours were required to transport all the men and goods to the other shore.

A short distance beyond, they reached the first range of mountains—a wild chaos of black, volcanic peaks, where only thorns and aloes grew. The path mounted or fell along the brink of precipitous abysses, and the loose stones and pebbles frequently slid and gave way under the feet of the natives, who were obliged to march in single file, so that an accident to one delayed all the others in the rear. The bleached bones of men, at the bottoms of the chasms, were a ghastly evidence of the dangers of the road. From time to time, among the higher cliffs, they saw the forms of the wild, predatory tribes of the hills, apparently mustering their strength, and deliberating whether an attack might be ventured. In spite of the great fatigue of the journey, Magyar was so impressed with the grand character of the scenery, and so refreshed by the purer atmosphere of the mountains, that he immediately began to receive his health and strength.

He describes two cataracts in the higher regions, one of which, called Kahi, is of an unusual character. The river slides down a rock, having a declivity of eighty degrees, for a distance of 150 feet, is then dashed into foam upon a transverse ledge, and falls 150 feet further into a black chasm, with a noise which may be heard for several miles. He also speaks of an active volcano, further to the northward. It is an isolated cone, rising high above the other mountains, and discharging low jets of steam and flame at regular intervals. The natives consider that the crater is the residence of the spirits of their dead, and never dare to approach the mountain.

The way led partly through wild passes, with running streams and luxuriant vegetation in their beds, partly over barren, stony hills, or across high tablelands, covered with a thick growth of grass.

In proportion as they advanced eastward, the tropical rains increased. Every afternoon the clouds gathered in dense masses, lightning and terrific thunder swept around the peaks, and rain, mixed with hail, poured in torrents. The mornings were cool and delightful, and the natives shivered in the showers shaken upon them by the wet foliage, until the sun was high enough to dry and warm them. On entering the Kissangi land, which is fertile and inhabited, the caravan constructed a rude fortified camp every evening, and temporary huts were erected as a shelter from the rains. The inhabitants, who build their villages on heights which are almost inaccessible, are inveterate robbers.

Magyar was requested by the natives to assume command, of the caravan, as they believed it would thus become more formidable. This imposed upon him the duty of looking after the goods, appointing the guards, and directing the daily marches; on the other hand, it gave him opportunities of learning the true method of dealing with the tribes of the interior. His first encounters with the chiefs of the villages were settled by some trifling presents; but, when the demands became more exorbitant, he was obliged to call the former leader of the caravan to his aid. It was necessary to put on a bold front, and more than once the members of the company armed themselves and prepared to resist an attack, which was probably prevented by their prompt show of courage.

The leader of a band of the Bailunda tribe, from whom hostilities were expected, contented himself with a moderate present of brandy, powder and flints, with the condition that the white man should bring him the articles in person. He sent two women as hostages, and Magyar, although not fully trusting the leader's word, felt bound to comply. He found the camp divided into four regular quarters, with the commander's tent in the centre, designated by a red flag. The latter was the son-in-law of the king, and was a tall, strong, and rather handsome man. He was surrounded with his guards, interpreters, and servants. He first addressed his troops, the musicians accompanying his words with the sound of their instruments. Then, turning to the traveller, he clapped his hands, and thrice gave the salutation, "Peace be with you!" He confessed that his officers had proposed to him to attack the caravan, but he had forbidden it, on account of his friendship for the white man.

While the troops were drinking the beer which they brew from maize, and beginning their savage dances, Magyar slipped away and returned to the caravan. His men feared that the Baihúndas would undertake an attack on their own account, in spite of the protection which their chief had promised; and, as these people usually attempt such undertakings in the early morning, the caravan was set in motion after night, marched unperceived past the Bailunda camp, and by morning was at a safe distance.

The next adventure was one of a more agreeable nature. In the neighborhood of a place called Kandala, two negro-girls, clad in a semi-European fashion, came to Magyar's tent, addressed him in Portuguese, and offered him a present of figs, pine-apples, and bananas. They brought him a greeting from Donna Isabel, their mistress, who lived near at hand, and who requested permission to visit him. Her presence was soon announced by the chanting of the hammock-bearers. She was a lady of about twenty-two, with negro features, but a bright mulatto complexion. She was born in Benguela, but had lived in Brazil, and, after returning to Africa, had married a native trader and settled in the interior. Now, as his widow, she carried on his business profitably, while a number of slaves cultivated his fields. When Magyar returned his visit, she entertained him with a meal in the European style. Seven years afterwards, he relates, her friendship was the means of saving his life.

Beyond the Kissangi land lies the splendid tropical valley of the Kubale River, filled with mountain streams and cataracts, and rejoicing in a most luxuriant vegetation. Then followed a broad and lofty table-land, stretching eastward to the base of another and higher range of mountains, called the Lingi-Lingi. Herds of buffaloes, zebras, and antelopes pastured on the rich grasses of the plain, and the natives immediately organized a hunting-party. The sight of the buffaloes, however, so alarmed Magyar that he climbed to the top of a huge ant-hill, and his nervous excitement was so great when the first beast stormed past, that he was unable to pull the trigger. He threw away the flint, and pretended to have lost it, lest the natives should detect his lack of the coolness necessary to a hunter. The former succeeded in killing seven of the animals, which gave them all a banquet of the tough flesh.

After encountering a terrific storm at the base of the Lingi-Lingi Mountains, they commenced the ascent. The path led for a time through huge forests, matted together with vines and parasitic plants, then slowly emerged upon open slopes, and wound in zigzags around the peaks, frequently along the verge of immense chasms. Magyar describes the scenery as imposing in its grandeur and the variety of its forms. The mountain peaks exhibited the most singular and grotesque forms. Some were clothed with pines; others were pinnacles of naked rock; and between them all the noise of cataracts resounded from the deeps. At the summit, about 5,000 feet above the sea, commenced another table-land, from the lofty

MAGYAR'S ASCENT OF THE COAST RANGE

level of which the mountain-ranges far to the east and west were visible, like lines of cloud.

The former of these ranges, called the Djamba, was the remaining barrier to be passed before reaching the country of Bihe. Between it and the Lingi-Lingi range lies the land of Hambo, not of great extent, but widely known for the warlike and plundering habits of its people. The march of the caravan across this region was fortunately not interrupted by any attack, but it was rendered slow and difficult by the rains, which had soaked the soil and swollen all the streams. At last they reached the wooded base-hills, above which tower the bald granite summits of the Djamba range. In spite of the difficulties of the ascent, the natives all shouted and sang at the prospect of so soon reaching their homes. Thunders from the peaks answered their songs, and in spite of their exertions, they were drenched by a furious rain long before reaching the summit. Magyar caught a fever from the exposure, but the caravan rested on the following day, and he was able to cure himself by a simple sudorific process.

The Djamba negroes, who inhabit the upper part of the mountains, and form an independent little republic of their own, came to visit the camp. They were a strong and finely-formed race, but rather impudent in their ways. One of them related to Magyar that he had formerly been the slave of a white man who lived in the mountains. This appeared to have been a Portuguese named Cota, an exile from Brazil, who, sixteen years before, had led an adventurous life in the interior. The Djamba stated that he had discovered gold in the mountains, and employed the natives to wash it out from the sands. On account of his cruelty and violence he had provoked their hostility, but succeeded in escaping to Benguela, whence he returned to Brazil.

The caravan now continued its journey across the highest table-land of Sambos, which is probably 6,000 feet above the sea. Here the dark, rich soil is of a sandy character, and the numerous streams form extensive swamps and pools. The plain is dotted with little hills, upon which the natives build their villages, which are shaded with groups of trees resembling the sycamore. Towards the close of the journey, they were visited by a hail-storm so severe that the ground was covered as with a crust of ice. But this was the last of their hardships: they had reached the frontiers of Bihe, and the company of nearly 2,000 persons began to divide into little squads and scatter towards their different homes. Messengers had been sent in advance, to announce their coming, so that the women could brew maize-beer, and even carry it to meet them on the last stage of the march.

Nearly all Magyar's servants and porters here left him, refusing to appear before their families in that character: only the *kissongo* and his relatives remained faithful, for they considered the white man as their guest, and their families had been instructed to prepare for his reception. They now pushed forward with great impatience, delayed only by too copious indulgence in beer, and in two or three days more arrived at their home. There Magyar was received with great kindness. After the first salutations were over, one of the porters commenced a recital of everything that had occurred during his absence of 116 days, omitting not the smallest incident.

Magyar's chief object being to establish his residence in Bihe as a base for further explorations, his first care was to send a messenger with presents to the king, asking his permission to build a house. The answer came in five days; the king sent a friendly greeting, and gave his permission, but added the request that the stranger could pay him a formal visit as soon as he had completed his dwelling.

Magyar was at liberty to take any piece of land which had not been already claimed and occupied by some one else. The country around the home of his *kissongo* was so attractive that his only difficulty was what point to select. He finally made choice of a beautiful little valley, with a clear swift rivulet in its bed. Forests and meadows alternated in the landscape, and every hill in the distance was crowned with a native village. The character of the scenery was so charming that he declared to his attendants that he would fix his residence there. To his great annoyance, the latter informed him that a notorious wizard had been executed on the spot, a year before, and since then the evil spirits had taken possession of the whole neighborhood. Foreseeing that the natives would resist his attempts to settle there, Magyar had recourse to one of their exorcising priests, to whom he presented a fat hog and several yards of cotton cloth, begging him to drive away the hateful spirits. The priest slaughtered a goat, marked several hieroglyphics with its blood on Magyar's arm and breast, blew three blasts through the horn of a gazelle, and the evil spirits immediately fled from the beautiful valley, leaving it free to human habitation.

As soon as the news became known, people came from all the neighboring villages, to be employed in the building of the house. The men felled trees in the forests, while the women and children cut the long grass of the meadows to thatch the roofs. In order to assure himself of the proper respect and consideration, it was necessary for the stranger to build a large dwelling, and employ at least fifty slaves or servants. In the material and character of the structure, he imitated the houses of the people, except that his was square, instead of being circular in form. First a large stockade was made of posts of iron-wood, with loop-holes for musketry. Inside of this were the slave-quarters and store-houses; then a second palisaded inclosure, with the house of the future lord and his family. The walls were of strong palisades, plastered with clay, and whitewashed, so that the residence had a semi-civilized appearance.

The people worked lustily to secure the white man a home before he could have time to change his mind. The women, especially, desired him to remain among them, not on account of his complexion and features, which were very disagreeable to them, but because he possessed such a store of trinkets, many of which they hoped to secure in the course of time. There was no trouble in procuring all the labor required. It is not advantageous, however, to employ those who are free, since they are only willing to render special services: the greater part of the labor falls upon slaves, or a class of retainers, whose work is purchased in advance, and who are bound to do whatever is required of them. For twenty yards of cotton cloth, apiece, Magyar purchased as many of the latter class as he needed, and the additional applications were so numerous that he was finally obliged to keep them forcibly at a distance. It is not more difficult to support such a retinue of followers, than to obtain them. The cultivation of the soil is carried on exclusively by the women, while the men build, hunt, and fish. As soon as a young man has earned the price of a wife he marries, in order to have his fields cultivated. The married slaves are obliged to help support the unmarried, as well as to furnish food for the master. The latter is only expected to clothe his slaves with a single narrow garment, and give them a few yards of cloth twice a year.

As soon as the residence was completed, Magyar made preparations to visit the king of Bihe, whose capital, Kombala, was about two days' journey distant. The nearer he drew, the more desolate and uninhabited the country became; the African rulers employ their power to plunder those of their subjects who are nearest at hand. The town was built, like the villages, on the summit of a hill, shadowed by huge trees. A narrow foot-path led up the steep and rocky height, to the gate of the town, where the traveller, with his native attendants, was obliged to wait an hour before entrance was allowed them. Within the gate there was a large grassy square, surrounded with trees, beyond which appeared the low, miserable huts and dirty streets of the town, crowded with a curious multitude of people.

Further on, he reached a shady square, with wooden benches, the place where the inhabitants were accustomed to meet and discuss public affairs. The people were more carefully dressed, and exhibited a greater refinement and tact in their manners, than those of the villages. After Magyar had again waited for a time, a messenger came to announce that the king would see him on the morrow; in the meantime he was invited to rest and refresh himself. A hut was given up to his use, provisions in abundance were brought, and only the troublesome curiosity of the natives prevented him from being comfortable.

The next morning an officer of the court came to conduct him to the palace, which was a large labyrinth of buildings, inclosed by a high palisade. The outer gate was profusely decorated with human heads, some of them bleached to the bone, others fresh as if just placed there. Having passed this, with a feeling that he was entering the den of a lion, Magyar was conducted by many winding ways to a door in an inner palisade-wall, through which he finally reached the royal court-yard. After waiting here for another half-hour, the sound of bells announced the approach of the king. He entered, took his seat on a sort of throne, over which was suspended a lion's hide, while a page knelt at his feet and a servant with a quagga's tail stood behind him. On either side the chiefs and warriors of the court, with their hair twisted into the shape of a helmet, arranged themselves in rows: as weapons they bore long guns, lances, and wooden clubs.

The king, whose name was Kayaya-Kayangula,

was about 50 years old, and of a tall, lean figure. His features were tolerably regular, and would have been agreeable, but for his keen, cunning eyes. He wore a kind of turban on his head, a wide blue robe, and a gayly-striped shawl over his shoulders. The claws of a lion, set in gold, hung as a talisman on his breast, and he held a small dagger in his hand. When he had taken his seat, he thrice greeted Magyar, who had also seated himself on a camp-stool, with the usual salutation: "Peace be with you!"—to which the latter answered, as he had been instructed: "Also with you, princely father!" while the warriors shouted in chorus: "Hail, mighty Lion! raging Lion!" Then Magyar's *kissongo* related all the incidents of the journey, and stated his master's wish to make his home in the land of Bihe, and to visit the other tribes of the interior. This statement lasted more than half an hour, because, although it was made in the language of the country, every word must be repeated to the king by one of his own officers.

The "raging Lion" listened patiently, and at the end expressed his satisfaction. His answer was: "You have honored me, white man, with the confidence you have placed in me, in giving up the comforts which you enjoyed at home, among your own people, and coming here to settle among us. Therefore, be welcome! I take you under my protection, and woe be to them who shall dare to injure your person or your property! I grant to you the right of hospitality which has been given by our ancestors, and my people must know and respect it." The twenty principal chiefs repeated their former salutation, as an acceptance of the king's words, and the traveller thus became an honorary citizen of Bihe.

The king, it appeared, had visited the coast, where he had seen ships, and was greatly impressed with the knowledge and courage of the European race. Magyar endeavored to persuade him that the negroes might procure for themselves many of the things for which they were most dependent on the whites, if they would only be more industrious. They might, for instance, raise and weave their own cotton, besides learning many other simple arts, which would be of great service. The king admitted the truth of this, but added that he was surrounded with such dishonest persons, that it would be impossible for him to introduce any such changes. At the end of the audience Magyar was conducted to his hut, and a festival, in which all the natives took part, closed the day.

CHAPTER XV.

MAGYAR'S JOURNEYS IN THE INTERIOR.

DURING the evening after his reception at the palace, Magyar was surprised by a visit from the king. The latter privately informed him of his intention to undertake a foray upon a neighboring tribe, and insisted on his accompanying the expedition. Under the circumstances, a refusal did not seem politic, and Magyar therefore temporarily agreed, in the hope that some means of escape from the unwelcome obligation would yet be found.

Before continuing the history of his personal adventures, we will here give his account of the manner in which the rule of the royal family of Bihe has been perpetuated for nearly three centuries. As soon as the king appears to be so ill that his death is probable, the chiefs nearest to him in authority separate him from his family and servants, and themselves carry on the government until his death. When this last circumstance is announced his many wives make a loud outcry, and thus proclaim it to the people of the capital. The heir to the throne is the eldest son of the king's eldest sister, because the people consider that the purity of blood is transmitted through woman, not through man. For this reason, when a male slave marries a free woman, his children are free. But the hereditary prince is not allowed to live in the neighborhood of the reigning king : he dare not even visit the latter ; and he is therefore quietly brought up in some remote part of the country. When the king is dead, the prince is escorted to the vicinity of the capital where a temporary camp is pitched, while the corpse, sewed up in a fresh ox-hide, is committed to the earth, in the midst of a number of slaughtered slaves.

The best warriors of the nation then assemble at the camp, and plan an expedition against some neighboring tribe, chiefly for the purpose of obtaining captives. When the foray has succeeded, and a sufficient number of prisoners, of both high and low rank, have been secured, the warriors return home. One of the former is then chosen as a special offering, but this is strictly kept secret from him. He is allowed a certain degree of liberty, is invited to all the festivals, fed and entertained in the best manner, and finally, in the midst of some inebriated dance, his head is suddenly struck off by a slave who steals behind him. His body is then cooked with the flesh of dogs and buffaloes, and eaten by the chiefs. Then, first, the new prince is proclaimed king, and enters on his reign.

Magyar returned to his settlement, and immediately began the cultivation of his fields. Something of his prestige was lost, however, when he took hold of the hoe and spade, in order to teach his slaves a better method of turning up the soil. It was therefore all the more necessary that he should conform to the prejudices of the people in other respects, especially in employing the native wizards, when any of his people were sick. This last expedient was the means of releasing him from the promise which he had made to the king. As the time for the expedition drew near, he complained of pains in the body, and bad dreams, which the wizards declared were produced by evil spirits. Magyar then explained to them that his participation in the foray was prohibited by the laws of his land, and this was probably a punishment sent upon him for intending to violate them.

The magicians, after a careful physical examination of the patient, retired into the forest to consult. They finally decided that an evil spirit had entered into Magyar's body, and would surely kill him if he should accompany the expedition; but the spirit could only be exorcised by slaughtering an ox, and sending presents to the king. The ox having been furnished, certain figures were painted with the blood on Magyar's forehead, breast and arms, and a piece of cotton with the same marks was forwarded to the king, together with a keg of powder and some bottles of brandy. The cure was effectual; the evil spirit departed, the king absolved the stranger from his promise, and—as a further evidence of his favor—sent him his daughter, the princess Osoro, as a wife.

Magyar found the second dilemma less formidable than the first. An unmarried man always excites suspicion and distrust among the African tribes, and the security of his later residence among the people was assured by his acceptance of the princess as a bride. The latter was 14 years old, tall and slender, and with as much grace and amiability as could be expected of any Bihe maiden. She came to him under the escort of two of her brothers, and followed by a numerous retinue of slaves, and the wedding was immediately celebrated. Magyar seems never to have regretted his compliance. The princess Osoro adapted herself to his habits, took care of his household, and became the mother of several children, one of whom was one of the prospective heirs to the throne of Bihe.

His experiments in agriculture were less successful. The people cultivate maize, manioc, and beans, but have a prejudice against potatoes and other vegetables which he introduced, and his only success was in substituting tobacco for the hemp which they had been accustomed to smoke. They raise cattle, sheep, pigs and fowls, and have great semi-annual hunts, when the men of the tribe assemble, surround a district of country and slaughter all the game which is caught in their toils. They are less skilled in fishing, since they do not know how to construct nets. They exhibit some natural skill as blacksmiths, but are deficient in all other mechanical arts.

The family life of the people presents some singular features. As soon as a young man is able to purchase a wife, he marries; and his ambition is to have at least two, since it is the wife's duty to support her husband, and the more wives he has, the better is his chance to be supported in idleness and luxury. The women favor polygamy, for the reason that it makes their own labor lighter. The husband has not the slightest authority over his own children. This belongs to the brother of the mother, who may do as he pleases with them,—even sell them as slaves. Divorces are easy and frequent, but the right is exercised more frequently by women than by men. The great delight of the latter is to lie on the ground, smoke and gossip all day, and listen or dance to music in the evening.

Magyar was obliged to wait for favorable opportunities of penetrating further into the interior, since he meant to combine trade with exploration. His choice of residence proved to be fortunate. The Kimbundas not only learn with much readiness the languages and habits of other tribes, but they are curious, adventurous, and always ready for journeys into new regions. The principal article of commerce is ivory, and, as neither the elephant nor the rhinoceros is found on the high table-lands of Bihe, a proposal to procure supplies further inland seemed quite reasonable to the natives.

Magyar had heard much of a country to the northeast, called Moluwa,—a temperate highland region, full of forests and with plentiful herds of elephants. In 1850, he succeeded in gathering together a caravan of about 400 persons, and set out on a journey to the Moluwa country. There had been no caravans thither from Bihe for several years, because former ones had come in conflict with the half-breed traders from Loanda, and suffered from the collision. But Magyar's proposal attracted a number of the best warriors and elephant-hunters, who volunteered to accompany him. The king gave his permission, although informed that the princess Osoro would accompany her husband. Starting in May, the caravan followed the old native foot-paths, leading eastward towards the Coanza River.

The country is covered with lakes and pools

during the rainy season, which become marshes in the dry months. The first district east of Bihe is called Kimbandi, a hilly, fertile country, watered by numerous affluents of the Coanza. The latter river is crossed at a place called Kujo, where the caravans usually halt, to supply themselves with provisions for the march through the wilderness beyond. The Kimbandi people are thievish and treacherous, but not hostile to travellers. Their territory is bounded on the east by the forests of Olowihenda, which form a belt of division between the western and the central regions of the continent.

These forests cover a mountain-chain which stretches north and south through several degrees of latitude. Towards its northern extremity (where Livingstone afterwards crossed,) they have a breadth of eight days' journey, but further south, a caravan requires sixteen days in order to pass them. The monotony of the dense woods is only occasionally broken by swampy meadows or large pools of water. On account of the streams and morasses, beasts of burden cannot be used, but all goods are slowly and painfully carried forward on the shoulders of men. The elephant and rhinoceros are here found in great herds, and the lion is also an old inhabitant.

The animal most feared is the buffalo. Magyar states that during his many journeys he lost but two of his men from lions, but a large number from the attacks of the buffaloes. It is true that the former is avoided, while the latter is followed on account of his flesh. If the first shot is not fatal, and the hunter does not succeed in instantly reaching a place of safety, he is inevitably tossed into the air, and then stamped to death by the sharp hoofs of the beast. The first impression made by these great tropical forests is solemn and imposing; the silence, the luxuriance of the vegetation, and its strange forms, excite the imagination; but in a short time the scenery becomes very monotonous and oppressive.

A singular race of human beings is sometimes encountered in this wilderness. They are called by the natives *Mu-Kankala*, and Magyar describes them as the most miserable creatures he ever beheld. They are not more than four feet in height, of a rusty yellow color, and with features which seem a caricature of the human face. Their legs are very thin; the round, protruding abdomen takes up one-third of the body; the lean neck bears a large head, with a perfectly flat face, in which wide mouth and nostrils, and small twinkling eyes are inserted. Their ears are like flaps, and their hair is very short and woolly. They appear to be a peaceable people, and unusually honest in their intercourse with strangers. They brought ivory, honey, wax, and dried meat to the caravan, and exchanged these articles for tobacco and glass beads. These poor people are hunted like wild beasts by the neighboring tribes, captured and sold as slaves. Some of the latter, whom Magyar bought, served him with great fidelity and did not leave him even while passing through their own country.

After reaching the eastern boundary of the Olowihenda forests, the highlands give place to a picturesque mountainous region, inhabited by the Chibokoe tribe, who gave Livingstone so much trouble when he passed through a portion of their territory. Magyar compares the region to Switzerland. The mountains are mostly isolated conical peaks, divided by deep, winding and moist valleys, which are very fruitful and inhabited by a dense population. The people raise maize, sorghum, beans and tobacco, and are much better mechanics than those of Bihe. The forests are rich in game and wild honey.

The climate of this region is cool rather than tropical. In July, Magyar sometimes found that vessels of water were covered with a thin crust of ice in the early morning, while the ground was once or twice white with frost. The mountain streams unite to form four considerable rivers which flow to the northward and appear to be affluents of the great river Kasay. None of the villages contain more than a thousand inhabitants: they are simply collections of straw huts, in the forests, and each one is known by the name of its chief.

The eastern portion of the Chibokoe country sinks into a great marshy plain which stretches to the Kasay River. Here commences the Moluwa kingdom, which Magyar declares to be the most powerful in Central Africa. He seems to confound it with that of Cazembe, the name of which is given by other travellers as Londa, while the king is called the Muata-janvo. Magyar's account of the Moluwa king corresponds with that given of the former by Portuguese traders. He enjoys more than human reverence: his subjects do not dare to approach him except creeping on all fours, and casting handfuls of earth upon their heads. His power over their goods and lives is absolute and cruelly exercised, and the people dare to disobey his commands only in the remote provinces. Magyar was unable to ascertain the exact boundaries of the kingdom, but conjectured that it reached to Lat. 4° N.—a length of nearly 1200 miles, with a breadth of about 400 from east to west. His geographical notes, however, are frequently confused, and the accounts he gives require to be tested by those of Livingstone and other travellers.

Since the falling off of the slave-trade, the principal article of commerce is ivory. Wax is very plentiful, but the difficulty of transport is too great to make it profitable. In the northern and eastern parts of the kingdom there are immense forests full of herds of elephants, the tusks of which often weigh 120 pounds each. The price of them is kept up by the competition of the Portuguese from the western and the Arab merchants from the eastern coast, although the two, or their agents, very rarely come in contact. Strings of cowries and white beads are used as money, as well as coils of copper wire, which the natives smelt from malachite. The have also iron of excellent quality, from which they forge swords and lances.

Magyar describes the Moluwa people as surpassing in intellectual capacity all the other South-African races. They have a tolerably well-organized social system, based upon certain traditions of their race, and are usually friendly and polite in their intercourse with strangers. On the other hand they are governed by the grossest forms of superstition, and still, on certain occasions, offer up human sacrifices.

He remained more than a year among them, taking up a temporary residence on the banks of the Kasay River, where he cultivated tobacco for his own use. The natives, who had previously smoked the leaves of hemp, soon learned to prefer the new plant, and began also to raise it. Further to the north, the people cultivate sugar-cane, pine-apples, bananas, and the oil-bearing palm. An unusual quantity of fruit is produced in the neighborhood of Kabebo, the capital town. This place contains a population of about 50,000, but covers, since each house stands within its own separate inclosure, an area of eight or ten square miles. It is built on an undulating plain, falling towards the east. Streams of fresh water flow through the streets, which are laid out at right angles, and shaded with rows of large trees. The houses are one story high and thatched with straw; those of the king and princes are larger and loftier, but none of them have two stories. There are also several spacious market-places, which are always crowded when a caravan arrives from the coast with European goods.

The dead kings are always buried in the town of Galanje, further to the northward. Each has his own particular vault, covered with a conical roof of straw: he is laid in the centre, dressed in his richest garments, and surrounded with the bodies of the slaves who are slain to accompany him. Two of the latter are always spared, to take care of the grave, which is kept open so long as the dead king's successor lives, when it is closed forever.

The Moluwa kingdom appears, nevertheless, to be but thinly populated: Magyar estimates the entire population at not more than one million. In the districts to the north-east the villages are large and near together, but there are other parts of the country where the traveller finds no settlement in a day's journey. The villages are generally built in the forests, but each is surrounded with its belt of cultivated land, which gives the impression of a bright oasis in the dark tropical wilderness. Towards the east the country becomes lower, the forests entirely disappear, and there are vast grassy plains, some of which become lakes during the rainy season. It is to be regretted that Magyar was unable to determine the latitude and longitude of the points he reached. His travels fill much of the space between that explored by Livingstone and the Lake Tanganyika, discovered by Burton; but he is not an exact reporter, and his explorations are thus deprived of their legitimate value.

During his residence in the Moluwa country, a son was born to him, to whom he gave the name of "Shah-Kilambe-Gonga." He seems to have been greatly flattered with the idea that a semi-Hungarian prince might one day inherit one of the barbaric thrones of Africa. And in fact, in the year 1854, he was visited by a special embassy from the rulers of Galangue and Sambos, claiming his child as their near relative, and endowing him with the rank and rights which appertained to a member of the royal house of Bihe.

In the year 1851 he called his caravan together, and set out on the return towards his adopted home, taking a more southern route, which led him through the district called Lobal, and across the upper end of the Zambesi valley, although he was not aware of the fact. He passed indeed over a small portion of the route afterwards traversed by Livingstone, skirting the Dilolo lake, and, like the latter traveller, leading his caravan through the marshes which surround it. He speaks of the lake as being full of fish, which the natives catch in great quantities, but, as they dry them without the use of salt, the taste is insupportable to a civilized palate. In the marshes around the lake there are also great snakes which are often found in companies of a dozen or more, coiled together in the grass. His followers did not show the least fear of the reptiles, but eagerly attacked them, and afterwards roasted and partook of their flesh as a great delicacy.

Magyar's description of the swampy plains around Lake Dilolo corresponds exactly with Livingstone's, of whose later visit to the same region he was apparently ignorant. He describes the land of Lobal, west of the lake, as a region of plains which are inundated during the rainy season, dotted with wooded hills, which then become islands. He speaks of the Niambedji River in the east, and this is undoubtedly the Leeambye of Livingstone. He estimates the population of Lobal at 200,000,—people of vigorous and well-proportioned physical character, but treacherous and unfriendly. They will receive the stranger with every show of hospitality, and the next day lie in wait to plunder him. Instead of forming a nation like that of Moluwa or Bihe, each region has its petty chief or chieftainess, whose relations with his or her neighbors are hostile rather than friendly. They frequently attack each other with the design of making slaves of the other's people, as if there were no relationship of blood between them. The caravans which pass through Lobal always pur-

AN EXPEDITION FROM BIHE.

chase a quantity of slaves from the petty chiefs, and afterwards exchange them for ivory with other tribes.

In some of his later journeys Magyar again visited the Lobal country. Some slaves whom he had purchased on his first visit accompanied him, but not one of them attempted to desert and remain in his native land. He describes one of the chiefs, named Kinjama, as a man more than a hundred years old, who received him with the greatest kindness. A strong contrast to him is another chief named the Parroquet, in the eastern part of the country, who is famous for his cruelty and his exactions upon travellers. The result was that the caravans, whenever it was possible, made a wide détour rather than pass through his territory.

Magyar took a south-western course through Lobal, and entered the Buunda region, passing its capital, Kissembo. Here he again struck the Olowihenda forests, which he crossed in a westerly direction, and returned to his residence in Bihe. For four or five years he seems to have made an extensive caravan journey every year, and to have followed his original plan of penetrating gradually further towards the east and south. Unfortunately, he has given us no detailed account of any of these journeys, the extent and character of which we can only conjecture from his fragmentary notes. The year after his return from the Moluwa kingdom, he made a journey to the country of the Kilengues, lying further to the south, and the year afterwards (1853) he claims to have reached the Kunene River, which was sought for so persistently by Anderson and Green, and to have explored a considerable portion of its course.

During this journey he visited the Portuguese "Presidio de Caconda," of which he gives a curious account. It lies far in the interior, not far from the head-waters of the Kunene River, and contains about 3,000 inhabitants. The fort and town are surrounded with walls of earth, and palisades, and defended by eight cannon, but the garrison consists of only a single company of negro soldiers, under the command of the Governor. Formerly there was an important trade between this point and the coast, but with the breaking up of the traffic in slaves it has fallen off. The climate is comparatively cool and healthy, whence the Portuguese traders who once settled here, took negro wives, and produced a race of mulattoes who still inhabit the place.

On his return from this southern journey, Magyar's caravan was attacked by a band of robbers, in the forests of Lusseke. After a prolonged fight, the enemy was driven off with considerable loss. He relates, however, that these predatory bands sometimes embrace whole tribes, and number from fifteen to twenty thousand fighting men. In such cases, they are irresistible; they burst upon the territories of weaker tribes, slay, lay waste and capture as they proceed, and leave a desert behind them.

We can only guess from Magyar's further notes that he remained upon his possessions in Bihe in 1854. But the next year he started again, crossed the Olowihenda wilderness, and reached the country of Lobal. How far his explorations extended cannot be ascertained. On his return he was again attacked by a large body of the natives, and only succeeded in repelling them, after a hard fight which lasted several hours. The supply of powder was thereby so reduced that the caravan was obliged to return to Bihe by forced marches.

In 1856 he undertook to revisit Benguela, since it was in this year that the Donna Isabel, whom he met during his inland journey in 1849, rescued him from death; but in what manner we are not informed. His death must have occurred about this time, or soon afterwards, and thus some of the most important geographical questions, upon which he might have thrown a great deal of light, are left unsolved. What information he has given, however, bears the stamp of truth. His system of exploration was bold, intelligent and successful; he, no less than Livingstone, has shown how much courage and an unflinching determination will accomplish.

CHAPTER XVI.

LIVINGSTONE'S EXPEDITION TO LAKE NYASSA.

LIVINGSTONE'S narrative of his journey across the African continent, published in 1857, excited the greatest interest throughout the civilized world. The importance of his discoveries was everywhere recognized, and his own determination to undertake a new journey of exploration met with a hearty support from the English Government and the Royal Geographical Society, as well as from private individuals. The object of this second expedition was to ascertain whether the Zambesi River was navigable to a point near the Makololo country, and to penetrate the regions north of that river, so as to connect Livingstone's discoveries with those of Burton and Speke, in Equatorial Africa.

The Earl of Clarendon, then Minister of Foreign Affairs, united with the Geographical Society in providing for the outfit of the expedition, and Dr. Livingstone was joined by his brother, the Rev. Charles Livingstone, who had been living as a clergyman in Massachusetts for some years, by Dr. Kirk, an accomplished botanist, and Mr. Thornton, who, however, left the party soon after their arrival in the Zambesi country, and joined Baron Van der Decker in his attempt to reach the mountain Kilimandjaro. The supplies were procured with especial reference to the regions to be traversed, and everything was done which promised to insure success in advance.

The expedition left England on the 10th of March, 1858, in the steamer *Pearl*, and, proceeding by the way of the Cape of Good Hope, reached the mouth of the Zambesi River in May. The navigation of this river, both as a highway for commerce and means for the christianization of Africa, was Livingstone's first object, and if he was finally disappointed therein, the results of his undertaking are none the less important in a geographical point of view. He brought with him a smaller steamer, in sections, which were then put together and launched, under the name of the *Ma-Robert* (mother of Robert),—a name which was given by the Makololo to Mrs. Livingstone, when she accompanied him on the first journey to Lake Ngami.

On reaching Mazaro, where the delta of the Zambesi begins and its arms branch off towards the sea, Livingstone found the Portuguese at war with a half-breed who had forcibly taken possession of the northern bank of the river as far as the Shire, and plundered at will.

A battle, of which he was a spectator, took place at Mazaro, but it fortunately ended in the defeat of the native chief, and he was able to go forward with safety. The steamer, driven by the heat of burned ebony and lignum vitæ, slowly ascended the river, passed Shupanga, which was to be the grave of Mrs. Livingstone three years later, and reached the mouth of the Shire. Here, however, no halt was made: Livingstone pushed on with difficulty, on account of the imperfect construction of the boat, which was scarcely able to stem the current, and on the 8th of September reached Tete, where he had left his faithful Makololos in 1856. They were still waiting for him, and their joy at his appearance was very great. Some fell upon his neck, while others exclaimed: "Do not touch him —you will soil his new clothes!" and the native minstrels struck up a chant of rejoicing.

As it was low water in the Zambesi, an examination of the Kebrabasi Rapids in the river, some forty or fifty miles above Tete, was made for the purpose of ascertaining whether the steamer would be able to pass them during high water. The result was entirely unfavorable; whereupon Dr. Livingstone wrote to England asking that a new and more powerful steamer should be sent, and meanwhile decided to undertake an exploration of the Shire, which river was wholly unknown to the Portuguese officials, who declared that they had been unable to navigate it on account of the density of the growth of water plants.

Livingstone entered the river in January, 1859, and found that the steamer was able to force its way through the aquatic vegetation, which gradually became less dense, and finally ceased, leaving a clear, deep stream. At the villages on the banks the natives collected in great numbers, brandishing their spears and making signs of attack, but when he explained to them that he was not a Portuguese, that he did not deal in slaves, and that his object was peaceful, their demeanor changed at once, and the signs of hostility ceased. Ere long the expedition reached a great isolated mountain, called Moramballa, about 4,000 feet in height, and wooded to its summit. High up on its side there was a native village, enjoying a pleasant and temperate climate. Beyond this point the river flows through great marshes, the waters of which are starred with the blossoms of the lily and lotus.

The navigation of the river through these marshes was very slow and difficult. The frequent shallows occasioned great delay to the steamer, and though the native villages appeared to be well supplied with goats and fowls, it was very difficult to procure provisions. After attaining a distance of a hundred miles in a straight line from the mouth of the river, all further progress with the steamer was suddenly cut off by a series of cataracts and rapids, 40 miles in extent, to the first and most important of which Livingstone gave the name of Murchison Falls. The difference of level between the lower valley of the Shire and the upper, beyond these rapids, is 1,200 feet. After establishing friendly relations with the chiefs in the neighborhood, Livingstone went back to Tete for further supplies, returned in March, and making the village of the native chief Shibisa his starting-point, set out on foot with Dr. Kirk and the Makololos for a new lake which was said to lie to the eastward. The natives of the country through which they passed made hostile demonstrations, and the greatest courage and prudence was necessary to avoid conflict with them.

Finally, on the 18th of April, 1859, Livingstone reached Lake Shirwa. The water was slightly brackish, and the shores bordered with reeds and papyrus plants. The lake has no outlet, although several small rivers empty into it. The eastern shore is hilly, while the western rises into a range of mountains, 7,000 feet in height, dividing the lake from the valley of the Shire. The breadth of this sheet of water was estimated at 20 miles; the length towards the north could not be exactly ascertained, but the explorers were assured that it was divided by a narrow strip of territory from another lake of much larger dimensions. Its elevation above the sea was about 1,200 feet. After remaining two days on the shore, Livingstone and Kirk postponed further explorations, returned to the steamer and descended to the mouth of the Zambesi for fresh supplies.

In August they again ascended the Shire, when they found the natives busily engaged in collecting the roots of the lotus, which they store away as an article of food. When roasted, the flavor is much like that of a chestnut. The progress up the river was slow, on account of the leaky condition of the *Ma-Robert*, while the travellers suffered terribly from the clouds of mosquitos which hung over the marshes. On reaching Shibisa's village they left the steamer and set out northwards, on foot, with thirty-six Makololos and two guides, towards the great lake Nyassa, which, although known through the reports of the Arab and Portuguese traders, had not yet been seen by any European.

They soon reached a table-land, 3,000 feet above the sea, with a better climate and purer atmosphere. The scenery was inspiring, for basaltic peaks, from one to five thousand feet in height, rose above the general level, and the distance was filled with lofty mountain-ranges. The tribe which inhabits this region is called the Mangandia. They appear to be related to the Kaffers, and are physically somewhat superior to the natives along the Zambesi. The women deform themselves hideously by covering their bodies with scars, and piercing their upper lips for the insertion of rings of wood or ivory, which are gradually increased in size until they reach two inches in diameter. This ornament, which is called the *pelele*, makes their natural ugliness almost frightful.

Following the upper valley of the Shire, the expedition soon reached the Pamalombe Lake, into which the river expands. It is ten miles in length by five in breadth, and swarms with fish. A native chief living near the lake assured them that there was no great body of water within two months' journey; yet they were then only, as it afterwards proved, one day's march from Lake Nyassa. On the 16th of September, in fact—in less than three weeks from the time they left the steamer—they reached the shore of the lake, at the point where the Shire issues from it, in lat. 14° 25′ S. The German traveller, Dr. Albert Roscher, who penetrated inland from Quiloa, and made his way to Lake Nyassa from the east, reached it on the 19th of October of the same year—only 33 days after Livingstone, but at the opposite extremity. Roscher was murdered soon afterwards, and his account of his journey is lost to the world.

The party remained but a short time at the southern end of Lake Nyassa, which they did not attempt to explore further. After a journey of forty days on foot, during which they suffered many privations and were accidentally poisoned by eating some cassava roots which were not properly prepared, they reached the steamer. Dr. Kirk and the engineer were sent in a direct course across the country to Tete, while Livingstone and his brother followed the river, arriving at the latter place on the 2d of February, 1860. His next plan was to retrace his old route in 1855 and '56, and return to the Makololo country in the upper Zambesi valley, but this obliged him to wait until the month of May before starting. One object of his journey was to take back the faithful Makololos who had accompanied him to Tete; the other to ascertain the condition of the missionary stations which, according to his advice, had been established in the upper Zambesi valley. He succeeded entirely, in the former particular; but the latter was far from meeting the sanguine expectations in which he had indulged.

Leaving Tete towards the end of May, 1860, Dr Livingstone, accompanied by his brother and Dr. Kirk, followed nearly the same route he had travelled more than four years before. His narrative contains some interesting particulars of the habits of the native tribes, but lacks the interest of his first journey. In September the party reached the great cataract of the Zambesi, and then went on to the town of Sesheke, where they found the chief Sekeletu still alive, but suffering from a leprous disease. At Linyanti, Livingstone's wagon still stood, with his scientific instruments and some goods, as he had left it seven years before! The English missionaries, who with their wives and children had reached the same spot only eight months before, were dead or departed. All that remained was seven graves: Mr. Helmore, his wife, Mrs. Price and their children had died of the fatal African fever, within reach of the supply of medicine which Livingstone had left in his wagon. The accounts of this unfortunate enterprise are conflicting. It seems that the missionary expedition had endured great suffering during the journey, and was poorly supplied; on the other hand, they were badly treated by the Makololos, and the chief Sekeletu prevented them from removing to a healthier part of the country.

On the return journey to Tete, the attempt was made to pass the Kebrabasa Rapids in canoes, the water being very low. It was an unfortunate failure, occasioning the loss of the instruments and Dr. Kirk's botanical collections. . After reaching the steamer they embarked for the mouth of the Zambesi, but on the 21st of December the leaky craft grounded on a sand-bank, and began to go to pieces. This was the end of the *Ma-Robert.*

In the meantime, notice of the discovery of Lakes Shirwa and Nyassa had reached England, and a missionary expedition, called the " Universities' Mission," was fitted out under the auspices of the Universities of Oxford and Cambridge. At its head was Bishop Mackenzie, formerly Archdeacon of Natal; he was assisted by the Rev. Messrs. Proctor, Scudamore, Burrup and Rowley, together with a physician, and some artists and scientific men. The object of the mission was to establish stations in Central Africa, from which Christianity could be gradually taught to the native tribes, together with agriculture and such other arts as might assist in breaking up the slave-trade. The members left in England in October, 1860, and reached the mouth of the Zambesi the following February, shortly after the arrival of the *Pioneer*, the new steamer which Livingstone had requested to have forwarded to him.

Although each expedition was independent of the other, it was advisable that the two should act in concert. The Bishop and his followers were desirous of reaching the cooler table-lands of the Shire, and there commencing their work, as soon as possible, while Livingstone strongly advised them to ascend the Rovuma River, which empties into the Indian Ocean between the parallels of 10° and 11° S., north of the Portuguese territory, and thence make the journey by land. This proposition was finally adopted, the *Pioneer* was given to the Universities' Mission, and entered the mouth of the Rovuma on the 11th of March. But the river was rapidly falling, and after an attempt of ten days, during which little progress was made, the boat turned back. In the meantime so much sickness had broken out on board, that the expedition sailed to the Comoro Islands to recruit.

Returning to the Zambesi, the *Pioneer* was found to be a good boat for the purpose, except that she drew too much water. Nevertheless, by the beginning of July, 1861, Livingstone and his party, with the Universities' Mission, reached the village of Shibisa, at the foot of the Murchison Cataracts, on the Shire. Here very unfavorable news awaited them. A tribe called the Ajawa had overrun the table-land inhabited by the Manganja, destroyed their villages, and carried off many of the people as slaves. Nevertheless the combined expedition set out, and marched for a few days without encountering any hostility. They then came upon a caravan of slaves, whom they liberated, following their instincts rather than calculating the possible consequences. Others were afterwards liberated, to the number of 148 in all, and the missionaries determined to keep them together and instruct them, as the beginning of their work.

Bishop Mackenzie accepted the invitation of one of Manganja chiefs, to establish his mission near the village of the latter, Magomero, a beautiful and apparently healthy place, not far from Lake Shirwa. Before this was done, the two parties were attacked by a band of the Ajawas, but drove off the enemy. There seems to have been some difference of opinion between Dr. Livingstone and Bishop Mackenzie as to the proper policy to be pursued, and the parties divided, the former returning to the steamer to make preparations for an exploration of Lake Nyassa, while the latter settled themselves at Magomero.

The *Pioneer* had brought out a four-oared boat in sections, which were carried around the cataracts and rapids of the Shire by the natives, after which it was put together by two or three English sailors, one of whom accompanied the two Livingstones and Dr. Kirk. They found the upper Shire a broad and deep stream, with no impediments to navigation. The evidence of malaria in the air obliged them to hasten on, and reach the fresher and cooler atmosphere of the great lake. The southern end of Nyassa, out of which the Shire flows, is about thirty miles long, by from ten to twelve in breadth. Beyond a high headland, to which Livingstone gave the name of Maclear, another arm stretches in a south-western direction for a distance of fifteen or twenty miles. The main body of the lake, at the junction of these two arms, has a breadth of about twenty miles, but gradually expands to the northwards until it reaches a breadth of fifty or sixty, so that from one side the opposite shore cannot be seen. The whole length of the lake is not less than 200 miles. It appears to be surrounded by mountains, but they are evidently only the fronts of lofty table-lands, like those described by Magyar in travelling inland from Benguela. The surface of the lake is 1,300 feet above the sea.

It was a stormy time of the year when they entered the lake, for which reason they were unable to cross it, while the air was so thick with cloud and haze that they had very rare views of the distant shores. Violent squalls burst upon them with hardly a moment's warning, and more than once their escape from shipwreck seemed almost miraculous. Livingstone asserts that he never beheld such waves as on Lake Nyassa. Fortunately the sailor who accompanied him was accustomed to similar storms on the coast of Ireland, and his skill in the management of the boat was of priceless service. The western shore, which they skirted, was densely populated. The people crowded the strand, by thousands, to witness the singular spectacle of a sail-boat, and gaze at the strange white men when they landed. In general they were friendly, and only once was any tribute demanded for passing their territory.

The Makololo and other native attendants on shore, who carried the supplies of the expedition, could only march very slowly, and as it had been arranged that they and the boat should meet every evening, the progress of the latter was greatly delayed. Besides, as they approached the northern end of the lake they found a state of war, and the safety of the land party became so uncertain that Livingstone turned about before quite reaching the extremity. His brother and Dr. Kirk reached the parallel of 11°, where they saw the mountains of the opposite shore closing in, and conjectured that the end of the lake was under Lat. 10°, but it may possibly extend a considerable distance further. After an exploration of nearly two months on and near the lake (on its western side, only,) the party returned to the steamer in November, 1861.

Soon after their arrival, Bishop Mackenzie made his appearance, with some English sailors who had gone to Magomero for their health. The Mission appeared to be flourishing: the hostile Ajawas had left the country, the native Manganjas were friendly, and there was every prospect that the missionaries would be able to support themselves, in the lack of supplies from England. It only remained to open a convenient road from their station to the head of navigation on the Shire, and this the Bishop undertook to do at once, in order to meet his sister and Mr. Burrup's wife, the following January.

The brief history of the Universities' Mission, as it is related by the only survivor, Mr. Rowley, is both interesting and instructive. In their zeal for immediately suppressing the slave trade, the missionaries allowed themselves to be persuaded by the Manganjas to join in a war against the Ajawas, whom they after found to be quite a peaceable people. But much valuable time had been lost before this discovery was made: the situation of Magomero proved to be unhealthy, and before good buildings could be completed the rainy season came on, with fever in its train. An attempt made by two of the members to reach the Zambesi failed, and the Bishop, having received word from Livingstone that he would come for him in his steamer on the 1st of January, 1862, left Magomero with one companion. He did not arrive until the 10th, when the steamer had left: and, worn out with fever and privations, died in two weeks afterwards.

Mr. Burrup followed him to the grave in less than a month. Messrs. Scudamore and Rowley then removed the Mission to the banks of the Shire, where the former, with Dr. Dickinson, the physician, soon afterwards died, and the few remaining members of the Mission left the country. Another victim to the terrible climate was Mrs. Livingstone, who, after joining her husband in January, died at Shupanga, on the lower Zambesi, on the 27th of April, and was buried there, under a majestic baobab-tree.

The third vessel sent to Livingstone, the *Lady Nyassa*, was put together and successfully launched at Shupanga, by the end of June. By this time the Shire River was so low that the new steamer could not ascend it, and the climate of the lower Zambesi was so unhealthy that it was not prudent to remain longer. Livingstone, therefore, determined to attempt the navigation of the Rovuma, wherein the Universities' Mission had failed, more than a year before. After visiting the island of Johanna, he entered the mouth of the river early in September, and commenced the ascent. Although the shores were bold and hilly, his progress was delayed by sand-bars and snags, and the stream, only thirty or forty miles from the coast, became so shallow that he was obliged to leave the steamer and push forward in smaller boats.

The natives along the Rovuma belong to a tribe called the Makonda, a shy, timid race, who feared the strangers too much to molest them. It was with difficulty that provisions could be procured from them. Further up the river, one band of these people ventured to shoot their poisoned arrows at the explorers, but a discharge of musketry immediately scattered them. Finally, on the 26th of September, having reached a point 156 miles from the sea, Livingstone found the stream so narrow, shallow and rapid, that it was impossible for him to advance further. The natives informed him that he was about 30 miles from a large village called Ngomans, whence it was a land journey of twelve days to Lake Nyassa.

The party returned down the river, re-embarked on the steamer, and after touching at the Portuguese town Quillimane, arrived at Shupanga, on the Zambesi, in December. His object, now was to transport the *Lady Nyassa* above the cataracts of the Shire, and undertake the complete exploration of the Nyassa lake. On entering the Shire River, he found everywhere the marks of death and desolation. The same half-breed, whose battle with the Portuguese he had witnessed at Mazaro, on his arrival in 1858, had overrun the country, slain, burned and plundered, until the once populous land had become a waste. In March, 1863, while the steamer was stayed on a sand-bank Livingstone was joined by Mr. Thornton, who had left him five years before, to undertake the journey to Kilimandjaro with Baron Van der Decken. He again offered his services, as geologist, but having undertaken to convey provisions to the few remaining missionaries in the Shire country, he succumbed to the hardships of the journey, and died in April.

Many of the native attendants had also died, and Dr. Kirk and Charles Livingstone were also so reduced by fever that on the 19th of May they left the chief of the expedition, and returned to England. In the meantime, news of the failure of the Universities' Mission had reached England; the part which Bishop Mackenzie had taken in the native wars gave offence to the Government, and on the 2d of July Livingstone received an order to return. Before obeying, however, he determined to make one final effort to explore Lake Nyassa and the country surrounding it.

He set out, with a much smaller party than before, and took a course northwards, on the west side of the Shire, and at some distance from the stream. This led to the discovery of a range of bare granite peaks, rising to a height of 5,000 feet above the sea, running parallel with the river. Following this range he came into the valley of Gova, which gently descends towards the south-western arm of Lake Nyassa. The country was well cultivated, and no serious difficulties were encountered from the inhabitants. Their greatest fear seemed to be concerning the "Mazitu," or Arab slave-traders, who, they related, built broad, flat boats in a bay toward the northern end of the lake, for the purpose of transporting their captives to the opposite side.

Livingstone followed the western shore as far as this bay, which he reached about the middle of September. He then turned inland, striking westward in the hope of being able to travel entirely around the lake, at a short distance from it. Ascending a mountain called Ndonda, which was 3,440 feet high, he came upon a broad scantily-watered table-land, where the air was so sharp and cool, that although to himself it gave new life, his native attendants fell sick, and one of them died. For three or four days more he pushed onward, and only turned about when compelled by the sufferings of his men and the want of nourishing food. He was upon the high-road from Lake Nyassa to Cazembe, the capital of the Londa country—the "Moluwa" of Magyar.

He returned by a more southerly route, striking the lake at a point about 30 miles south of that where he had left. He reached the steamer in November, after a journey of nearly 700 miles, and after resting from his hardships, and waiting for the rains, left the Shire towards the end of January, 1864. In a month he reached the mouth of the Zambesi, where his little steamer was taken in tow by an English man-of-war, and carried to Zanzibar. From the latter port he returned to England by way of Bombay.

This expedition occupied nearly six years of time, and—in connection with the Universities' Mission—cost some valuable lives. The English Government seems to have been disappointed in its results, which, nevertheless, are of sufficient importance, when we consider what was accomplished for geographical and natural science. The suppression of the slave-trade, the Christianization of the native tribes, and the substitution of English for Portuguese and Arab commercial interests require a much longer period of time. Had Dr. Livingstone's task been limited to exploration, he would undoubtedly have done much more; and his subsequent history is the proof that, in this respect, he was far from being satisfied.

CHAPTER XVII.

LIVINGSTONE'S LAST JOURNEY.

IN the preface to his last work, "Narrative of an Expedition to the Zambesi and its Tributaries," written in April, 1865, Livingstone announces his intention of starting upon a new journey of exploration.

He says: "I propose to go inland, north of the territory which the Portuguese in Europe claim, and endeavor to commence that system on the east which has been so successful on the west coast. . . . I hope to ascend the Rovuma, or some other river north of Cape Delgado, and, in addition to my other work, shall strive, by passing along the northern end of Lake Nyassa, and round the southern end of Lake Tagnanyika, to ascertain the water-shed of that part of Africa. In so doing, I have no wish to unsettle what with so much toil and danger was accomplished by Speke and Grant, but rather to confirm their illustrious discoveries."

In order to carry out this new design, Livingstone was obliged to depend upon narrower means and arrange his plans in a simpler manner. The Royal Geographical Society contributed £500, the English Government an equal amount, and a friend whose name is not mentioned, £1,000. Livingstone was appointed Consul for Central Africa, with power to make treaties with the native tribes, and an annual salary of £500. Thus the means for a small yet sufficiently appointed expedition were procured. The importance of the geographical questions to be solved fully justified Livingstone in the undertaking, and the hopes and good wishes of the principal scientific men of Europe and America accompanied him when he left England, towards the close of the year 1865.

He first went to Bombay, and sailed thence for Zanzibar on the 2nd of January, 1866. On his arrival at the latter port he procured boats for the navigation of the Rovuma River, and several camels for the land journey thence to Lake Nyassa. His attendants were chiefly natives of Johanna, one of the Comoro Islands, and Mahometans. On reaching the mouth of the Rovuma, it was found that the paths through the mangrove swamps were impracticable for camels, whereupon the boats were compelled to go some distance up the river. About 25 miles from the sea a good landing-place was found: the expedition was here organized, and proceeded up the southern bank of the river to the mouth of a large affluent called the Loendi, 30 miles further than the point reached by Livingstone in 1862.

There at the village of Ngomano, he was so well received by the chief, that he determined to remain until the best route to Lake Nyassa should be ascertained. The Rovuma valley is here bordered by ranges of hills from four to six hundred feet in height, and covered with dense thickets. The Makonda people were industrious, and helpful in opening a way for the party.

In June or July, Livingstone started with his Johanna servants, and reached the eastern shore of Lake Nyassa, probably near its northern extremity. It seems, however, that he was unable to find a boat to

ZANZIBAR.

transport his party across to the western shore, and was compelled to make a long journey around the southern end of the lake, and up the western side, over the same ground which he had traversed in 1861 and '63.

The next information received of his fortunes reached Zanzibar in March, 1867, and came from some of the Johanna men, who, with their leader, Moussa, returned to the coast, and related a story which for a time was believed. They stated that Livingstone had crossed the lake, reached a place called Kampunda, and pushed on in to a region infested by the hostile Mazitus. Here, while they were in the rear, resting with the baggage, the traveller and his servants were suddenly attacked by an ambushed party. Livingstone fired and killed three of the enemy; but some of the others, under cover of the powder-smoke, approached him from behind, and killed him with the blow of an axe on his head. The Johanna men hid themselves in the bushes, and were not seen. The next day they returned to the spot, found the bodies of Livingstone and four of his attendants, which they buried, and then made their way back to Kampunda, where they arrived in fourteen days. Here they waited until a caravan offered them the opportunity of reaching the coast. When this news was brought to Zanzibar, all the flags were lowered, and there was a universal sorrow for the supposed loss of the intrepid explorer.

Some few, however,—and chief among them Sir Roderick Murchison, President of the Royal Geographical Society,—refused to believe the story. At his instigation, it was determined to send out an expedition to ascertain, at least, whether there was any foundation for it. Mr. Young, who had commanded Livingstone's steamer, the *Pioneer*, was appointed; a small iron boat, in sections, was built and sent to the Cape of Good Hope, and by the 27th of July, 1867, the expedition had reached the mouth of the Zambesi. On arriving at the village of Shibisa, where Young was recognized and cordially welcomed, he found a very different state of things. The Manganja and Ajawa tribes had become friendly, and both were united in a common cause against the slave-robbing Mazitus, who were coming down upon them from the north. Some of Livingstone's Makololos were also at the place, and a few of them at once offered their services as boatmen and guides.

On the 19th of August Young reached the Murchison Cataracts, where his boat must be taken to pieces, and every piece, together with all the supplies of the expedition, transported a distance of 60 miles, to the upper valley of the Shire. On account of the ravages of war, he experienced the greatest difficulty, not only in procuring the 180 porters who were required for this labor, but also in feeding them during the time. When at last, with great difficulty, 150 men were gathered together, the bargaining in regard to pay, which must be separately repeated with each, seemed as if it would never come to an end. Young was obliged to exercise the greatest skill and patience, in order to accomplish his purpose without losing much valuable time.

He left two Kroomen at the falls, with orders to remain there until the 15th of November, when, if they should hear no news of him, they were to descend the Zambesi and communicate with the English frigate which was expected off the mouth of that river, about the 1st of December. In case his own return should be interrupted by the Mazitus, he designed to make his way directly from the lake to the Eastern coast.

The transport of the boat, in spite of all difficulties, was successfully accomplished, and while the sections were being put together, some natives brought word that, some time before, a white man had passed the Pamalombe lake, and gone on in a westerly direction. This intelligence was puzzling to Young, who, supposing that Livingstone had gone around the northern end of Lake Nyassa, did not suspect that he was actually receiving news of the lost traveller.

On the 31st of August he started in the boat, but was much annoyed by the Makololos, who were not only bad oarsmen, but became so excited by the rumors of the fierce Mazitus, that they were anxious to return. Young, however, pushed on with them, and, on approaching the Pamalombe lake, again heard of the recent visit of the white man, with the additional information that he was not an Arab, but an Englishman. Now, for the first time, he began to suspect that this might be Livingstone. With full sails the boat sped through the smaller lake, traversed the brief additional reach of the Shire River, and on the 6th of September entered Lake Nyassa. After resting for a night on an island, where they were safe from the curiosity or hostility of the natives, Young sailed across to the eastern shore, which had not been visited before, during the previous expeditions.

By a wonderful chance, he received news of Livingstone at the very first village where he landed. A single native stood on the shore, and showed the greatest astonishment and terror at the approach of the strange boat: but when Young addressed him, and explained that he was an Englishman, all his fear vanished and he answered: "The English are good people." When asked why he said so, he declared that an Englishman had passed through the villages along the lake, and had given many presents to the people. Young then questioned him more closely, and soon became convinced that he was indeed on the track of Livingstone.

The man stated that he lived at an Arab settlement, in the neighborhood. Young immediately went to the place, and announced himself as an Englishman, whereupon the people clapped their hands and cried: "That is good!" The chief asked him whether he knew the Englishman who had passed by there during the previous cold season. Then followed a long examination: the people answered Young's questions without hesitation, not only minutely describing Livingstone's personal appearance, and his method of taking astronomical observations, but mentioning the names of two boys, Chuma and Wako, whom he had taken along for servants. They also stated that the chief of his porters was a stout man called Moussa. They informed Young that the Englishman wanted to cross Lake Nyassa, but, not being able to find a boat, had gone southward to a village near the Pamalombe lake.

The details of Livingstone's journey increased

rapidly, and the evidences of his having passed around the lake became more certain. The natives picked out his photograph from a collection of fifty, they brought small articles which he had given away, and marked out several of his days' journeys, showing the places where he had rested or slept. A company of Makololos, sent out to follow his route towards the Rovuma, found no difficulty in doing so, until they were prevented from going further by reports of war between the tribes. By this time a large number of natives were collected, and, as many of them were armed with fire-arms, Young judged it prudent to sleep on board his boat, and to keep her at a safe distance from the shore.

Having learned all that could be ascertained on the eastern side, he crossed to a place called Chinsamba, on the western side, about fifty miles from the southern end of the lake. Here he heard the same story: a white man had been in the village of Marenga, and had gone on, in a westerly direction. He also found porters, who had assisted in carrying the white man's baggage, but no one had heard of a murder, or even of an attack. Yet he was now very near the point, where, according to the accounts of the Johanna men, Livingstone had been slain. The people stated, moreover, that he only had seven attendants with him: so the treacherous bearers of the evil tidings must have already deserted him.

Young's next movement was to the village of Marenga, where he was heartily welcomed by the chief, who immediately asked after Livingstone. He voluntarily related that the latter had visited him, had been carried in his boat further up the lake, while the Johanna porters went on by land. Two days afterwards he was surprised by the return of the latter, who declared that they were going home. Livingstone, however, had quietly continued his journey inland towards the north-west, and the chief produced several porters who had accompanied him a part of the way. All doubt was now dispelled; both Livingstone's safety and his success up to this point were established, and there seemed better grounds than ever for hoping that he would finally carry out his great undertaking.

After several days of festivity in Marenga's village, Young started on his return on the 20th of September. He doubled Cape Maclear, which divides the two southern arms of the lake, rising 2,000 feet above the water, and then sailed to Mapunda, where the Shires issues from Lake Nyassa. Here he learned that Livingstone's boy, Wako, had been left, on account of an injury to his leg, which afterwards healed. The boy was then absent, but the natives showed Young a book in which he had written his name. Young left a letter for him, and then commenced the descent of the Shire.

On reaching the commencement of the rapids, where it was necessary to take the boat to pieces, there were no natives to be seen. The party were suffering from hunger, and in the desolated and depopulated region around, no supplies were to be had. A dead hippopotamus which came floating down the stream was seized and eagerly devoured by the natives. However, when the arrival of the party became known, 150 men soon appeared, eager to be employed in carrying the pieces of the boat to the lower river. With a heat of 110° in the shade, when the iron sections scorched the hand which touched them, these men made the transport of sixty miles in four days and a half. They were to be paid from the supplies of cotton goods which had been left below the rapids, but the men who had these in charge had neglected to protect them from the water, and they were nearly all rotten. Young, nevertheless, succeeded in satisfying the natives: he then reconstructed the boat, descended the Shire and the Zambesi, and on the 1st of December was picked up by an English frigate. In four months' time he had made the journey from the ocean to Lake Nyassa and back, and ascertained the truth concerning Livingstone, at a small expense, and without losing a man.

Not long afterwards, some Arab merchants brought news to Zanzibar, from which it appeared that Livingstone had penetrated the unknown regions west of Lake Nyassa. It was reported that he had crossed the Loangwe River, a large northern affluent of the Zambesi, which drains the western slope of the great table-land of Maravi (lying west of Lake Nyassa), and had entered the land of the Babisa. The whole country had been devastated by the slave-hunters, the villages were destroyed, even game had become scarce, and the brave explorer had suffered much from hunger.

After some months, some brief and fragmentary despatches from Livingstone himself reached Zanzibar. He had arrived in a country called Bamba, or Lobamba, lying nearly midway between the Nyassa and Tanganyika Lakes, in February, 1867. Here the chief received him kindly, and he remained for some time to rest and recruit his strength. In October of the same year he reached the Marunga country, near the southern end of Tanganyika. His progress was greatly delayed by the exhaustion of his stock of goods and medicines, and though many efforts were made to supply him from Zanzibar, the intermediate region is always so unsettled, from the continual wars between the tribes, that there was no certainty that any supplies had reached him.

Early in 1869 new letters for Dr. Kirk and Sir Roderick Murchison reached the coast, and gave most welcome if scanty news of Livingstone's explorations. He was on the western side of Lake Tanganyika, anxiously waiting for supplies, and still determined to carry out his original plan of pushing onward to the Luta N'zige (Albert Nyanza), discovered by Baker. He had suffered a great deal from hunger, exposure and fever, but had lost none of his courage and resolution.

Since then we have received frequent reports of his situation through the native traders who now and then visit Zanzibar, but nothing direct from himself. The greater part of the intervening period between 1868 and 1871 seems to have been spent by him in the regions west of Lake Tanganyika. The natives report that he made one journey of three hundred miles in that direction, but they say nothing of journeys to the northward. It was known, in 1870, that supplies for him had safely reached Ujiji, on the eastern shore of the lake, and nearly opposite his temporary home.

His long experience of the native African tribes, and his wonderful success in dealing with them, diminish in his case the risks to which every traveller must be exposed, and those who know him best have been most sanguine of his final return to the world, with a richer store of knowledge than any traveller has yet brought from the heart of Africa.

In 1871 Mr. Stanley set out from Zanzibar, with the intention of reaching Livingstone, and towards the close of the year the sum of £5,000 was raised in England to fit out an expedition, which, at the time these lines are written (March 1st, 1872), is on its way to Africa. The latest news received at Zanzibar, which has an air of authenticity, and seems to be accepted as reliable by Livingstone's friends, represents him as being midway between Ujiji and Unyanyembe,— therefore about 150 miles east of lake Tanganyika— on his way to the coast. If this be true, and no misfortune comes to mar the close of the most daring and important journey in the annals of exploration, he may be expected to reach England during the summer of 1872.

POSTSCRIPT.

SIX months have passed since the closing paragraphs of the last chapter were written. The belief there expressed that Livingston was still alive has been happily justified, though the hope that he would soon return to tell the story of his adventures has not been fulfilled. His self-imposed task is not yet accomplished: a space of perhaps two hundred miles remains to be explored before the long hidden secret of the Nile is revealed, and he will not return until he has made it his own. The story of his discovery and relief by Mr. Stanley, forms one of the most romantic episodes of African adventure, not less from the peculiar character of the expedition, and the boldness of its conception, than the personal heroism, pluck, and persistence manifested in its execution, and the rare good fortune with which it was rewarded.

The report that Livingston was pushing eastward from Ujiji toward Unyanyembe, proved to be without foundation. Mr. Stanley left the latter place late in September, 1871, and early in the following November, — spite of wars and rumors of wars, treacherous servants, blackmailing chiefs, mountain fever, and all the other obstacles to African travel, — he arrived at Ujiji, whither Livingston had just come from a tramp of more than four hundred miles beneath a vertical tropical sun, "a mere ruckle of bones," to use his own words, " dying on his feet," " baffled, worried, and defeated," having been turned back from his exploration of the Manyema country, by the refusal of his cowardly and mutinous servant to go on. The arrival of Mr. Stanley was most opportune. The supplies that had been sent by the English Government to Ujiji, on which Livingston depended for the prosecution of his researches, had been stolen by the agent to whom they had been intrusted; and the sorely disappointed, almost disheartened explorer, found himself at Ujiji, sixteen days before Mr. Stanley came, travel-worn, ill, and dejected, and reduced almost to beggary. His letters to the coast had been so often destroyed by the Arabs, who dreaded any exposure of their horrid practices in obtaining slaves, that he had relinquished all hope of ever obtaining help from Zanzibar, and had determined, when he became stronger, " to work his way down to Mteza or Baker for help and men."

But assistance came when least expected. A vague rumor had reached Ujiji, shortly before his arrival there, that an Englishman had come to Unyanyembe with boats, horses, men, and goods in abundance. " It was in vain," Dr. Livingston writes, " to conjecture who this could be ; and my eager inquiries were met by answers so contradictory that I began to doubt if any stranger had come at all. But one day, I cannot say which, for I was three weeks too fast in my reckoning, my man Susi came dashing up in great excitement, and gasped out, " An Englishman coming ; see him !" and off he ran to meet him. The American flag at the head of the caravan told me the nationality of the stranger. It was Henry M. Stanley, the travelling correspondent of the *New York Herald*, sent by the son of the editor, James Gordon Bennett, Jr., at an expense of £4,000, to obtain correct information about me if living, and if dead to bring home my bones. The kindness was extreme, and made my whole frame thrill with excitement and gratitude."

This sudden change of fortune had the happiest effect on the forlorn explorer. The possession of supplies, the strange news that the deliverer had to tell of the events of the past six years, and more than all the assurance that he was neither abandoned nor forgotten by his friends at home, brought new life and strength and hope to him. " It was, indeed, overwhelming " he wrote to the proprietor of the *Herald*, " and I said in my soul, ' Let the richest blessings descend from the Highest on you and yours.' "

As stated (page 302), Dr. Livingston left the coast early in 1866, with an expedition consisting of twelve Sepoys, nine Johanna men, seven liberated slaves, and two Zambezi men, with six camels, three buffaloes, two mules, and three donkeys. The Sepoys armed with Enfield rifles were to serve as guards. The expedition pursued a difficult route up the left bank of the Rovuma River, through jungles impenetrable to the camels. The way had to be hewn out with axes, and progress was constantly retarded by the unwillingness of the Sepoys and the Johanna men to work. The Sepoys were rebellious from the outset, and soon proved themselves utterly worthless as an escort. To stop the advance of the expedition, they maltreated the animals, so that in a few days not one remained alive. Failing to gain their end in this way, they began to tamper with the natives, setting them against their commander by false reports of strange practices on his part.

Finding the Sepoys useless as guards and dangerous as members of the expedition, Livingston paid them their wages, and sent them back to the coast. With his diminished company he pushed on through an uninhabited wilderness, suffering much from hunger and desertion, until he reached a village belonging to a Mahiya chief, eight days' march south of the Rovuma, and overlooking the watershed of Lake Nyassa. Two of the liberated slaves deserted while on the road to Mponda's country, near the lake, where he arrived early in August. At this point his ungrateful *protégé* Wakotani demanded his discharge, falsely alleging that he had found a sister in Mponda's favorite wife, that his " big brother " lived near there, and that his family lived across the lake. Though convinced that these stories were untrue, Livingston released him, and pushed on to the lake, to minister to a Babisa chief who required medicine for a skin disease. While at the village of this chief a half-caste Arab arrived from the western shore of the lake, and reported that he had been plundered by a band of Mazitus, at a place which Livingston knew to be a hundred and fifty miles distant, north-northwest. Musa, the chief of the Johanna men, was equally well aware of the absence of danger, yet the Arab's story afforded a pretext for refusing to proceed, and he made the most of it. Livingston endeavored to compromise the matter by promising to go due west beyond the range of the Mazitus, but it was of no use : the Johanna men ran away in a body, returned to the coast, as already noticed, and deceived the majority of Livingston's admirers by their lying story of his death.

Fortunately Livingston was now in a country that had never been cursed by slave hunters, and the people were, — as he always found them in such cases, — kind and hospitable. For small payments of cloth and beads they carried his baggage from village to village, and gave him other assistance which made it possible for him to proceed with his meagre force. But this could not last always. Toward the close of 1866, the limit of this kindly region was reached, and the expedition entered upon a country that had been devastated by marauding Mazitus. The land was stripped of provisions and cattle, and the inhabitants had migrated beyond the reach of their ferocious enemies. Here the expedition was reduced to great extremity, plagued by famine and lessened by desertion. Robbed of his personal baggage, which his unfaithful servants had made off with, beset by dangers and distresses, yet undaunted in spirit, the explorer pushed on through the countries of the Babisi, the Bobemba, the Barungu, and the Baulungu, into Londa, the dominion of prince Cazembe, first made known to Europeans by the Portuguese traveller, Dr. Lacerda. Here Livingston met with a kind reception, and was freely granted permission to pursue his search for "great waters."

The reports of the next two years' exploration are

of the briefest character, though the results of them are unsurpassed in the history of African adventure.

Just before he arrived at Cazembe's, Livingston crossed an important stream called the Chambezi. All the Portuguese explorers who had preceded him had described the river as the Zambezi. Misled by the similarity of the name, and trusting too much to the Portuguese authorities, Livingston assumed it to be the head stream of the river he had already explored, and paid no attention to it. This error cost him many months of tedious labor and travel. Finding as he proceeded the books and maps of the Portuguese seriously at variance with his observations, he retraced his steps, traversed and retraversed the broad region watered by the numerous branches of the Chambezi, until he was convinced that it marked a new and hitherto unsuspected line of drainage sloping northward.

In the course of his researches he came upon a lake, northeast of Cazembe's, called the Liemba, from the country bordering it on the east and south. Following this lake northward he found it to be no other than Tanganyika, whose southern extremity reaches to a latitude about 9° south. This great lake extends north and south, a distance of three hundred and sixty geographical miles, and has an outline very much like that of Italy.

Livingston next pushed his explorations westward, crossing the Marungu country with great difficulty, and almost at the cost of his life, until he came to a large lake, Moero by name, shut in by lofty mountains. Its surplus waters he found to escape toward the north through a deep rent in the mountains, pouring an impetuous torrent through the chasm with the roar of a cataract. From the south it receives the waters of a broad river, the Luapula, which Livingston ascended along a tortuous course until he found it to be the outlet of a still larger lake which the natives called Bangwelo. The largest of the many feeders to this lake proved to be the Chambezi, which Livingston ascended to the country of King Cazembe. Evidently this grand river, whose northward course Livingston had traced under changing appellations through three degrees of latitude, could have no connection with the Zambezi. Where did it flow?

The most intelligent natives and traders in the upper part of the Chambezi valley thought that the rivers of that region ran into Tanganyika. But to do that they must run up hill, as the deep trough of the valley into which the waters of all the great rivers and lakes converged, lay a full thousand feet lower than the Upper Tanganyika. Was the Chambezi the head stream of the Nile? So Livingston strongly suspected, but he could not be certain until he had followed its waters through the unknown region north of the great lakes he had discovered. That was the next task he set himself to do.

Instead of retracing his course down the river, Livingston, for reasons which he has not explained, struck across the country northward to Ujiji, harassed almost to death by his miserable attendants, who, under the corrupting influence of an ungrateful Arab, made the long and painful journey a period of peculiar and exasperating misery. While at Ujiji, in the summer of 1869, he wrote the letters mentioned on page 310, and others which the Arab traders treacherously destroyed, lest they should expose their iniquitous proceedings in connection with the slave trade.

As soon as he was strong enough to travel, Livingston descended the Tanganyika about sixty miles, crossed over to Uguhha, on the western shore, and set off northwestward through the Manyema country, intending to strike the river flowing out of Lake Moero, and then follow down the central line of drainage he had discovered. At first he was able to travel but two hours a day; but by persevering he gained strength, and in July he came up with the trading party of Muhamad Bogharib, who by native medicines and carriage had saved his life when prostrated by a severe attack of pneumonia in the Marungu country. With this company he journeyed into the interior, descending the Luamo, a river from one to two hundred yards wide, rising in the mountains opposite Ujiji, and flowing westward. Approaching its confluence with the Lualaba — the outlet of Lake Moero — he found himself among a people who had lately been maltreated by a company of ivory hunters. The feeling against all strangers was very strong, especially among the women. The worst the men did was to turn out in force, fully armed, and escort the party out of their district. Glad that no collision had taken place, Livingston returned to a place called Bambarre, about 150 miles west of Ujiji, and, in company with his friend Muhamad, struck away due north, Muhamad to buy ivory, Livingston to reach another part of the Lualaba and buy a canoe. The country was extremely beautiful but difficult to penetrate. Mountains of light gray granite stood like islands in new red sandstone, both mountains and valleys clad in a mantle of varied green. Vegetation was indescribably rank. The dense spiry grass, with stalks half an inch in diameter and twelve feet high, was impassible to everything except elephants; and while the party wormed their way along the elephant walks, the rough edges of the grass tore their faces and rasped the skin from their hands. In November heavy rains set in, making the difficult travelling all the harder by deepening the mud. In many cases the heavy weight of the elephants had broken through the subsoil, making deep mud holes into which the travellers would slump up to their waists, or bury themselves, ivory and all. The valleys were deeply undulating, and in the bottoms of each innumerable small streams had to be crossed, and though there might be only a thread of water, the mire was "grievous."

"Some of the numerous rivers which in this region flow into Lualaba are covered with living vegetable bridges — a species of dark, glossy-leaved grass, which with its roots and leaves, felts itself into a mat that covers the whole stream. When stepped upon it yields twelve or fifteen inches, and that amount of water rises up on the leg. At every step the foot has to be raised high enough to place it on the unbent mass in front. This high stepping fatigues like walking on deep snow. Here and there holes appear which we could not sound with a stick six feet long; they gave the impression that anywhere one might plump through and finish the chapter. Where the water is shallow, the lotus, or sacred lily, sends its roots to the bottom, and spreads its broad leaves over the floating bridge so as to make believe that them at is its own; but the grass referred to is the real felting and supporting agent, for it often performs duty as bridge where no lilies grow. The bridge is called by Manyema "kintefwetefwe," as if he who first coined it was gasping for breath after plunging over a mile of it."

Everywhere in this primeval wilderness the accumulated ivory of ages lay rotting on the ground, and the unsophisticated natives were willing to collect it for nominal payments of beads and copper bracelets. News of such abundance of cheap ivory no sooner reached Ujiji than a " rush " set in for the Manyema country, and Livingston was soon overtaken by a horde numbering six hundred muskets, every man eager for the precious tusks. Unwilling to bear the new-comers' company, and suffering from the effects of bad water and frequent wetting, the explorer returned seven days' journey southwest to a camp formed by the head men of the ivory traders, and on the 7th of February went into winter quarters. He had no medicine, but rest, shelter, boiling all the water he used, and a new potato found among the natives, served as restoratives, and he soon regained his health. The rains continued into July; fifty-two inches fell, and the mud from the clayey soil was awful, exhausting the strongest men notwithstanding their intense eagerness for ivory.

As soon as it was possible to travel, Livingston lost

no time in preparing to follow the river; but his attendants preferred the easy life of the camp, where they were fed and lodged by the slave women whose husbands were away in search of ivory. At first they pretended to fear going into a canoe. Livingston consented to go without one. Then they pretended to fear the people, though the inhabitants along the Lualaba were reported by the slaves to be remarkably friendly. Elsewhere he could employ the country people as carriers, and was comparatively independent though deserted by his attendants. But in Manyema no one could be induced to go into the next district for fear of being killed and eaten. He was at the mercy of those who had been Moslem slaves, and who knew that in thwarting him they had the sympathy of all the Moslems in the country, and they took advantage of the situation. With only three attendants he went on towards the northwest in ignorance that the great river flowed west by south; and there was no one who could correct his mistake.

Muhamad's people went further on in the forest than he could, and came to the mountainous country of the Balegga, who collected in large numbers, and demanded of the strangers why they came. "We came to buy ivory," was the reply, "and if you have none no harm is done; we shall return." "Nay," they shouted, "you came to die, and this day is your last; you came to die — you came to die." When forced to fire on the Balegga their terror was like their insolence — extreme; and next day, when sent for to take away the women and children who were captured, no one appeared.

In their journeying Muhamad's party crossed many large rivers. One was so tortuous that they were five hours in water, waist, and sometimes neck deep, with a man in a small canoe sounding for places which they could pass. In another case they were two hours in the water, and they could see nothing in the forest, and nothing in the Balegga country but one "mountain packed closely to the back of another, without end, and a very hot fountain in one of the valleys."

Livingston suffered grievously from continual wading in the mud, and for the first time in his life his feet failed him. When torn by travel, instead of healing kindly as heretofore, they were afflicted with irritable eating ulcers. The people, however, were civil and kind, his reputation for goodness having preceded him everywhere. On one occasion he had a striking proof of their confidence in him. While he was sleeping with his three attendants in a village, a member of a trading party, in camp close by, was pinned to the ground by a spear. Nine villages had been burned and at least forty men killed, because a Manyema man had tried to steal a string of beads; and the midnight assassination was in revenge for the loss of friends there. It was evident that a reaction against the bloody slaving had set in; and convinced by the accounts given by Muhamad's people that nothing would be gained by going further in that direction, Livingston, now very lame, limped back to Bambarre, where he was laid up many months with ulcers on his feet. These distressing ulcers are common in the Manyema country, and kill many slaves. If the foot is placed on the ground blood flows, and every night a discharge of bloody ichor takes place, with pain that prevents sleep. The wailing of the poor slaves with ulcers that eat through everything, even bone, is one of the night sounds of a slave camp.

In this horrid place Livingston remained from August, 1870, until the close of the year, prevented by the ulcers from setting a foot on the ground.

"I lived," he writes (1870), "in what may be called the Tipperary of Manyema, and they are certainly a bloody people among themselves. But they are very far from being in appearance like the ugly negroes on the west coast. Finely formed heads are common, and generally the men and women are vastly superior to the slaves of Zanzibar and elsewhere. We must go deeper than phrenology to account for their low moral tone. If they are cannibals they are not ostentatiously so. The neighboring tribes all assert that they are men-eaters, and they themselves laughingly admit the charge. But they like to impose on the credulous, and they showed the skull of a recent victim to horrify one of my people. I found it to be the skull of a gorilla, or soko — the first I knew of its existence here — and this they do eat."

Satisfactory progress in the exploration of the river could be made only in canoes with men accustomed to work. Livingston tried hard to get such men from Ujiji; but all the traders were eager to secure the carriers for themselves, and circulated the report that he would go from Manyema to his own country and leave the men to shift for themselves. He offered a thousand dollars to some traders for the loan of ten of their people, — more than that number of men ever obtained, — but the ivory fever was so high that none would consent to his proposition, so long as the hope of getting ivory remained.

At last, in February, 1871, seven Banian slaves that had been dispatched in 1869, with goods for his relief, arrived in Bambarre with so much of the supplies as had not been plundered on the way from the coast: "a few coarse beads, evidently exchanged for my beautiful and dear beads," Livingston writes with justifiable bitterness, "a little calico, and in great mercy, some of my coffee and sugar." His tent, which they had used all the way, was so rotten and full of holes that he could not use it. " They had been sixteen months on the way from Zanzibar instead of three, and now, like their head men, refused to go any further. They swore so positively that the Consul had told them to force me back, and on no account to go forward, that I actually looked again at their engagement, to be sure my eyes had not deceived me. Fear alone made them consent to go; but had I not been aided by Muhamad Bogharib, they would have gained their point by sheer brazen-faced falsehood."

How the unfortunate explorer was baffled and worried, and finally defeated by these wretched slaves, who had been sent him contrary to his express orders to send none but free men, we have not space to recount: they were one of the bitterest misfortunes that he has had to contend against. His medicines had been unaccountably detained by the Governor of Unyanyembe since 1868, though he had twice sent for them with calico to prepay the carriers. He succeeded, however, in curing the ulcers on his feet with a piece of malachite, rubbed down with water on a stone, and as soon as he could travel he set off in a northerly direction in search of the Lualaba. After several days' journey he found the river, and by exceeding pertinacity he contrived to follow its erratic course, until it entered a lake called Kamolondo, in about 6 deg. 30 min. south. Then he retraced the river southward to where he had seen it issue from Lake Moero. Descending the Lualaba again — a broad and curiously tortuous stream — he returned to Lake Kamolondo, explored it, and then pushed his investigations down the stream, which issues from it. He found it to bear the same name below as above the lake, and to distinguish the upper portion he called it Webb's Lualaba, in honor of one of his oldest and most consistent friends. Away to southwest of Kamolondo is another large lake which discharges its waters into the Lualaba, through a large river called the Loeki, or Lomami. To this lake, which is known as Chebungo by the natives, Livingston gave the name of Lincoln, in honor of our martyred President. A large river called the Lufira, flows into the Lualaba, a little north of Lake Kamolondo ; and many other important streams help to swell its waters, as it sweeps through many and crooked windings northward to another great lake, which Livingston was unable to reach. His Banian slaves refused to go on, fearing they said to enter a country where there were no Moslems. He waited three months for the arrival of a friend named Dugumbe, who was on the way from Ujiji with a caravan of two hundred guns and nine under-traders with their people. As soon as he came,

Livingston endeavored to hire ten men and a canoe, that he might finish his geographical work without the Banians. His proposition was agreed to, but Dugumbe required a few days to consult his associates. Two days after, June 13th, a massacre was perpetrated, which filled Livingston with such intolerable loathing that he resolved to yield to the Banian slaves, return to Ujiji, get men from the coast, and try to finish his work by going outside the area of Ujijian bloodshed, instead of vainly trying from its interior outwards. We quote at length his description of that dreadful affair, for the double view it gives of native life, and the horrors of slave hunting: —

"Dugumbe's people built their huts on the right bank of the Lualaba, at a market place called Nyanwe. On hearing that the head slave of a trader at Ujiji had, in order to get canoes cheap, mixed blood with the head men of the Bagenya on the left bank, they were disgusted with his assurance, and resolved to punish him and make an impression in the country in favor of their own greatness by an assault on the market people, and on all the Bagenya who had dared to make friendship with any but themselves. Tagamoio, the principal under-trader of Dugumbe's party, was the perpetrator. The market was attended every fourth day by between two thousand and three thousand people. It was held on a long slope of land which, down at the river, ended in a creek capable of containing between fifty and sixty large canoes. The majority of the market people were women, many of them very pretty. The people west of the river brought fish, salt, pepper, oil, grass-cloth, iron, fowls, goats, sheep, pigs, in great numbers, to exchange with those east of the river for cassava grain, potatoes, and other farinaceous products. They have a strong sense of natural justice, and all unite in forcing each other to fair dealing. At first my presence made them all afraid, but wishing to gain their confidence, which my enemies tried to undermine or prevent, I went among them frequently, and when they saw no harm in me became very gracious; the bargaining was the finest acting I ever saw. I understood but few of the words that flew off the glib tongues of the women, but their gestures spoke plainly. I took sketches of the fifteen varieties of fish brought in, to compare them with those of the Nile farther down, and all were eager to tell their names. But on the date referred to I had left the market only a minute or two when three men whom I had seen with guns, and felt inclined to reprove them for bringing them into the market place, but had refrained by attributing it to ignorance in new-comers, began to fire into the dense crowd around them. Another party, down at the canoes, rained their balls on the panic-struck multitude that rushed into these vessels. All threw away their goods, the men forgot their paddles, the canoes were jammed in the creek and could not be got out quick enough, so many men and women sprung into the water. The women of the left bank are expert divers for oysters, and a long line of heads showed a crowd striking out for an island a mile off; to gain it they had to turn the left shoulder against a current of between a mile and a half to two miles an hour. Had they gone diagonally with the current, though that would have been three miles, many would have gained the shore. It was horrible to see one head after another disappear, some calmly, others throwing their arms high up towards the Great Father of all, and going down. Some of the men who got canoes out of the crowd paddled quick, with hands and arms, to help their friends; three took people in till they all sank together. One man had clearly lost his head, for he paddled a canoe, which would have held fifty people, straight up stream nowhere. The Arabs estimated the loss at between four and five hundred souls. Dugumbe sent out some of his men in one of thirty canoes, which the owners in their fright could not extricate, to save the sinking. One lady refused to be taken on board because she thought that she was to be made a slave; but he rescued twenty-one, and of his own accord sent them next day home. Many escaped and came to me, and were restored to their friends. When the firing began on the terror-stricken crowd at the canoes, Tagamoio's band began their assault on the people on the west of the river, and continued the fire all day.

I counted seventeen villages in flames, and next day six. Dugumbe's power over the underlings is limited, but he ordered them to cease shooting. Those in the market were so reckless they shot two of their own number. Tagamoio's crew came back next day, in canoes, shouting and firing off their guns as if believing that they were worthy of renown.

"Next day about twenty head men fled from the west bank and came to my house. There was no occasion now to tell them that the English had no desire for human blood. They begged hard that I should go over with them and settle with them, and arrange where the new dwellings of each should be. I was so ashamed of the bloody Moslem company in which I found myself that I was unable to look at the Manyema. I confessed my grief and shame, and was entreated, if I must go, not to leave them now. Dugumbe spoke kindly to them, and would protect them as well as he could against his own people; but when I went to Tagamoio to ask back the wives and daughters of some of the head men, he always ran off and hid himself.

"This massacre was the most terrible scene I ever saw. I cannot describe my feelings, and am thankful that I did not give way to them, but by Dugumbe's advice, avoided a bloody feud with men who, for the time, seemed turned into demons. The whole transaction was the more deplorable, inasmuch as we have always heard from the Manyema that though the men of the districts may be engaged in actual hostilities, the women pass from one market place to another with their wares, and were never known to be molested. The change has come only with these alien bloodhounds, and all the bloodshed has taken place in order that captives might be seized where it could be done without danger, and in order that the slaving privileges of a petty sultan should produce abundant fruit."

Heartsore and depressed in spirit by these terrible instances of "man's inhumanity to man," Livingston turned his back on the object of his hopes, and started on a long and weary tramp to Ujiji, under a blazing tropical sun. Almost every step of those wretched five hundred miles was in pain. "I felt as if dying on my feet," he writes ; and he came very near death in a more summary way.

Outrage after outrage was heaped on the poor Manyema people by the trading companies until they could endure it no longer. As soon as trouble began the scattered camps of ivory seekers begged to be taken into Livingston's company, and he could not refuse them. No more could he restrain their excesses, or escape sharing the blame of them. On one occasion the party had to pass through five hours of forest thronged with exasperated natives, bent on revenging the enslavement and death of their relatives. The vegetation was so dense that they could not see their foes.

"Our people in front peered into every little opening in the dense thicket before they would venture past it; this detained the rear, and two persons near to me were slain. A large spear lunged past close behind ; another missed me by about a foot in front. Coming to a part of the forest of about a hundred yards cleared for cultivation, I observed that fire had been applied to one of the gigantic trees, made still higher by growing on an ant-hill twenty or more feet high. Hearing the crack that told the fire had eaten through, I felt that there was no danger, it looked so far away, till it appeared coming right down toward me. I ran a few paces back, and it came to the ground only one yard off, broke in several lengths, and covered me with a cloud of dust. My attendants ran back, exclaiming, ' Peace, peace! you will finish your work in spite of all these people, and in spite of everything.' I, too, took it as an omen of good that I had three narrow escapes from death in one day.

"The Manyema are expert at throwing the spear, and as I had a glance of him whose spear missed by less than an inch behind, and he was not ten yards off, I was saved clearly by the good hand of the Almighty Preserver of men. I can say this devoutly now, but in running the terrible gauntlet for five weary hours among furies all eager to signalize themselves by slaying one they sincerely believed to have been guilty of a horrid outrage, no elevated sentiments entered the mind. The excitement gave way to overpowering weariness, and I felt as I suppose soldiers do on the field of battle — not courageous, but perfectly indifferent whether I were killed or not."

The abject condition of the illustrious explorer on his return to Ujiji has already been described. The results of the years of unparalleled labor and suffering which he has undergone since he disappeared from the ken of civilization, he sums up briefly as follows: —

"I have ascertained that the water-shed of the Nile is a broad upland between ten degrees and twelve degrees south latitude, and from 4,000 to 5,000 feet above the level of the sea. Mountains stand on it at various points, which, though not apparently very high, are between 6,000 and 7,000 feet of actual altitude. The water-shed is over 700 miles in length, from west to east. The springs that rise on it are almost innumerable — that is, it would take a large part of a man's life to count them. A bird's-eye view of some parts of the water-shed would resemble the frost vegetation on window panes. They all begin in an ooze at the head of a slightly depressed valley. A few hundred yards down, the quantity of water from oozing earthen sponge forms a brisk perennial burn or brook a few feet broad, and deep enough to require a bridge. These are the ultimate or primary sources of the great rivers that flow to the north in the great Nile valley. The primaries unite and form streams in general larger than the Isis at Oxford, or Avon at Hamilton, and may be called secondary sources. They never dry, but unite again into four large lines of drainage, the head waters or mains of the river of Egypt. These four are each called by the natives Lualaba, which, if not too pedantic, may be spoken of as lacustrine rivers, extant specimens of those which, in prehistoric times, abounded in Africa, and which in the south are still called by Bechuanas 'Melapo,' in the north, by Arabs, 'Wadys,' both words meaning the same thing — river bed in which no water ever now flows. Two of the four great rivers mentioned fall into the central Lualaba, or Webb's Lake River, and then we have but two main lines of drainage as depicted nearly by Ptolemy.

"The prevailing winds on the water-shed are from the southeast. This is easily observed by the direction of the branches, and the humidity of the climate is apparent in the numbers of lichens which make the upland forest look like the mangrove swamps on the coast.

"In passing over sixty miles of latitude, I waded thirty-two primary sources from calf to waist deep, and requiring from twenty minutes to an hour and a quarter to cross stream and sponge. This would give about one source to every two miles.

"A Suaheli friend, in passing along part of the Lake Bangweolo. during six days counted twenty-two from thigh to waist deep. This lake is on the water-shed, for the village at which I observed on its northwest shore was a few seconds into eleven degrees south, and its southern shores, and springs, and rivulets, are certainly in twelve degrees south. I tried to cross it in order to measure the breadth accurately. The first stage to an inhabited island was about twenty-four miles. From the highest point here the tops of the trees, evidently lifted by the mirage, could be seen on the second stage and the third stage; the mainland was said to be as far as this beyond it. But my canoe men had stolen the canoe and got a hint that the real owners were in pursuit, and got into a flurry to return home. 'They would come back for me in a few days, truly,' but I had only my coverlet left to hire another craft if they should leave me in this wide expanse of water, and being 4,000 feet above the sea it was very cold; so I returned.

"The length of this lake is, at a very moderate estimate, 150 miles. It gives forth a large body of water in the Luapula; yet lakes are in no sense sources, for no large river begins in a lake; but this and others serve an important purpose in the phenomena of the Nile. It is one large lake, and (unlike the Okara, which, according to Suaheli, who travelled long in our company, is three or four lakes run into one huge Victoria Nyanza) gives out a large river, which, on departing out of Moero, is still larger. These men had spent many years east of Okara, and could scarcely be mistaken in saying that of the three or four lakes there, only one (the Okara) gives off its waters to the north. . . .

"The great river, Webb's Lualaba, in the centre of the Nile valley, makes a great bend to the west, soon after leaving Lake Moero, of at least one hundred and eighty miles; then, turning to the north for some distance, it makes another large sweep west of about one hundred and twenty miles, in the course of which about thirty miles of southing are made; it then draws around to northeast, receives the Lomani, or Loeki, a large river which flows through Lake Lincoln. After the union a large lake is formed, with many inhabited islands in it; but this has still to be explored. It is the fourth large lake in the central line of drainage, and cannot be Lake Albert; for, assuming Speke's longitude of Ujiji to be pretty correct, and my reckoning not enormously wrong, the great central lacustrine river is about five degrees west of Upper and Lower Tanganyika. . . .

"Beyond the fourth lake the water passes, it is said, into large reedy lakes, and is in all probability Petherick's branch — the main stream of the Nile — in distinction from the smaller eastern arm which Speke, Grant, and Baker took to be the river of Egypt.[1]

"The Manyema could give no information about their country because they never travel. Blood feuds often prevent them from

---

[1] Dr. Charles Beke and others, widely known in connection with African geography, dispute the possibility of any connection between the Lualaba and the Nile, certainly through Petherick's branch. It is, they say, a question of fact, not of theory. Since Livingston left England a German botanist, Dr. G. Schweinfurth, has explored the basin of the western arm of the Nile, proving it to be not the "main branch," as Livingston supposes. Dr. Schweinfurth claims not only to have visited "Petherick's Nile" — the river Djur — but to have passed beyond it, finding in latitude 3 35′ north, and longitude 28° east, a large river, the Uelle, running directly across the course which Livingston supposes the Lualaba to take. Having its course on the western side of the Blue Mountains, flanking the Albert Nyanza on the northwest, somewhere about latitude 2′ north, and longitude 30° east, the Uelle runs from east to west, and is supposed to be the upper course of the Shary, running into Lake Chad. Such a river, in such a position and with such a course, it is said, must shut up the basin of the Nile in that direction, and preclude the passage into it of any waters from the south.

visiting villages three or four miles off, and many at a distance of about thirty miles did not know the great river, though named to them. No traders had gone so far as I had, and their people cared only for ivory.

"In my attempts to penetrate further and further, I had but little hope of ultimate success, for the great amount of westing led to a continued effort to suspend the judgment, lest, after all, I might be exploring the Congo instead of the Nile, and it was only after the two great western drains fell into the central main, and left but the two great lacustrine rivers of Ptolemy, that I felt pretty sure of being on the right track."

Soon after Mr. Stanley's arrival at Ujiji, he proposed an expedition to the northern end of Tanganyika, to settle the disputed question of its relation to the Albert Nyanza. Though sorely weakened by disease, and much cast down by the disappointments of his last journey and the outrageous robbery of his supplies, Livingston heartily seconded the proposition, and instantly set about making ready for the start. A canoe was procured, and by means of the supplies which Mr. Stanley had brought, a company was soon organized and equipped for what proved to be a rare pleasure excursion to the travel worn explorer. Discovering that the Rusizi, the river at the end of the lake, flowed into instead of out of Tanganyika, and finding no outlet in that direction, the party returned from their month's cruise satisfied that Tanganyika was of no interest, except in a very remote degree, in connection with the sources of the Nile.

On Mr. Stanley's return to the coast, Dr. Livingston accompanied him as far as Unyanyembe, where he remained until Mr. Stanley should be able to send him men and supplies from the coast. On the receipt of these his purpose was to set off immediately for the prosecution of his great work.

"It is only a sense of duty, which I trust your lordship will approve," he writes to Earl Granville, "that makes me remain, and if possible finish the geographical question of my mission. After being thwarted, baffled, robbed, worried almost to death in following the central line of drainage down, I have a sore longing for home; have had a perfect surfeit of seeing strange, new lands and people, grand mountains, lovely valleys, the glorious vegetation of primeval forests, wild beasts, and an endless succession of beautiful man; besides great rivers and vast lakes — the last most interesting from their huge outflowings, which explain some of the phenomena of the grand old Nile."

His plan of operation for the coming years he sketches as follows: —

"I shall at present avoid Ujiji, and go about southwest from this to Fipa, which is east of and near the south end of Tanganyika; then round the same south end, only touching it again at Pambette; thence resuming the southwest course to cross the Chambeze, and proceed alone to the southern shores of Lake Bangweolo, which being in latitude twelve degrees south, the course will be due west to the ancient fountains of Herodotus. From them it is about ten days north to Katanga, the copper mines of which have been worked for ages. The malachite ore is described as so abundant it can only be mentioned by the coalheavers' phrase 'practically inexhaustible.'

"About ten days northeast of Katanga very extensive underground rock excavations deserve attention as very ancient, the natives ascribing their formation to the Deity alone. They are remarkable for all having water laid on in running streams, and the inhabitants of large districts can all take refuge in them in case of invasion. Returning from them to Katanga, twelve days north-northwest, take to the southern end of Lake Lincoln. I wish to go down through it to the Lomani, and into Webb's Lualaba, and home."

Nothing remains but to speak of the English Search

and Relief Expedition. Its work was forestalled. Before it was ready to leave the coast, Mr. Stanley arrived with the unexpected intelligence that Livingston had been found and relieved, and bearing a letter from Livingston directing the return of any company that might be on the way with men or supplies for him. With no one to search for and no one to relieve, the members of the English Expedition did the only thing left for them to do — they disbanded and returned.

A NEW AND VALUABLE SERIES

For Readers of all Ages and for the School and Family Library.

The Illustrated Library
OF
TRAVEL, EXPLORATION,
AND ADVENTURE.
EDITED BY
BAYARD TAYLOR.

The extraordinary popularity of the ILLUSTRATED LIBRARY OF WONDERS (nearly *one and a half million* copies having been sold in this country and in France) is considered by the publishers a sufficient guarantee of the success of an ILLUSTRATED LIBRARY OF TRAVEL, EXPLORATION, AND ADVENTURE, embracing the same decidedly interesting and permanently valuable features. Upon this new enterprise the publishers will bring to bear all their wide and constantly increasing resources. Neither pains nor expense will be spared in making their new Library not only one of the most elegantly and profusely illustrated works of the day, but at the same time one of the most graphic and fascinating in narrative and description.

Each volume will be complete in itself, and will contain, first, a brief preliminary sketch of the country to which it is devoted; next, such an outline of previous explorations as may be necessary to explain what has been achieved by later ones; and finally, a condensation of one or more of the most important narratives of recent travel, accompanied with illustrations of the scenery, architecture, and life of the races, drawn only from the most authentic sources. An occasional volume will also be introduced in the LIBRARY, detailing the exploits of individual adventurers. The entire series will thus furnish a clear, picturesque, and practical survey of our present knowledge of lands and races as supplied by the accounts of travellers and explorers. The LIBRARY will therefore be both entertaining and instructive to young as well as old, and the publishers intend to make it a necessity in every family of culture and in every private and public library in America. The name of BAYARD TAYLOR as editor is an assurance of the accuracy and high literary character of the publication.

The following volumes are now ready:—

JAPAN, ARABIA,
WILD MEN AND WILD BEASTS.

Will be published soon:—

SOUTH AFRICA, CENTRAL AFRICA,
WONDERS OF THE YELLOWSTONE.

The volumes will be uniform in size (12mo), and in price, $1.50 each.
Catalogues, with Specimen Illustrations, sent on application.
SCRIBNER, ARMSTRONG, & CO., 654 *Broadway*, N. Y.

WILFRID CUMBERMEDE.

BY

GEORGE MACDONALD,

Author of "*Alec Forbes,*" "*Annals of a Quiet Neighborhood,*" "*Robert Falconer,*" &c., &c.

Complete in One Vol. 12mo, with 14 full-page illustrations, Cloth, $1.75.

WILFRID CUMBERMEDE is the latest and ripest work of one who is now acknowledged, by a large and constantly increasing public, to be the greatest living master of fiction, equalling DICKENS in his vivid depiction of character, glorious in imagination, and intense in religious fervor.

WILFRID CUMBERMEDE is absorbingly interesting in plot, full of adventure, pure and strong in every point of incident and style, and written with a power which places it entirely by itself among the novels of the day.

CRITICAL NOTICES.

"The charms and value of Mr. Macdonald's work need not be sought. They present themselves unasked for, in the tender beauty of his descriptions, whether of nature or life and character, in his almost superhuman insight into the workings of the human heart, and in his unceasing fertility of thought and happy exactitude of illustration."—*London Pall Mall Gazette.*

"This book is full of intellectual wealth. It will teach us as many wise thoughts, and nurture as many noble feelings, as either 'Robert Falconer' or 'Alec Forbes.'"—*British Quarterly Review.*

"It is simple, natural, pathetic, and playful by turns, interesting in plot and development of character, and written in such limpid English as it does one good to meet with."—*N. Y. Journal of Commerce.*

"After all, the supreme interest of Macdonald's novels is found, neither in the delineation of character nor in the narration of incident, but in the personality of the writer, revealed everywhere in lofty or subtle thought, in noble sentiment, and in lovely feeling."—*Boston Daily Transcript.*

"The best story of him who is the best of living story-writers. It may be enjoyed almost in perfection by one who has not read the beginning, and who will never read the sequel; and it will remain in the memory like a beautiful song."—*N. Y. Independent.*

"Mr. Macdonald's writings are beautiful in style, powerful in description, pathetic and pure in their design."—*Christian Intelligencer.*

WITHIN AND WITHOUT.

BY

GEORGE MACDONALD.

One vol. 12mo. $1.50.

This, which is the longest poem and one of the most important works of this popular author, is, in fact, a *Thrilling Story in Verse.*

It deals in a graphic and masterly manner with the deepest human passion, is beautiful with imagination, and intensely interesting in plot. Macdonald is one of the most original and charming of living poets, and the many American readers of his prose works will be delighted at this opportunity of becoming acquainted with his poetry.

☞ *These works sent post-paid, upon receipt of the price, by*

SCRIBNER, ARMSTRONG & CO.,
Successors to CHARLES SCRIBNER & CO.,
654 Broadway, New York

A NEW SERIES OF
The Illustrated Library of Wonders,

ENLARGED IN SIZE, IN A NEW STYLE OF BINDING, AND EDITED BY PROMINENT AMERICAN AUTHORS.

The extraordinary success of the ILLUSTRATED LIBRARY OF WONDERS has encouraged the publishers to still further efforts to increase the attractions and value of these admirable books. In the new series, which has just been commenced with THE WONDERS OF WATER, the size of the volumes is increased, the style of binding changed, and the successive volumes are edited by distinguished American authors and scientists.

The following volumes will introduce

THE SECOND SERIES OF THE
ILLUSTRATED LIBRARY OF WONDERS.

MOUNTAIN ADVENTURES. (39 Illustrations.) Edited by J. T. HEADLEY.

WONDERS OF ELECTRICITY. Edited by Dr. J. W. ARMSTRONG, President of the State Normal School, Fredonia, N. Y.

WONDERS OF VEGETATION. (Over 40 Illustrations.) Edited by Prof. SCHELE DE VERE.

WONDERS OF WATER. (64 Illustrations.) Edited by Prof. SCHELE DE VERE.

WONDERS OF ENGRAVING. (34 Illustrations.)

THE FIRST SERIES OF
The Illustrated Library of Wonders

Comprises Twenty Volumes, containing over 1,000 Beautiful Illustrations.

These twenty volumes in cloth, or in half roan, gilt top, are furnished in a black walnut case for $30.00 (the case gratis), or they may be bought singly or in libraries, classified according to their subjects as below, each 1 vol. 12mo. Price per vol. $1.50.

WONDERS OF NATURE.
	No. Illus.
THE HUMAN BODY	43
THE SUBLIME IN NATURE	44
INTELLIGENCE OF ANIMALS	54
THUNDER AND LIGHTNING	39
BOTTOM OF THE SEA	68
THE HEAVENS	48

6 Vols. in a neat box, $9.

WONDERS OF ART.
	No. Illus.
ITALIAN ART	28
EUROPEAN ART	11
ARCHITECTURE	60
GLASS-MAKING	63
WONDERS OF POMPEII	22
EGYPT 3,300 YEARS AGO	40

6 Vols. in a neat box, $9.

WONDERS OF SCIENCE.
	No. Illus.
THE SUN. By Guillemin	58
WONDERS OF HEAT	93
OPTICAL WONDERS	71
WONDERS OF ACOUSTICS	110

4 Vols. in a neat box, $6.

ADVENTURES & EXPLOITS.
	No. Illus.
WONDERFUL ESCAPES	26
BODILY STRENGTH & SKILL	70
BALLOON ASCENTS	30
GREAT HUNTS	22

4 Vols. in a neat box, $6.

☞ Any or all the volumes of the ILLUSTRATED LIBRARY OF WONDERS sent to any address, post or express charges paid, on receipt of the price.

A descriptive Catalogue of the Wonder Library, with specimen illustrations, sent to any address on application.

SCRIBNER, ARMSTRONG, & CO. 654 Broadway, N.Y.

POPULAR AND STANDARD BOOKS

PUBLISHED BY

SCRIBNER, ARMSTRONG & CO.

(SUCCESSORS TO CHARLES SCRIBNER & CO.)

No. 654 Broadway, New York,

IN 1871.

BIBLE COMMENTARY (THE). Vol. I. The Pentateuch. 1 Vol. Royal 8vo, with occasional Illustrations,..........................$5.00
CURTIUS, Prof. Dr. ERNST. The History of Greece. Volume III. Cr. 8vo, per vol..........................$2.50
DE VERE, Prof. M. SCHELE. Americanisms. 1 vol., cr. 8vo, $3.00
ERCKMANN—CHATRIAN NOVELS (THE). Each 1 vol., 16mo. With Illustrations..........................cloth $1.25—paper 75c.
—————————— The Blockade of Phalsburg.
—————————— The Invasion of France in 1844.
FROUDE, J. A. History of England. *Popular Edition.* In twelve vols. 12mo. The Set..........................$15.00
—————————— Short Studies on Great Subjects. Second Series. 1 vol. cr. 8vo..........................$2.50
HARLAND (MARION). Common Sense in the Household. 1 vol., 12mo..........................$1.75
HARRIS (Mrs. S. S.) Richard Vandermarck. 1 vol., 12mo., $1.50
HODGE, Dr. CHARLES. Systematic Theology. Vols. I. and II. 8vo. per vol..........................$4.50
ILLUSTRATED LIBRARY OF WONDERS (THE). First Series. In 20 vols. Each 1 vol. 16mo., per vol. $1.50 With numerous Illustrations. The Set in a neat case for..........................$30.00
—————————— Second Series. Each 1 vol, 12mo., with numerous Illustrations, per vol..........................$1.50
—————————— —————————— Mountain Adventures.
—————————— —————————— The Wonders of Water.
—————————— —————————— The Wonders of Vegetation.
ILLUSTRATED LIBRARY OF TRAVEL, EXPLORATION, AND ADVENTURE (THE). Edited by Bayard Taylor. Each 1 vol., 12mo. With numerous Illustrations. Per vol..........................$1.50
—————————— Japan (with a Map).
—————————— Wild Men and Wild Beasts.
JOWETT, Prof. B. The Dialogues of Plato. In four vols., cr. 8vo., $12.00
LANGE'S COMMENTARY. Edited by Dr. P. Schaff. Each 1 vol. 8vo., $5.00
—————————— Jeremiah.
—————————— John.
—————————— Joshua, Judges, and Ruth.
MACDONALD (GEORGE). Wilfrid Cumbermede. 1 vol., 12mo. With 14 full page Illustrations..........................$1.75
MULLER, Prof. MAX. Chips from a German Workshop. Vol. III. 1 vol., cr. 8vo..........................$2.50
—————————— Lectures on the Science of Religion. 1 vol. cr. 8vo..........................$2.00
PORTER, Pres. NOAH. Elements of Intellectual Philosophy. 1 vol. cr. 8vo..........................$3.00
—————————— Books and Reading. *New Edition.* 1 vol. cr. 8vo..........................$2.00
TRENCH, R. C. English Past and Present. *Revised Edition.* 1 vol. 12mo..........................$1.25
UEBERWEG, (Prof.) History of Philosophy. Vol. I, 8vo......$3.50
WOOD (Rev. J. G.) Insects at Home. Illustrated. 1 vol. 8vo......$5.00

These books sent post-paid by the publishers on receipt of the price.

The Erckmann-Chatrian Novels.

THE CONSCRIPT: A Tale of the French War of
1813. With four full-page Illustrations. One vol. 12mo. Price, in paper, 75 cents; cloth, $1.25.

From the Cincinnati Daily Commercial.
"It is hardly fiction,—it is history in the guise of fiction, and that part of history which historians hardly write, concerning the disaster, the ruin, the sickness, the poverty, and the utter misery and suffering which war brings upon the people."

WATERLOO: A Story of the Hundred Days. Being a Sequel to "*The Conscript.*" With four full-page Illustrations. One vol. 12mo. Price, in paper, 75 cents; cloth, $1.25.

From the New York Daily Herald.
"Written in that charming style of simplicity which has made the ERCKMANN-CHATRIAN *works popular in every language in which they have been published.*"

THE BLOCKADE OF PHALSBURG. An Episode of the Fall of the First French Empire. With four full-page Illustrations and a Portrait of the authors. One vol. 12mo. Price, in paper, 75 cents; cloth, $1.25.

From the Philadelphia Daily Inquirer.
"Not only are they interesting historically, but intrinsically a pleasant, well-constructed plot, serving in each case to connect the great events which they so graphically treat, and the style being as vigorous and charming as it is pure and refreshing."

INVASION OF FRANCE IN 1814. With the Night March past Phalsburg. With a Memoir of the Authors. With four full-page Illustrations. One vol. 12mo. Price, in paper, 75 cents; cloth, $1.25.

From the New York Evening Mail.
"All their novels are noted for the same admirable qualities,—simple and effective realism of plot, incident, and language, and a disclosure of the horrid individual aspects of war. They are absolutely perfect of their kind."

MADAME THERESE; or, The Volunteers '92. With four full-page Illustrations. One vol. 12mo. Price, in paper, 75 cents; cloth, $1.25.

From the Boston Commonwealth.
"It is a boy's story—that is, supposed to be written by a boy—and has all the freshness, the unconscious simplicity and *naïveté* which the imagined authorship should imply; while nothing more graphic, more clearly and vividly pictorial, has been brought before the public for many a day."

Any or all of the above volumes sent, post-paid, upon receipt of the price by the publishers,

SCRIBNER, ARMSTRONG & CO.,
(Successors to CHARLES SCRIBNER & CO.),
654 Broadway, New York.

A NEW BOOK BY MAX MULLER.

Lectures on the Science of Religion;

WITH PAPERS ON BUDDHISM, AND A TRANSLATION OF THE
DHAMMAPADA, OR PATH OF VIRTUE.

By F. MAX MULLER,

Author of "Lectures on the Science of Language," "Chips from a German Workshop," &c., &c.   1 vol. crown 8vo. $2.00.

These "Lectures on the Science of Religion," by this eminent scholar, although they attracted wide attention at the time of their delivery, have never before been produced in book form. In connection with them are given a lecture on "Buddhist Nihilism," and a translation of the original of the "Dhammapada, or Path of Virtue," an important part of the Buddhistic canon, together with an introduction explaining its importance. The interest lately awakened in the Oriental religions gives peculiar value to these contributions to the literature relating to them, by one who is perhaps more competent to give an account of them than any other living scholar.

PROF. PORTER'S "HUMAN INTELLECT" ABRIDGED.

Elements of Intellectual Philosophy.

A MANUAL FOR SCHOOLS AND COLLEGES.

Abridged from "The Human Intellect." By NOAH PORTER, D.D., LL.D., President of Yale College.   1 vol. crown 8vo, nearly 600 pages, cloth.   Price $3.00.

President PORTER'S great work upon the *Human Intellect* at once secured for him a foremost place among living metaphysicians. The demand for this work—even in its expensive form—as a text-book, has induced the preparation of this abridged and cheaper edition, which contains all the matter of the larger work necessary for use in the class-room.

FROUDE'S SHORT STUDIES, SECOND SERIES.

THE SECOND SERIES OF

Short Studies on Great Subjects.

By J. A. FROUDE, LL.D., Author of the "History of England."

1 vol. crown 8vo, on laid tinted paper, in brown cloth, $2.50.

The papers in this series of "Short Studies" are quite as popular as those comprised in the first volume, and fully as characteristic of their distinguished author. Among them are the address on "Calvinism," which has caused so much discussion and comment; papers on "The Condition and Prospects of Protestantism," on "Progress," "Education," the "Scientific Method Applied to History," &c., &c., with several which, although lighter and more ephemeral, add greatly to the entertaining character of the volume.

These works sent, post-paid, on receipt of the price, by

SCRIBNER, ARMSTRONG, & CO. 654 Broadway, N. Y.

www.ingramcontent.com/pod-product-compliance
Lightning Source LLC
Chambersburg PA
CBHW020731240426
43664CB00053B/263